A GUIDE TO THE NATURE RESERVES

OF

SOUTHERN ENGLAND

Researched and written by
Linda Bennett

Based on accounts of the reserves researched and written by
Jeremy Hywel-Davies and Valerie Thom

MACMILLAN
PRESS

This edition published 1989 by The Macmillan Press Ltd
a division of Macmillan Publishers Limited
Stockton House 1 Melbourne Place London WC2B 4LF
and Basingstoke.

Associated companies in Auckland, Delhi, Dublin, Gaborone,
Hamburg, Harare, Hong Kong, Johannesburg, Kuala Lumpur, Lagos,
Manzini, Melbourne, Mexico City, Nairobi, New York, Singapore
and Tokyo.

British Library Cataloguing in Publication Data
A Guide to the nature reserves of Southern England.
  1. Southern England. Nature reserves
  639.9'09422

  ISBN 0-333-51494-7

Filmset in Palatino by Photo·graphics, Honiton
Originated by Adroit Photo Litho Limited, Birmingham
Printed in Great Britain by Butler & Tanner Ltd, Frome, Somerset

Picture research: Juliet Brightmore
Design: Robert Updegraff
Maps: Hilary Evans

Cover: Ivinghoe Beacon, Buckinghamshire.
Photo © E.A. Janes/NHPA

Contents

Contributors

Editorial Advisers
Robert E. Boote CVO *Vice-President of the Royal Society for Nature Conservation, and Council Member of a number of voluntary bodies.*
Dr Franklyn Perring OBE *Former General Secretary of the Royal Society for Nature Conservation, Vice-President of the Botanical Society of the British Isles, writer and broadcaster.*

Research Officers
Jeremy Hywel-Davies *Writer on wildlife and the countryside.*
Linda Bennett *Editor of* Natural World, *the magazine of the Royal Society for Nature Conservation.*

Authors of the Introductions
Rennie Bere CMG *Past president of the Cornwall Trust for Nature Conservation and former Director and Chief Warden of the Uganda National Parks.*
Dr H.J.M. Bowen *Member of the Botanical Society of the British Isles and the British Lichenological Society, and author of* The Flora of Berkshire.
P. Evans *Conservation Officer of the Kent Trust for Nature Conservation.*
Richard Fitter *Author, broadcaster, Chairman of the Fauna and Flora Preservation Society, Past President of BBONT, and Committee or Council Member of several national and international wildlife organisations.*
Ian Mercer *Chairman of the Devon Wildlife Trust and Chief Officer, Dartmoor National Park.*
Steve Micklewright *Marketing Officer of the Avon Wildlife Trust and member of the Bristol University's Avon Gorge Project.*
Dr Pat Morris *Writer, Lecturer in Zoology at Royal Holloway College, University of London, Vice-president of the London Wildlife Trust and Patron of the Avon Wildlife Trust.*
The late Morley Penistan *Chartered Forester and Chairman of the Gloucestershire Trust for Nature Conservation.*
John Price *Vice-Chairman of the Wiltshire Trust for Nature Conservation.*
Dr C.E.D. Smith *Chairman of the Somerset Trust for Nature Conservation.*
Bob Smyth *Journalist, author of* City Wildspace *and editor of the journal* Urban Wildlife.
Dr Fay R. Stranack *Council Member of the Hampshire and Isle of Wight Naturalists' Trust, and a Fellow of the Zoological Society of London.*
David Streeter *Author, broadcaster, Reader in Ecology at the University of Sussex, and Deputy President of the Sussex Wildlife Trust.*
W.G. Teagle *Life Fellow of the RSPB and a Scientific Fellow of the Zoological Society of London*

Picture Acknowledgements

Aquila Photographics: 5 photo H.A. Hems; 79 E.A. Janes. Ardea: 55, 59 *below*, 63, photos J.B. and S. Bottomley; 110 photo Bob Gibbons; 111 photo John Mason; 127 photo Bob Gibbons; 142–143 photo John Mason. John S. Beswick: 31, 42–43, 54, 58. John Cleare: 170. Bruce Coleman: 18 photo Roger Wilmshurst; 71 photo Eric Crichton. Robin Crane: 167. Exmoor National Park Authority: 147 photo F.B. Pearce. David Gantzel: 27. K.F. Giles: 15. A.F. Kersting: 23, 72, 119, 172-3. London Wildlife Trust: 94, 95. John Mason: 106, 118 *above*. National Trust: 38–39, 67, 107. Nature Conservancy Council: 35, 41, 47, 50, 75, 102 *below*, 122, 135, 139, 146, 149, 163, 166, 171, 178. Nature Photographers: 34 photo J.V. and G.R. Harrison; 51 photo S.C. Bisserôt, 66 photo Andrew Cleave; 70 photo M.D.E. Oates; 123 photo Andrew Cleave; 154 photo Frank V. Blackburn; 155 photo Derek Washington; 158 photo Frank V. Blackburn. NPHA: Cover photo E.A. Janes. Premaphotos Wildlife: 78 photo K.G. Preston-Mafham. R.K. Pilsbury: 102 *above*. Dr D.A. Ratcliffe: 82–83, 90, 103, 131. Richard Revels: 14, 59 *above*, 134. Michael Rose: 91. Royal Society for the Protection of Birds: 118 *below* photo Michael W. Richards.

Foreword

It doesn't seem all that long ago, when people and organisations who showed concern for the environment and the natural world were considered just a trifle 'cranky'. Not any more. There is increasing public awareness of environmental issues and of the dangers that come from upsetting the ecological pyramid, and increasing concern at the loss for all time of species of flora, fauna and indeed sadly, entire habitats. There is enormous support for protecting and conserving as much as possible of our natural heritage.

Much of the credit for this public appreciation of what is happening around us belongs to the scores of organisations that have been established to protect or conserve various elements of our natural heritage. Almost entirely charitable and supported by volunteers, these organisations have done immense work in educating the public, raising funds to preserve species and to purchase and maintain valuable habitats. Some of the evidence of their success can be seen on the pages of the five regional editions that together make up *The Macmillan Guide to Britain's Nature Reserves*.

British Gas is delighted to sponsor these regional editions, for the Company has itself a long-standing commitment to protect the environment. Of course the product it supplies, natural gas, is the least pollutive of the fossil fuels, burning without soot, smoke or smell, and contributing least to the acid-rain problem and the greenhouse effect. Much of the progress made in Britain with clean air in the 1960s and 1970s was because of natural gas.

Similarly the transportation of natural gas need make little impact on the landscape – or indeed the townscape. The first natural gas pipeline was laid from Canvey Island, Essex, to Leeds and was completed in 1963. Since then, some 3,400 miles of underground transmission pipelines have been laid, networked across the country, transversing environmentally sensitive moorlands, forests, mountains and bogs as well as some of the country's richest farmland.

The British Gas pipeliners have restored the routes to their former status and in some cases have improved conditions with the advice of local naturalists. Although the Company has its own teams of specialists, it takes considerable heed and co-operates closely with local expertise on environmental matters.

The Company's onshore terminals and other vital installations are invariably sited in rural areas – sometimes in places that are outstanding in terms of habitat. However this has always been taken into consideration with natural landscaping and screening and the planting of indigenous trees and shrubs. Indeed, there is actually a nature trail round the perimeter of one of the onshore terminals. Another terminal also was built a half-mile from its ideal position in industrial terms, to accommodate wildlife considerations.

Within the boundaries of gas installations across the country there is an enormous variety of wildlife which has been allowed to develop without the hindrance of man. A typical example is in Derbyshire where a test centre for controlled explosions, combustion and venting of gases in confined spaces has also become a veritable treasure of wildlife. Among the flowers are yellow toadflax, rose-bay willowherb, white field rose, ladies bedstraw and wild orchids as well as the better-known oxeye daisies, foxglove, primroses and cowslips. In this environment the abundance and variety of the flora has attracted a good population of butterflies: red admirals, tortoishells, peacocks, commas, brimstones, white and painted ladies, and if the chatter of wildlife is momentarily silenced by the occasional experimental controlled explosion, the chances are that it will be broken afterwards by the raps of one of the three species of woodpeckers there – green, greater-spotted and lesser-spotted. While the few staff based at the site are regaled by the cabarets given by hares, stoats, weasels and rabbits, their favourite residents must undoubtedly be those stars of the nocturnal world – badgers.

The enclosed land around the Company's compressor stations have also become mini-reserves in their own right and nature lovers working on these installations have reported some interesting sightings.

At one compressor station the Company is establishing an experimental wildflower meadow and conservation area, with the involvement of the local branch of the British Trust for Conservation Volunteers. The site is becoming a haven for a wide variety of species to thrive, in a part of the country where intensive farming, the use of chemical fertilisers and pesticides, the grubbing of hedges and woodland, and the drainage of wetlands have resulted in a serious loss of natural habitat.

British Gas is just one of the many industries proving that if we go about things the right way, industry and nature can co-habitate. It takes a little bit of extra effort and it costs more too. But we think it's a small price to pay for saving something that we have enjoyed for future generations.

Introduction

The publishers are grateful to British Gas plc whose support for these regional guides have made their publication possible.

The entries are based upon detailed work and research by Jeremy Hywel-Davies and since revised and rewritten by Linda Bennett. Their work would not have been possible without the unstinting co-operation of the Royal Society for Nature Conservation, the NCC and many other bodies concerned with conservation.

Our basis for inclusion of a site is that members of the public should have access either by common law rights, or by membership of a club or trust which gives access by right of membership or by special permit. (All sites in the latter category are marked *Permit only* in the text.) Exceptions have been made on two criteria: where we believe that an endangered or rare species would be threatened by publication of any information about the site where it is found, or where the owner of a site at present allowing access to a limited section of the public would be unwilling to continue such arrangements if an account were published here. We have taken the best advice available on these delicate issues, but in the last resort have made our own judgement.

Our aim has been to be comprehensive and 500 sites have been added to the 1984 list. We have taken pains to ensure that the information was accurate at the time of compilation in mid 1988. It has not been possible to evaluate and include all the sites owned or managed by the Forestry Commission, the Woodland Trust, the Ministry of Defence and the various water authorities. Readers should apply for information to the appropriate addresses (see p.184).

Every entry has been shown to a representative of the owner or managing body to ensure accuracy and the text has been read by two other advisers in addition to our own staff.

Throughout England we have had to take a pragmatic approach, using a combination of old and modern counties in our section titles, and basing our structure in general on the areas covered by the nature conservation trusts, many of which still retain titles relating to the pre-1974 administrative counties. The geographical area of each section is coloured green on the map.

Each section is introduced by a well-known naturalist living in the area and possessing an extensive knowledge of its characteristics. The longer entries in each section have been selected for their perspective on the magnificent diversity of habitats in Britain, and because they are large enough to sustain much public use; many of them offer interpretative facilities. The increasing emphasis on and support for wildlife in cities is reflected in this Guide.

Readers will no doubt wish to support the work of the trusts and other organisations involved in the management of many of the sites included here. The addresses of the relevant bodies are on p.184.

At a time when public interest in our natural heritage has never been stronger, but when paradoxically threats to its future seem to be gathering force, we hope that this Guide will encourage both the sensitive use and enjoyment of Britain's wildlife.

How to Use the Guide

Entries are arranged alphabetically under counties or regions of England, Wales and Scotland. The precise order is shown in the Contents list.

Each county or regional section contains a map showing sites open to the general public, with details of size, population, physical features, climate and major land use. An introduction highlights the main points of interest and characteristics of each county or region.

Factual information is given at the beginning of each entry, in this form:

> 1   2   3
> SC 946562: 43ha: Great Bookworthy BC
> 4 Limestone cliffs, grassland, heath and scrub
> 5 Restricted access to old quarry: apply to warden
> 6 Booklet and nature trail leaflet from car park
> 7 *Spring, early summer*

Key

1 Ordnance Survey map reference (every OS map contains clear instructions on how to read it) or, in the case of very large sites, reference to the map. For sites marked *Permit only* apply to the managing body (see addresses on p.184) unless otherwise stated.
2 Area in hectares, or length in kilometres, as appropriate. (One hectare is approx. 2½ acres; one kilometre is approx. five-eighths of a mile.)
3 Manager/owner of site (for key to abbreviations, see p.182).
4 Brief description of site.
5 Details of any restrictions.
6 Availability of leaflets or other information.
7 Best season(s) for visiting site.

Sites with access limited to members of trusts or other bodies, or to holders of special permits, are not shown on the map or given OS references.

Cross references to other sites mentioned in the text are shown in CAPITALS on their first mention in any entry. These may include sites not in this region but which may be found in the other companion books in this series.

A list of addresses of nature conservation trusts, wildlife organisations and other managing bodies of sites is on p.184.

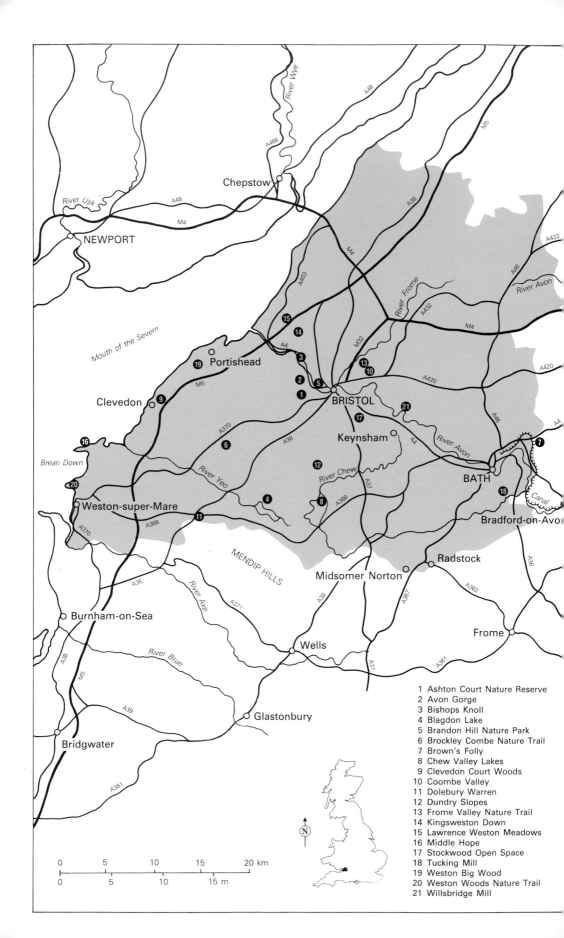

1 Ashton Court Nature Reserve
2 Avon Gorge
3 Bishops Knoll
4 Blagdon Lake
5 Brandon Hill Nature Park
6 Brockley Combe Nature Trail
7 Brown's Folly
8 Chew Valley Lakes
9 Clevedon Court Woods
10 Coombe Valley
11 Dolebury Warren
12 Dundry Slopes
13 Frome Valley Nature Trail
14 Kingsweston Down
15 Lawrence Weston Meadows
16 Middle Hope
17 Stockwood Open Space
18 Tucking Mill
19 Weston Big Wood
20 Weston Woods Nature Trail
21 Willsbridge Mill

Avon

With the cosmopolitan city of Bristol at its heart, Avon can appear very urban in character. The county also boasts the ancient Roman city of Bath on its eastern edge which is almost entirely surrounded by seven hills. However, Avon's complicated geology has bestowed upon it an incredibly varied landscape for such a small county. There are ridges of carboniferous limestone hills to the south of Bristol and their associated damp valleys form an extension of the famous Somerset Levels. Limestone country also occurs in the north of the county with the Cotswold ridge producing very dramatic vistas to the east and north of Chipping Sodbury.

Avon can also appear very bleak. The Severn Estuary with its dark cloudy water and desolate mud banks provides a lonely wilderness on a stormy day. This contrasts with the Avon valley which offers a gentle and relaxed journey for any boatman; that is until it reaches the AVON GORGE near Bristol with its precipitous cliffs of stark, bare limestone.

All this variety provides great opportunities for wildlife, even within the cities of Avon. Bristol has many sites to visit, not least the BRANDON HILL NATURE PARK in the centre of the town. This is being converted from a traditional urban park into a high quality nature reserve boasting hay meadows and a heathland imported from Somerset. Bristol also has many 'natural' reserves of which the most celebrated are the limestone grasslands and ancient woodlands of the AVON GORGE. The Gorge contains no less than 36 rare or uncommon plants, including a type of tree which is only found here in the whole world; to celebrate this fact, it is called the Bristol whitebeam. In Bath, BROWN'S FOLLY reserve contains a similar variety of habitats coupled with a superb view and a colony of the greater horseshoe bat in the mines beneath.

Outside the cities wildlife is also in abundance. The county is particularly rich in ancient woodlands. In the north there are some remarkable damp woodlands including the WETMOOR and MIDGER nature reserves. These woods boast a prolific flora and fauna, including a patch of wild daffodils in one of them.

The southern carboniferous limestone ridges also support some excellent woodlands, many containing large stands of old coppiced small-leaved lime. LIMEBREACH WOOD near Nailsea is a fine example, but almost any woody place on these hilltops will contain at least one patch of this uncommon tree.

The dry, springy limestone grasslands of Avon provide excellent habitats for wildlife. One of the best sites is DOLEBURY WARREN; here sheets of summer flowers provide nectar-rich food for clouds of colourful butterflies. There is even an area of rare and unusual limestone heathland which is festooned with purple heather and wild strawberries. But not all of Avon's grasslands are so hospitable: WESTON MOOR in the Gordano Valley can be damp and unwelcoming, but it is always worth a visit because it is full of wetland flowers and wild creatures. Nothing can compete with the spectacle of the southern marsh-orchid and ragged-Robin in full bloom together. The ditches or 'rhynes' of this site and of the Avon Levels generally provide an excellent habitat for all kinds of water plants and animals, especially frogs, dragonflies and the ubiquitous heron.

Man has also played his part in creating places for wildlife in Avon; CHEW VALLEY and BLAGDON LAKES are reservoirs which are managed with nature in mind. These lakes provide excellent refuges for wintering wildfowl as does the whole of the Severn Estuary which can be teeming with many species of waders and ducks during the winter. The Estuary supports so many migratory visitors that it is regarded as internationally important for wetland birds.

Avon is also fortunate to have a dynamic organisation caring for nature. The Avon Wildlife Trust cares for the county's wildlife and is committed to setting up reserves which the public can visit. To encourage everyone to become interested in its work it has set up a visitor centre at WILLSBRIDGE MILL on the edge of Bristol. The imaginative displays present wildlife and conservation in an enjoyable way and are well worth a visit.

STEVE MICKLEWRIGHT

Ashton Court Nature Reserve

ST 544721; 3.5ha; AWT reserve
Grassland and scrub, with nature trail
Trail booklet from ST554726, BNS or Bristol CC
Summer

Plants in this herb-rich limestone grassland include a huge colony of common spotted-orchid and lots of broomrape. Small and large skippers, common blue and small heath are among the butterflies which can be seen.

The Ashton Court Estate Nature Trail (2.5–3.7 km) passes through this reserve.

Avon Gorge

ST 553731; 105ha; NT–NCC reserve
Wooded limestone gorge
Leaflet from NCC
Spring, early summer

The reserve lies on the western side of the Avon Gorge, clothed with woodland and scrub, quarried out into slabby scallops and topped with the ancient Leigh Woods. The general feel of the woodland is of high oak forest with ash and beech over a thin shrub layer of dogwood, hawthorn, hazel, spindle and yew. There are dark areas of impenetrable yew and holly as well as old coppiced small-leaved lime. The Avon Gorge is important for the endemic Bristol whitebeam and Bristol rock-cress, and species of biogeographical importance such as honewort, hutchinsia and spiked speedwell.

Nightingale Valley, a gorge within a gorge, runs down from the plateau to the river below, showing yet another face of the reserve. Here huge old oaks stand over slopes of bramble and thickets of young ash trees. Steeper slopes of unstable scree spread below rocky faces, cascaded with ivy, and form stony gardens of pink herb-Robert, yellow corydalis and dense plumes of hart's-tongue.

Where the saplings grow, with bramble, on the less steep slopes, the scree is stable enough for a shallow soil to form and so for typical woodland plants to find a footing. The ground cover in the plateau woods above is chiefly bramble, with bracken, honeysuckle and species such as wood sage and bluebell. On the slopes, more rich in lime, dog's mercury and enchanter's-nightshade grow with traveller's-joy and wild madder. Less usual plants include columbine, green hellebore, ivy broomrape, toothwort and bird's-nest orchid.

Other slopes, rocky and scrub-covered, have a mixture of lime-loving shrubs such as privet, wayfaring-tree, dogwood, common and less common whitebeam species, with a rich variety of herbs, including the unusual spring cinquefoil.

Avonmouth Sewage Works

Permit only; 10ha; AWT reserve
Bird-rich lagoons
Autumn, winter

Lying in the Severn Estuary flight line, the reserve attracts a wide range of waterbirds with maximum interest at migration times.

Bishops Knoll

ST 553754; 2.4ha; WdT reserve
Mixed woodland
Spring, summer

An attractive wood at the western end of the AVON GORGE, mature trees and new planting enhance the scenery leading to the Clifton Suspension Bridge.

Blagdon Lake

Described under CHEW VALLEY LAKES.

Blake's Pools

Permit only; 8ha; AWT reserve
Brackish pool
Autumn, winter

A series of three brackish pools created as part of the recent sea defence improvements, their proximity to the Severn Estuary makes them an ideal stop-off point for migrant birds. Over 100 species have been seen since the first pool was flooded in 1983.

Brandon Hill Nature Park

ST 579728; 2ha; AWT reserve
Newly created meadow, pond and woodland
Nature trail leaflet from AWT
Spring, summer

This wildlife area has been created in a city centre park in Bristol. It includes ponds, gardens for butterfly and other wildlife, woodland and a meadow close to the Trust's headquarters.

Brockley Combe

ST 478665; 50ha; Fountain Forestry Ltd
Woodland, grassland and heath
Leaflets from AWT or Avon County Planning Dept., Avon House North, St James Barton, Bristol BS99 7EU
All year

The deep winding gorge cuts through carboniferous limestone and is noted for its badgers' setts. The woodland is a mixture of oak, ash, beech and yew. There are remains of old quarries and mines where limestone heath with common rock-rose, common spotted-orchid and yellow rattle can be seen. A nature trail set up by AWT runs through the wood.

Brown's Folly

ST 798664; 38.5ha; AWT reserve
Limestone downland, woodland and scrub
No entry to old mine shafts
Spring, summer

A great shoulder of rock from which the famous Bath stone was quarried, Brown's Folly stands high above the valley of the River Avon, terraced by the benches of the old mine workings whose scars are covered now with a rich mix of woodland, scrub and grassland. The key to the general pattern is the underlying limestone, encouraging a colourful and varied range of plants and animals. The downland benches, open to the sun, sheltered by the slopes behind them and the scrub around, are opulent with limestone flowers and filled with the quick movement of insects. Wild thyme, common rock-rose, common bird's-foot-trefoil, harebell and lady's bedstraw attract the butterflies common blue and marbled white, the caterpillar of the common blue feeding on clovers, trefoils and vetches and that of the marbled white on grasses. Green hairstreak butterflies may also be seen.

The benches overlook mixed woodland and, sitting on a cushion of herb-rich grassland, one can look out into the canopy of ash, beech, birch and oak. The woods are very varied and range from mature woodland to newly planted trees or to dark thickets of tangling thorns. The woodland shows typical limestone shrub species, while the scrub and grassland areas are also rich in species including both cowslip and the spectacular woolly thistle.

The reserve is a site of special scientific interest scheduled for its geological importance because of its strata of oolitic limestone. The old mines are extensive and house an important colony of greater horseshoe bat.

Chew Valley Lakes

ST 570615; 656ha; Bristol Waterworks Co.—AWT reserve
Large reservoirs
Permits required for hides
Booklet from BWC
Information centre at ST 573613
All year

Chew Valley Lake, some 489ha in size, and BLAGDON LAKE (at ST 516596, permit only from Bristol Waterworks Co.) form together a large area of water which attracts a wide variety of birds. Blagdon is smaller, deeper and more enclosed, with clearer water and a wider variety of water animals associated with an abundance of sub-merged water plants.

The natural banks and the island on Chew Valley Lake make it a fine site for nesting waterbirds such as gadwall, mallard, pochard, ruddy duck, shelduck, tufted duck and heron. Outside the breeding season duck tend to move between the two reservoirs. To lessen the impact of recreation a sanctuary area, the Chew Valley Lake reserve, has been established in the most southerly bay.

At any time of year the lakes and their surrounds may hold varying numbers of gadwall, great crested grebe, ruddy duck, kingfisher, little owl, kestrel and all three native woodpeckers. In spring wintering duck, waders and other birds move north to breed and the lakes become staging posts for passage birds or breeding sites for southern-wintering species. Swallow, sand and house martin, sedge and reed warbler and yellow wagtail fly in to breed while common sandpiper, dunlin and sanderling pass through. Occasionally predators such as osprey and marsh harrier may be seen, while the resident sparrowhawks look forward to the influx of smaller birds, some of which may remain to breed, birds such as whitethroat and lesser whitethroat and garden warbler.

By autumn the migrant breeders will begin to leave and a return passage will sweep back southwards through the reservoirs. Osprey may be reinforced by peregrine and hobby. Terns may pause to hunt across the waters while waders feed on the muddy edges.

In winter many goosander, goldeneye and wigeon may be seen, with increased numbers of mallard, pochard, tufted duck and teal, with Bewick's and a wide variety of predators, waders, sheltering seaduck and finch flocks.

Chivers Knoll

ST 657569; 0.2ha; WdT reserve
Mixed woodland
Spring, summer

This small but prominent wood is an important landmark in the area. It originated as the spoil heap of a small coal-mine that operated for a short time in the eighteenth century.

Cleeve Heronry

Permit only; 3.2ha; AWT reserve
Woodland
Spring, early summer

The reserve has been established to protect one of the most important heronries in the south west, a site which may hold over 30 breeding pairs.

Clevedon Court Woods

ST 425724; 118ha; AWT reserve
Woodland and grassland
Use footbridge across motorway at eastern end of reserve
Spring, summer

Ornamental trees have been planted among the beech and oak of this former estate woodland. There is also an area of scrub and limestone grassland called the Warren where careful management is re-establishing a diversity of plants.

Coombe Valley

ST 632748; 1.6ha; AWT reserve
Scrub woodland and stream
Spring, summer

The steep-sided valley with a stream at the bottom provides an attractive urban site for common birds and plants close to the city of Bristol.

Dolebury Warren

ST 450590; 93ha; AWT—NT reserve
Acid heath, limestone grassland and scrub
Spring, early summer

Heather, bell heather, western gorse and bilberry characterise the acid area below slopes of lime-stone grassland with typical species such as common rock-rose. Thirty-five species of butterfly have been recorded here including good populations of little blue and dark green fritillary.

Dundry Slopes

ST 582669; 3.6ha; AWT reserve
Wet meadow and scrub
Spring, summer

With areas of scrub developing towards woodland, there is a surprising range of habitat for such a small area which includes an attractive variety of wetland plants and insects.

Frome Valley Nature Trail

ST 622765; 4.5km; Bristol Naturalists' Soc.
Riverside trail
Booklet from site or Bristol City Council
Spring, summer

The fast-flowing river contains attractive water-plants such as arrowhead and river water-crow-foot, while the trail includes several areas of other interest where plants such as ivy broomrape and yellow archangel occur. Over 70 bird species have been recorded here including heron, kingfisher and grey wagtail, with redstart, spotted flycatcher, sparrowhawk and kestrel.

Goblin Combe

ST 476652; 9ha; AWT reserve
Steep valley woodland and limestone grassland
Spring, summer

The approach to the reserve is along a woodland footpath deep in the bed of the combe. Tall ash trees, beech, sycamore and yew stand above hazel and box; the ground cover has the richness expected of limestone with deep beds of dog's mercury and enchanter's-nightshade fringed with wood melick. The shrub layer includes privet and field maple, while rubbly screes fanning downwards from unseen cliffs above may show stinking hellebore. Where the crags do show between the trees they are hung with ivy and decorated with the lifting crowns of hart's-tongue.

Within the reserve an area of dense old coppice woodland, under some large old oak trees, gives way to more scree and then to craggy downland. The screes are bare of plants, or colonised by bramble, wild madder and wild rose, with privet and sapling yew beginning to stabilise them. Wood sage and marjoram show as the scree

Goblin Combe: small copper butterfly on marjoram.

consolidates into grassland and the smaller herbs appear.

These downland slopes are shallow-turfed but support an amazing variety of small, colourful plants which include quaking-grass, common rock-rose, yellow-wort, and dwarf thistle. Along with many other butterflies common blue, small copper and marbled white may be seen on the sunlit slopes.

Above the slopes the grassland levels out, a most spectacular viewpoint from which the combe is overlooked, a vista of mixed woodland, dark yew contrasting with ash, beech and oak, against the sloping uniform dark background of the conifer plantations to the west. Here, above the broken slopes with thickets of hawthorn, whitebeam, yew, ash, spindle and wayfaring-tree, the more acid-loving birch and oak take over and bell heather shows in the grassland, adding a heathland touch to this beautiful reserve.

Kingsweston Down

ST 553781; 25ha; AWT reserve
Grassland and woodland
Summer

A flat hilltop site of unimproved limestone grass-land surrounded by woods provides an ideal habitat for many butterflies including purple hairstreak, holly blue and brimstone. There is also a good variety of flowers such as harebell, yellow rattle, red bartsia and wild basil.

Lawrence Weston Meadows

ST 545792; 11.9ha; AWT reserve
Grassland and wetland
Summer

It is extraordinary to find such excellent hay meadows in an urban area. The neutral and acid grassland contains meadow-rue, ragged-Robin, creeping-Jenny and meadowsweet. There are breeding reed warblers and tree sparrows, and both green and great spotted woodpecker, lesser whitethroats and long-tailed tits visit the reserve. The site supports many species of the more common butterflies.

Limebreach Wood

ST 466725; 6ha; AWT reserve
Old coppiced woodland
Spring, early summer

A block of important ancient woodland containing old coppiced small-leaved lime, the reserve is being re-coppiced to maintain its richness.

Littleton Brickpits

Permit only; 6ha; AWT reserve
Extensive reedbed
Can be overlooked from sea wall at ST 590912
Spring, autumn

The reserve is a good site for migrant birds and typical reedbed species such as reed bunting, and reed and sedge warbler.

Middle Hope

ST 330660; 8ha; NT–AWT reserve
Limestone grassland, scrub and saltings
Access by foot only from Sand Bay car park
All year

The limestone flowers are attractive in spring and early summer, with bird interest in Sand Bay and the Severn Estuary all year round but particularly at migration times.

Midger

Permit only; c. 9ha; GTNC reserve
Limestone woodland
Permit may be extended to cover 32ha of neighbouring estate
Leaflet from GTNC or AWT
Spring, early summer

The mixed woodland contains a good range of tree and shrub species and a rich ground cover including the lime-loving specialities green hellebore, columbine and herb-Paris. Bird interest is increased by the presence of streamside species.

Steepholm

Permit only; 20ha; Kenneth Allsop Memorial Trust reserve
Steep-cliffed limestone island
Access by boat from Weston-super-Mare
Leaflets from KAMT
Day trips Saturdays April–October

This fascinating island reserve supports an interesting range of plants, including wild leek and peony. Animals include slow-worm, which may grow half a metre long, breeding cormorant, lesser and great black-backed gull, and an important colony of herring gulls. Peregrine falcons have now returned to the island. There is a small colony of muntjac and a large number of hedgehogs.

Stockwood Open Space

ST 625693; 24.5ha; AWT reserve
Grassland, woodland and wetland
Leaflets from AWT
Summer

Moschatel, wood anemone, yellow archangel and Bath asparagus are found in the mixed broadleaved woodland, while the limestone grassland supports common spotted-orchid, dyer's greenweed, cowslip and yellow rattle. Tawny and little owls, cuckoo, lesser whitethroat and blackcap all breed, and many common butterflies occur.

Tucking Mill

Permit only; 1ha; AWT reserve
Grassland and woodland
Trail leaflet available
Spring, summer

Appropriately for a reserve on the outskirts of Bath, the wood contains Bath asparagus as well as ramsons, bluebells and woodruff. In the unimproved grassland cowslips are followed by pyrami-

Peony grows wild on Steepholm.

dal and bee orchids, and later clustered bellflower, devil's-bit scabious and autumn gentian come into flower. Sparrowhawk, green and great spotted woodpeckers and treecreeper can be seen in the woods, while the variety of flowers attracts dark green fritillary and marbled white butterflies.

Upton Cheyney

ST 699704; 2.8ha; WdT reserve
Mixed woodland
Spring, summer

Three fields have been planted up with mixed broadleaf trees to create a small woodland characteristic of the rolling countryside of the area.

Weston Big Wood

ST 455750; 38ha; AWT reserve
Ancient woodland
Spring

This oak, ash and lime woodland has an outstanding ground flora including herb-Paris, twayblade, early-purple orchid, toothwort and woodruff.

Weston Moor

Permit only; 4ha; AWT reserve
Rich wetland reedbed
All year

This is the last remaining reedbed in the Gordano Valley and is managed to retain its breeding populations of reed, sedge and grasshopper warbler. Because of agricultural drainage, the wetland has been drying out, severely threatening the reedbeds, but the AWT has now erected a windpump which will lift water into the reserve and encourage a stronger growth of the vital common reed.

Drying out of the peat has meant that many of the beautiful and important plants have been suppressed by the invasion of bramble, hemp agrimony and rosebay and great willowherb. Even in its generally drier state the reserve is still an exciting rich wetland with the reedbeds full of yellow iris and purple-loosestrife, greater bird's-foot-trefoil and meadowsweet. Tussocks of purple moor-grass replace some areas of reed and these are bright with tormentil, marsh thistle, devil's-bit scabious, marsh pennywort and water mint. The drier areas are taken over by bracken.

A number of shrubs have grown up, spreading from the strip of woodland on the east edge of the reserve. These include birch and hawthorn, willow, guelder-rose, alder and a particularly good growth of alder buckthorn, important as a foodplant of the brimstone butterfly. The woodland belt itself is chiefly alder, with sycamore, hawthorn, willow and ash, and stands above a ground cover of ivy with ferns such as broad buckler-fern and lady-fern.

Weston Woods Nature Trail

ST 327627; 1–3km; Woodspring DC
Mixed woodland
Leaflet from WDC
Spring, early summer

The woodland is largely a planted area of sycamore with oak, ash, sweet chestnut and poplar trees above a rather limited ground cover which includes toothwort. Birds include woodland species such as warblers, goldcrest and kestrel, while sunlit clearings are enjoyed by butterflies such as brimstone, comma and peacock.

Wetmoor

Permit only; 20ha; GTNC reserve
Damp ancient woodland
Booklet and leaflet from GTNC
Spring, early summer

The fine coppiced woodland has rich butterfly, moth and insect life, a good variety of spring flowers and abundant nightingales.

Willsbridge Mill

ST 665707; 8ha; AWT reserve
Wildlife and countryside centre open April–October
Leaflet from visitor centre
All year

The steep-sided valley of the Siston Brook contains a disused quarry and a deep old railway cutting which show the geological interest of the area, while woodland, scrub, meadowland and ponds display a good range of wildlife.

A heron nesting. Cleeve Heronry in Avon is one of the most important breeding sites for herons.

Bluebells bring spring colour to woodland glades.

Berkshire

The Royal County of Berkshire extends over the region once called the Royal Forest of Windsor, which stretched from Windsor to Hungerford, and includes the lower reaches of two Thames tributary streams, the Kennet and the Loddon; the Loddon has given its name to two rare and beautiful plants, a lily and a pondweed. In the north west and extreme south west, chalk, which underlies so much of the county, gives rise to rolling waterless downland similar to the whalebacked South Downs. In the east the dominant soils, supporting a rather monotonous plant life, have formed on heavy, ill-drained London clay. In parts of the south and south east there are large infertile tracts of plateau gravels and sandy Eocene beds that support heath vegetation, which reverts to birch and oak woodland if not regularly burnt. Exposed rock is extremely rare in the county though sandstone boulders, called sarsens, occur very locally near Lambourn and support interesting lichens.

Historical records show that by AD 1600 only a tenth of the county was still wooded, and the proportion of woodland has changed very little in the last four centuries. The natural forest was probably oak, with alder in the wetter valleys and some beech around Streatley and Bisham. Beech does not appear to have extended along the Berkshire Downs. From the evidence of certain plants, lichens and bark beetles, fragments of ancient forest have been located at Windsor, Ashridge Wood, Clay Hill, Snelsmore, Hamstead Park, Riva Copse (which has the rare snail *Ena montana*) and other sites. One old-woodland plant, the wild service-tree, is widespread east of Reading. Elms have long been a feature of the hedgerows, but only sucker shoots have survived the recent outbreak of disease. This has had a disastrous effect on associated species, such as bark lichens and the large tortoiseshell and white-letter hairstreak butterflies.

Heathland has declined in area following its use for building, gravel extraction and conifer plantation. The abandoned gravelpits, however, can provide nesting sites for sand martin or little ringed plover and, near Ascot, an old brickpit has developed into a *Sphagnum* bog. Dwarf gorse does not occur further west than Berkshire, nor does the bent *Agrostis curtisii* occur much further east, but both grow at INKPEN COMMON.

The relative proportions of grassland and arable have fluctuated dramatically since the early eighteenth century. Today, there is more than twice as much arable as grassland, but 50 years ago the reverse was true. It is now hard to find old permanent meadows and pastures, though most of them have traces of ridge and furrow. All types of grassland can still be seen in the county, however, from the acid ridges of WINDSOR GREAT PARK, with their flora of dwarf ephemeral plants, mosses, ferns and lichens, to the orchid-rich chalk turf of the Berkshire Downs, Inkpen Downs or Winter Hill near Maidenhead. On the chalk, there are at least two good colonies of pasqueflower, and a few sites for rarities like the stone curlew, and the Adonis blue and silver-spotted skipper butterflies. Rich alluvial meadows are found by the Thames between Streatley and Reading and near Cookham, by the upper Loddon where there is a fine fritillary field, and especially along the Kennet. The Kennet is the favoured habitat of the tiny snail *Vertigo moulinsiana*. At least one reedbed along the Kennet has had bearded tits nesting on occasion.

The clear streams of the Pang and Kennet, with their sheets of common water-crowfoot in summer, contrast with the muddy Thames where all submerged vegetation is shredded by power-boats. The Thames still has one rare mollusc, *Gyraulis acronicus*, found nowhere else in Britain, but the river's aquatic plants are now confined to backwaters. Another freshwater mollusc, the tiny *Pisidium tenuilineatum*, has only been found on the Loddon. A large gravelpit at Sandhurst is remarkable for its wealth of aquatic plants, which include six-stamened waterwort and needle spike-rush, which forms a fringing turf kept short by grazing Canada geese. By the lower Loddon many huge gravelpits are now being dug, and it is to be hoped that an equally rich aquatic flora will spread there.

The weedy vegetation of Berkshire is extensive, but the widespread use of weedkillers has made good fields hard to find. Areas close to towns affected by planning blight are often weed refuges. On the chalk wild candytuft, pheasant's-eye, the small fumitories and broad-fruited cornsalad are extremely local, but may be survivors of three millennia of arable farming. On acid soils mouse-tail, lesser snapdragon and lamb's succory are sporadic. A few corncockle plants are kept going each year by a co-operative farmer. Among the rather large number of alien plants established in Berkshire are yellow figwort, the dock-like beet *Beta trigyna*, and spring crocus which colours a whole field at Inkpen each year.

H.J.M. BOWEN

Avery's Pightle

SU 435651; 1.3ha; BBONT reserve
Meadow
Summer

The species-rich, low-lying paddock contains notable plants such as pepper saxifrage, dyer's greenweed, broad-leaved helleborine, adder's-tongue, heath-grass and whorl-grass.

Blackwater Reach Meadow

SU 843608; 1ha; BBONT–Sandhurst Town Council reserve
Meadow
Summer

The rough, wet meadow contains a large number of plant species for so small an area. These include sneezewort, meadow thistle, ragged-Robin, betony, devil's-bit scabious, marsh stitchwort and five species of sedge.

Bowdown Woods

SU 504657; 20ha; BBONT reserve
Mixed woodland
Open to public along path only
Spring, summer

The wooded scarp which drops down to the floor of the Kennet Valley is deeply incised with numerous valleys carrying small, spring-fed, nutrient-poor streams. They are clothed mainly with alder, which grows from large old coppice stools. The higher ground supports oak, birch, hazel, rowan and cherry. The ground flora is rich and includes an unusual number of woodland plant species indicative of its ancient woodland status.

Broadmoor Bottom

See OWLSMOOR BOG AND HEATHS

Dinton Pastures Country Park

SU 785718; 111ha; Wokingham DC
Flooded gravelpits
Leaflets from WDC or site
Spring, early summer

Even so close to the motorway the lakes draw a good variety of birds, while the plant life of meadow, lakeside and water is attractively varied and includes the delicate summer snowflake, a plant locally called the Loddon lily. A nature trail guide illustrates much of the interest of the park and demonstrates the wildlife importance of these gravel pits which now form chains along so many of our major river valleys.

Edgbarrow Woods

SU 837632; 31.2ha; Bracknell DC reserve
Lowland heath
Leaflet from BDC
Spring, summer

The higher ground is wooded with planted or self-sown Scots pine, birch and rowan, but the dry heaths carry a good range of characteristic species such as heather, bell heather, gorse and dwarf gorse, while the wetter areas are distinguished by cross-leaved heath, purple moor-grass and bog asphodel. Among the butterflies recorded regularly are grayling and silver-studded blue, and both fox and emperor moths may be found on the dry heath.

Englemere Pond Nature Trail

SU 902684; 1.2km; Bracknell DC
Lake and heathland
Leaflet from BDC
Spring, summer

Waterbirds, reedbed birds and insect takers such as swallow and sand martin may be seen at the lake, which has considerable stands of common reed and grades through fringes of *Sphagnum* mosses, common cottongrass and the attractive marsh St John's-wort to spreads of heath and invading woodland, rich in many forms of typical wildlife.

Hurley Chalk Pit

SU 813820; 1.4ha; BBONT reserve
Disused chalkpit
Spring, summer

Open chalk, scree, scrub grassland and a narrow beech woodland all contribute to the variety of this tiny reserve, rich in plant species such as bee, fragrant and pyramidal orchid and the strange-looking earth-star fungus.

Inkpen Common

SU 382641; 10.4ha; BBONT reserve
Heathland with small bog
Spring, early summer

Although gorse may sometimes look as brash and vivid as yellow-wort or cowslip, in a heathland setting, moderated by the colours of heather, bell heather and paler cross-leaved heath, it seems to glow like captured sunshine. Inkpen Common shows both the subtle colours of the heathlands and also the gemlike smaller plants adapted to such areas.

Gorse and birch form a scrub which shelters the common, providing, with hawthorn, a choice of nesting sites suitable for linnet and nightingale and, perhaps, ground-nesting nightjar. Much of the common is kept open, mown from time to time to keep the scrub from taking over, the effect being that of areas of coarse grass, with regrowing heather being separated by gorse hedges. The grassland contains typical acid heathland plants such as sheep's sorrel, heath bedstraw and tormentil with heath milkwort and lousewort.

The common has suffered badly from fire damage in the past, allowing in invaders such as rosebay willowherb, but heather is regrowing now, a contrast in its tender greenness with the unburned uncut areas where gorse and birch scrub stand above the coarse and leggy old heather plants. The damper ground supports common spotted-orchid and, by the stream, a belt of wet woodland, full of willow, is bright with marsh-marigold, lesser spearwort and ragged-Robin.

On the drier areas bracken may alternate with the grassland, and seedling oak trees have become established with rowan but, as with most heathland areas, the most attractive plants are in the wetter parts. Among the other small bog plants at Inkpen are the typical bog asphodel and bogbean, far more attractive than its name.

A speciality of the reserve is the presence, in the grassy paths, of pale dog-violet which is not known to occur at any other site in Berkshire.

Lily Hill Park Trail

SU 887694; 34.8ha; Bracknell DC
Ornamental parkland
Tree trail leaflet from BDC
Spring, early summer

A wide variety of exotic tree and shrub species forms most of the park woodland, but sufficient native trees have invaded to improve the resident wildlife and the range of birds includes greenfinch, nuthatch, treecreeper and long-tailed tit.

Moor Copse

SU 635742; 22.4ha; BBONT reserve
Damp woodland and riverside
Spring, early summer

Three areas of woodland make up the major part of this reserve, which is bisected by a river. The woods are surprisingly different from each other, providing a range of type over a small area, while the river adds further interest.

Little grebe, water rail and moorhen breed along the river, together with mallard and tufted duck, and the sheltered banks provide ideal sites for water vole and water shrew. One of the specialities of the reserve is the richness of its Lepidoptera, with upwards of 300 species recorded.

Northerams Woods

SU 856682; 3ha; BBONT reserve
Woodland and grassland
Spring, summer

The reserve consists of mixed deciduous woodland on London Clay with small areas of damp meadow, improved grassland and scrub. Over 100 plant species and 17 butterflies have been recorded, and the area is also excellent for birds.

Owlsmoor Bog and Heaths

SU 845632; 26ha; BBONT reserve
Heath and mixed woodland
Spring, summer

The reserve is adjacent to EDGBARROW WOODS and together with Broadmoor Bottom forms the largest and most important area of heathland in east Berkshire. Flowers include two species of sundew, bog asphodel and white-beaked sedge, while at BROADMOOR BOTTOM (SU 855627) there is ideal habitat for woodlark, stonechat and hobby.

Ridgeway Path

SU 464848–595807; 15km; CC
Part of ancient chalkland way
Leaflet from CC and booklet from HMSO bookshops
Spring, summer

Based on an age-old route along the top of the hills, the Ridgeway Path gives a superb picture of chalk downland north of the Thames, with its wide high skies and rich pattern of colourful chalkland flowers.

Snelsmore Common Country Park

SU 463711; 58.4ha; Newbury DC
Lowland heath
Leaflet from NDC
Spring, summer

Woodland, heathland and valley bog are the main aspects of the common, encouraging a good range of bird life which includes nightjar, grasshopper warbler and woodcock, with occasional visits from sparrowhawk and hobby. Plants include bog asphodel and bogbean.

Thatcham Reedbeds

SU 501673; 12.8ha; Newbury DC reserve
Reedbeds, marsh and wet woodland
Permit only off rights of way
All year

The reserve is part of a more extensive area which makes up one of the largest and most important reedbeds in southern England. Its continuity as a wetland area and the deep beds of common reed make Thatcham Reedbeds a very important staging post for migrant birds and a reservoir of winter food and shelter.

The reserve is mainly reedbed, marsh and wet woodland, where the marsh is a mix of grasses, sedges and tall herbs and the wet woodland consists chiefly of alder and willow species standing over a damp ground cover of pendulous sedge and great horsetail.

The importance of the reedbeds can be seen in the presence of several uncommon moths, the larvae of which all live on or in common reed alone – moths such as brown-veined, obscure, silky, southern and twin spot wainscot. The marshes are also very important for other moths and an expert might need only to look at a list of Thatcham's moths to describe some of the marsh plants there: the blackneck moth predicts tufted vetch, the butterbur moth tells of spreads of the butterbur plant, the dentated pug of yellow loosestrife, the scarce burnished brass of hemp-agrimony and the scarlet tiger of comfrey. All are rare moths, and all are present here because of the large populations of their food plants.

In spring and autumn, Thatcham may be flocked with migrants, including warblers, swallows and martins. In summer, too, warblers abound and the reedbeds, marshes and scrub hold large breeding numbers of reed and sedge warbler, together with grasshopper warbler, nightingale, water rail, little grebe and tufted duck.

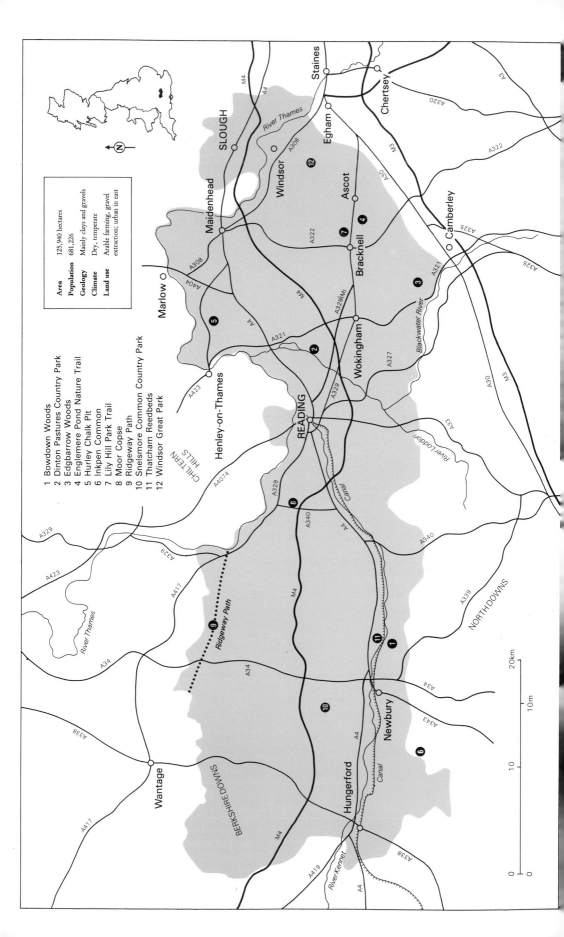

Area 125,940 hectares
Population 681,226
Geology Mainly clays and gravels
Climate Dry, temperate
Land use Arable farming, gravel extraction; urban in east

1 Bowdown Woods
2 Dinton Pastures Country Park
3 Edgbarrow Woods
4 Englemere Pond Nature Trail
5 Hurley Chalk Pit
6 Inkpen Common
7 Lily Hill Park Trail
8 Moor Copse
9 Ridgeway Path
10 Snelsmore Common Country Park
11 Thatcham Reedbeds
12 Windsor Great Park

In winter, some 50 bird species have been recorded, including up to 1000 wrens, with flocks of goldcrest, treecreeper and tit species, with gatherings of finches, with siskin and redpoll, redwing and fieldfare, and pochard, teal, wigeon, snipe and jack snipe.

The reedbeds have attracted uncommon species such as great reed warbler, Baillon's crake and spotted crake, while the area is the only known Berkshire site for the stonefly *Leuctra geniculata* and the beetles *Leistus rufescens* and *Phyllobius viridicollis*.

Windsor Great Park

SU 953735; 6000ha; Crown Estate Commissioners
Ancient hunting forest
Booklet from NCC
Spring, early summer

An oak tree near Forest Gate is reputed to be some 800 years old. Many of the other old oak trees, hollow, riven, seemingly stunted, are thought to be some 500 years old. The large mature oaks in the park were planted from Elizabethan times onwards to supply timber for the ships of the navy. This continuity of woodland life, shared only with a very few old forests, preserves at Windsor a wonderful community of plants and animals, rivalled in variety and interest only by the NEW FOREST (Hampshire and the Isle of Wight).

Roughly half of the present area of the Great Park and Forest is wooded, a mixture of ancient pollards with park trees, high-forest woodland, coppice, mixed woodland and coniferous trees. Old beech woodland supplements the importance of the oak and the NCC have declared an 18ha block of the finest surviving original oak–beech woods as a forest nature reserve. Oak is the food plant for over 280 species of insects and beech too has its complement of important species.

The area has long been famous for its bird life with breeding species including sparrowhawk and little owl, a number of warblers, all three British woodpeckers and other insect-takers such as nuthatch, treecreeper and redstart. On the heathland fringe to the south hobby, nightjar, woodlark and stonechat breed, while Virginia Water, renowned for its wildfowl, is one of the foremost sites for mandarin duck, now a British breeding species, together with gadwall, pochard, shoveler, shelduck, tufted duck, teal and wigeon. Over 30 butterfly species are recorded including silver-studded and holly blue, painted lady, white admiral and five species of skipper. Red and fallow deer are present but rarely seen and there are populations of roe and muntjac. Some 400ha of the Great Park is now a deer park; 19 red hinds were brought from Balmoral in 1979 and the herd has now multiplied to over 300.

The greatest interest to naturalists probably lies in the fungi and insects associated with the ancient trees. The fungi include rare species of *Boletus* while over 2000 beetle species have been identified here, together with a number of rare Diptera, including *Chrysopilus lactus* and *Rainieria calceata* at their only known British locality.

Typical rolling chalkland of the Berkshire Downs, rich in orchids.

Buckinghamshire

Like Caesar's Gaul, Buckinghamshire is divided into three parts: a northern region that is part of the Midlands; the Vale of Aylesbury in the middle, considered by many to be the most English part of the English countryside; and the core of the Chilterns in the south, sandwiched between Oxfordshire and Hertfordshire and sloping down to the opulent towns and villages of the Thames Valley.

Northern Buckinghamshire lies largely on oolitic limestone, although it is not marked by the characteristic stone walls of the Cotswolds to the south west or Northamptonshire to the north east. It is very agricultural limestone countryside, from which any rolling lime-rich downland has long since been eliminated by the plough and the government grant.

But it is also still very wooded, with some fine fragments of the extensive oak forest that once covered most of the Midlands – SALCEY FOREST, which is half in Northamptonshire (where it is described), as is Whittlewood Forest, and Whaddon Chase. The eastern side of this region is now being slowly engulfed in the new town of Milton Keynes, leaving an isolated fragment of rural Buckinghamshire north of the Ouse around the eighteenth-century poet William Cowper's magical little town of Olney, perhaps the only place in the county with an echo of the flavour of an eighteenth- or nineteenth-century market town.

Despite the rapid growth of the town of Aylesbury, the Vale is still very rural and you can still find gated roads and splendid minor roads that take you through the green countryside, deserted since the Enclosures, straight to the old county town of Buckingham. Here is as good a place to search for deserted villages as anywhere in the Midlands. Again the Vale is very agricultural, with only scattered woodlands to vary the hedged landscape of green and brown fields. But it is still a hedged landscape, and the farmers and landowners deserve praise for resisting the temptation to rip out hedges as others have done elsewhere in England. At the eastern end of the Vale, on the borders of Bedfordshire, is one of the few areas north of the Thames where the greensand becomes an important landscape feature. The mini-escarpments and fragments of heathland still surviving around the Brickhills are similar to those of Wealden Sussex.

To many people Buckinghamshire means the Chilterns, and it was the Chilterns that gave the county its nickname, 'Beechy Bucks', which nowadays has faint echoes of John Betjeman's Metroland and the early motoring era, when venturesome London motorists discovered the wealth of woodland on their doorstep. The Chilterns form an astonishingly rural area so near to London, with more single-track roads than you will find elsewhere until you reach the Pennines or the Welsh Marches. There are still plenty of trees, most of them beeches, and more rare orchids than anywhere else in England west of the Medway.

Although the Chilterns are chalk hills, there is very little typical chalk grassland, for the tops of the hills are covered with a thick layer of clay with flints. Going south towards the Thames, the chalk is covered with various tertiary sands and gravels, culminating in Burnham Beeches with its ancient pollard trees including a few oaks. What little chalk downland there is lies mainly between IVINGHOE BEACON and the Chequers estate to the south. This stretch still has such treasures as pasqueflower and musk orchid, not to mention one of the three boxwoods in England that may be native.

The Thames itself is very respectable and sedate in Buckinghamshire, but there are still towpath walks around Great and Little Marlow, and the towering cliff of Cliveden bows the river out into what is now Berkshire on both banks. Even this tamed part of the Thames can still offer a fine stand of the Thames's special flower, summer snowflake, sometimes called the Loddon lily.

If the two-thirds of the county that lie north of the Chiltern escarpment have little semi-natural habitat left, except for a few oakwoods and a handful of marshy meadows, the Chilterns make up for the deficiency. Their well-known beechwoods and rolling chalk grasslands, many of them belonging to or managed by the National Trust and BBONT, put them high among the parts of southern England that every naturalist ought to know.

R.S.R. FITTER

Amersham Main Substation Nature Trail

Permit only; 2km; CEGB
Circular trail in substation grounds
Restricted site for use by Bucks Education Authority and BBONT. Leaflet from CEGB or BBONT
Spring, early summer

This varied trail runs through woodland and grassland rich in plant and animal life. Numerous bird species include blackcap, coal and marsh tit, goldcrest, kestrel and nuthatch.

Bernwood Forest

Permit only; 409ha; NCC–FC reserve
Invertebrate reserve
Spring, autumn

This large tract of mixed woodland includes a ride system.

Big Round Green

SU 972015; 5.7ha; WdT
Deciduous woodland
Spring, summer

Despite its name, this reserve is triangular in shape. It contains a mixture of ancient oak and hornbeam coppice and pollards, as well as field maple, wild cherry and holly.

Black Park Nature Trail

TQ 005833; 0.8km; BCC
Nature walk in country park
Booklet from site or BCC
Spring, early summer

The trail contrasts broad-leaved woodland with coniferous plantations and the plants and animals of the acid gravels with those of the lake.

Boarstall Decoy

SP 623151; 7.2ha; BBONT–NT reserve
Duck decoy in mixed woodland
Limited opening Good Friday–August Bank Holiday. No access at other times
Spring, summer

The practical working of a traditional decoy is demonstrated here, where the curious duck are worked down a narrowing netted channel by the antics of a trained decoying dog.

Buckingham Canal

SP 728357; 0.5km; BBONT reserve
Disused canal
Spring, summer

Open water and marshy areas make this reserve a good one for wetland plants and insects.

Buttler's Hangings

SU 818962; 4ha; BBONT reserve
Chalk grassland
Spring, summer

Rich downland with plants such as wild candytuft and blue fleabane; 26 species of butterfly have been recorded.

Calvert Jubilee

SP 684252; 37ha; BBONT reserve
Flooded claypit
Dangerous without a guide
All year

The pit is a deep islanded pool partly surrounded by sheltering trees and scrub. Some of the land around has been cleared, providing an open plateau which is being recolonised by vegetation, while the undisturbed margins are rich in scrub and meadow species with good numbers of common spotted-orchid.

The depth of the pool provides a more suitable site for divers than for dabblers, and probably explains the only infrequent visits of heron and kingfisher, but numbers generally should increase as the protected nature of the reserve is recognised. Even now well over 100 species have been recorded including great grey shrike and osprey.

Regular breeding species include great crested grebe, moorhen and coot on the pool, with the trees and scrubland providing nest sites for green woodpecker, magpie and bullfinch, and warblers such as blackcap and garden, sedge and willow warbler. Grasshopper warbler and nightingale are probable breeders.

Despite the lack of ideal shallows, the reserve may still draw visits from the passage waders – greenshank, redshank and common sandpiper, with rarer occurrences of other species. Black and common tern have also been recorded.

Tufted duck have two peaks, one in late summer when birds gather in the safety of the reserve to go through their moult, another when winter numbers build. Winter brings in the largest numbers of waterbirds. Regular wintering species include mallard, pochard and wigeon with smaller numbers of teal and with occasional gadwall, pintail, scaup and shoveler, goldeneye and goosander. The pool may be visited by Slavonian or black-necked grebe, and when the duck fly out to feed in the evening, it forms an important winter gull roost.

Chalkdell Wood

SP 900012; 1ha; WdT reserve
Small beech woodland
Spring, early summer

The woodland surrounds an old chalk quarry. Mainly beech, it includes lime and Scots pine above a typically varied Chiltern shrub layer. A rookery adds to the interest.

Chesham Bois Wood

SP 960003; 16ha; WdT reserve
Beech woodland
Spring, early summer

The wood is rich in species such as bluebell, together with coralroot, adapted to the shade.

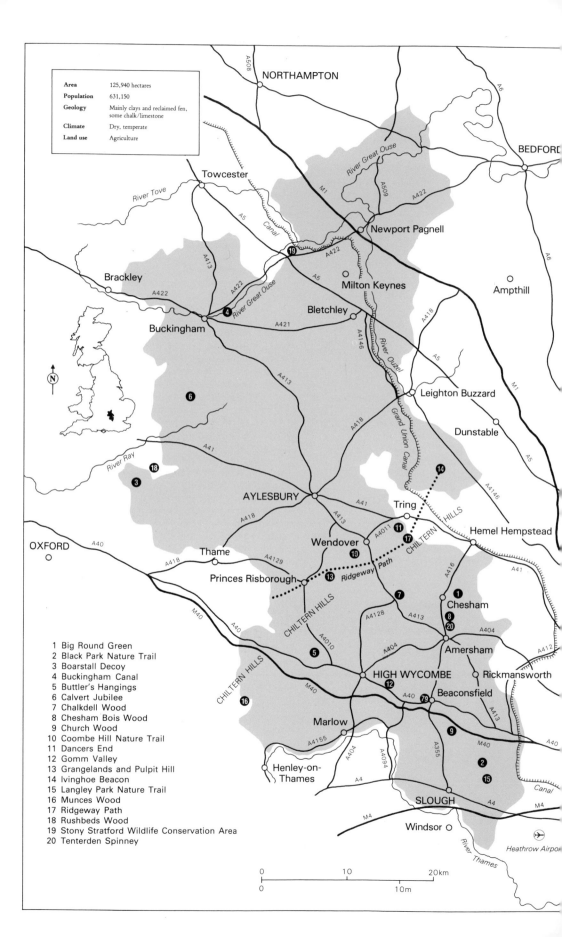

Area	125,940 hectares
Population	631,150
Geology	Mainly clays and reclaimed fen, some chalk/limestone
Climate	Dry, temperate
Land use	Agriculture

NORTHAMPTON

BEDFORD

River Tove

Towcester

River Great Ouse

Newport Pagnell

Brackley

Milton Keynes

Ampthill

Bletchley

Buckingham

Leighton Buzzard

River Ouzel

River Ray

Dunstable

AYLESBURY

Tring

Hemel Hempstead

OXFORD

Thame

Wendover

CHILTERN HILLS

Princes Risborough

Ridgeway Path

Chesham

Amersham

HIGH WYCOMBE

Rickmansworth

Beaconsfield

Marlow

CHILTERN HILLS

Henley-on-Thames

SLOUGH

Windsor

Heathrow Airport

River Thames

Grand Union Canal

1 Big Round Green
2 Black Park Nature Trail
3 Boarstall Decoy
4 Buckingham Canal
5 Buttler's Hangings
6 Calvert Jubilee
7 Chalkdell Wood
8 Chesham Bois Wood
9 Church Wood
10 Coombe Hill Nature Trail
11 Dancers End
12 Gomm Valley
13 Grangelands and Pulpit Hill
14 Ivinghoe Beacon
15 Langley Park Nature Trail
16 Munces Wood
17 Ridgeway Path
18 Rushbeds Wood
19 Stony Stratford Wildlife Conservation Area
20 Tenterden Spinney

0   10   20km

0   10m

Church Wood

SU 973873; 14ha; RSPB reserve
Mixed woodland, and scrub grassland
Spring, early summer

Woodland and grassy scrub, together with a recently built pond, provide a wide range of suitable sites for birds in the reserve and this has resulted in some 80 recorded species, over half of which breed. The wood, on a slope of flinty clay above a chalky bedrock, is very varied, chiefly of birch but with areas of oak, beech, and ash and mixed throughout with other species including tall exotic conifers. Much of the ground cover is dense bramble, providing ideal nest sites for many small birds, but clearings and more open areas allow a good variety of woodland plants to flourish. The grassland area, the paddock, has been invaded by willow and aspen, tangled with bramble, or has an open scrub of hawthorn, again providing convenient nest sites and singing posts.

Some 200 plant species have been identified, which show both the rather acid nature of the clays, with birch–oak–bramble as a natural cover, and the effect of chalk in adding more interesting species such as hornbeam, yew and box. Butcher's-broom is found in clumps within the wood, as are green hellebore and Solomon's-seal. Primrose, bugle, wood spurge and violets grow in the open rides, while damper clearings show ragged-Robin and common spotted-orchid. The pool adds plants such as sedges, rushes and yellow iris.

A good variety of butterflies includes white admiral, purple and white-letter hairstreak and the beautiful holly blue; mammals include muntjac deer, fox and weasel, together with grey squirrel.

The major management at Church Wood is for the birds which share the habitats. Blackcap and garden warbler nest in the less dense woodland and tall bramble; magpie and jay prefer the taller trees; pheasant and woodcock nest upon the ground; hole-nesting birds find, or make, holes in the standing trees or use the nest boxes provided. The pool encourages water-loving species; mallard and moorhen will breed there, heron visit, pied and sometimes grey wagtail work the edges, and snipe probe the marshy ground. The wood sees the spring and autumn passage of many other species, with wintering flocks of fieldfare and redwing, siskin and redpoll.

Coombe Hill Nature Trail

SP 853063; 2km; NT
Chiltern Hills walk
Leaflet from NT
Spring, summer

Acid plants such as broom, gorse and heather contrast with the chalk-loving species such as juniper, yew and whitebeam below. The trail affords superb views across the clay vale and to the Cotswolds and the Berkshire Downs.

Dancers End

SP 900095; 31ha; BBONT reserve
Wood, scrub and grassland
Spring, summer

A very rich variety of plant species, with abundant Chiltern gentian, and of associated insects, may be seen in this area which has an interesting contrast between acid clay with flints above and chalk richness below.

Gomm Valley

SU 898922; 4ha; BBONT reserve
Chalk grassland, scrub and woodland
Spring, summer

Rather overgrown with scrub, the reserve is notable for its butterflies with over 30 species recorded.

Gomm Valley: an area of woodland adds to the wide variety of the reserve, famous for its chalkland butterflies.

Grangelands and Pulpit Hill

SP 827049; 26ha; BBONT–NT reserve
Chalk downland, scrub and beech woodland
Spring, summer

This complex of three areas is rich in plant species such as bird's-nest orchid and narrow-lipped helleborine, *Epipactis leptochila*, with a good variety of butterflies and birds.

Ivinghoe Beacon

SP 961168; 400ha; NT
Chalk grassland and scrub
Spring, summer

The slopes of the Beacon are grassed or trodden into chalky pathways while the hills have an open scrub of hawthorn, with species such as wayfaring-tree and whitebeam, over deep or thinner grassland depending on the steepness of the slope. Competition from the coarser grasses tends to smother the small chalk plants where the soil is deeper, so the richest areas are those steep slopes where the soil is shallowest. Salad burnet and common rock-rose are widespread and there are good numbers of cowslip, even under the denser areas of scrub, but the banks of the old cart-tracks and the steepest slopes of the hills hold the richest collection of plants and attract the widest range of chalkland butterflies.

Kidney vetch and horseshoe vetch, both important food plants for blue butterfly species, grow with common bird's-foot-trefoil, milkwort and wild thyme. Bladder campion, wild mignonette, yellow rattle and quaking-grass also occur, together with common-spotted orchid, fragrant orchid and, here and there, adder's-tongue.

Deep coarse grasses, gorse and mixed scrub on the hilltops show where the chalk is topped by clay with flints and mark the upper level of the chalkland richness. In the natural course of events the whole area would return to woodland, only small areas remaining as herb-rich grasslands with chalkland flowers, areas too steep for scrub to gain a foothold. Grazing and scrub clearance are the usual methods for keeping grassland open, often at the expense of excluding public access.

The public are so often accused of damage through trampling and flower picking that the points of greatest interest here are not only that some trampling acts as a grass control, in the absence of grazing, and allows the smaller plants to gain a foothold, but also that some of the finest shows of fragrant orchid stand beside and in a much-used pathway – with not a sign of damage.

Langley Park Nature Trail

TQ 016824; 1.6km; BCC
Parkland and woodland including gardens
Booklet from BCC
Spring, early summer

A number of ancient oak trees with many exotics and coniferous plantations add interest to the trail which is laid out in part of the County Council's green belt estate.

Munces Wood

SU 746893; 2.1ha; WdT reserve
Mixed woodland
Spring, summer

The wood is split into two parts and includes an interesting range of trees and shrubs such as beech, wild cherry, whitebeam, holly and yew.

Ridgeway Path

SP 770013–961168; 30km; CC
Part of ancient chalkland way
Leaflet from CC and booklet from HMSO bookshops
Spring, summer

The final, eastern section of this fascinating long-distance way passes briefly through a limb of Hertfordshire before ending at the steep chalk knoll of IVINGHOE BEACON. As well as the beauties of its flora and fauna the path gives spectacular views across the plain of the Vale of Aylesbury.

Rushbeds Wood

SP 668157; 45ha; BBONT reserve
Ancient woodland
Spring, summer

Nearly 100 species of flowering plants have been recorded, reflecting the reserve's ancient status. The wood is excellent for butterflies, with purple emperor, black hairstreak and white admiral. Fallow deer are occasionally seen and there are thriving populations of both fox and muntjac.

Stony Stratford Wildlife Conservation Area

SP 785412; 22.3ha; BBONT reserve
Disused gravel workings
Permit only to main reserve area
All year

Opened in 1980, this reserve was restored and designed first and foremost for breeding redshank and other waders. Considerable work has been carried out, including the erection of a hide and nesting boxes, and the transfer of water plants from the nearby Grand Union Canal. Shingle and mud islands have been established in the now water-filled pits, along with the scrub islands which provide cover for nesting. Sand martin and kingfisher banks have also been constructed. A good selection of waders and wildfowl now make use of the reserve, including ringed plover, curlew and redshank.

Tenterden Spinney

SU 967995; 2ha; WdT reserve
Mixed woodland
Spring, summer

A mixed woodland now surrounded by houses. A footpath provides good access.

Whitecross Green Wood

Described under Oxfordshire.

Cornwall and the Isles of Scilly

Cornwall is the most southerly county in Britain and the most westerly in England. Almost an island, cut off from the rest of the country by the River Tamar, it is over 120km long with no part of it more than 24km from the sea. This shape and situation mean that Cornwall has a relatively warm and wet climate, with tearing salt-laden winds constantly sweeping across a landscape full of strong contrasts: bare cliff faces scorched by the wind, then followed suddenly by great swathes of brightly coloured flowers; stark, desolate moors with pockets of wetland alive with their own glorious plant life; ancient oakwoods in the valleys; deep-cut lanes; and the ever-changing shoreline.

The soils themselves are mostly derived from Devonian and carboniferous sedimentary rocks known as the Cornish killas, and from the granite spine which runs through the length of Cornwall, though exposed only on the higher moors: Bodmin Moor, Hensbarrow, Carnmenellis and West Penwith, where the granite actually meets the sea. China clay and the lodes of tin and copper are derivatives of the granite; their excavation and exploitation have created a strange 'lunar' landscape which presents formidable conservation problems.

The highest hills are on Bodmin Moor (Brown Willy, 420m, and Rough Tor, 400m), an area of open moorland, tors, clitter slopes, bogs and streams. There is less heather than there used to be because of grazing pressure and improvement schemes, but orchids, insect-eating sundews, bogbean and other wetland plants may be found, as well as rare mosses and lichens. Mysterious, isolated Dozmary Pool, an upland tarn steeped in Cornish legend, nestles among the hills and attracts wintering wildfowl and wading birds, as do certain recently constructed reservoirs, notably Crowdy which already looks convincingly natural and is a favourite haunt of ornithologists.

The granite of the moors reappears from the ocean as the ISLES OF SCILLY, a group of 145 rocks and islands, only five of which are inhabited. The Scillies are famed for their breeding colonies of seabirds and for rare migrants, grey seals and the Scilly shrew which, unlike most of its kind, favours stony beaches. The island of Annet is a nature reserve, and the whole group is carefully protected.

The moorland and plateau surfaces of THE LIZARD, the heel of Cornwall, are not part of the granite but consist of alkaline soils derived from Pre-Cambrian serpentinite rocks and boulder-strewn gabbro. They support a unique plant life including Cornish heath and a number of lime-loving plants which are rare in Cornwall. This important area is now well protected by the LOWER PREDANNACK reserves.

The Lizard is only a small though by no means insignificant part of Cornwall's greatest glory, the 650km long coast which reaches its climax in the bare rocks and towering cliffs of north Cornwall, High Cliff (223m) being the highest point. The line of harsh, wild north-coast cliffs is broken only at a few places: the CAMEL ESTUARY, rich in bird life; the HAYLE ESTUARY, a favourite refuge for migrating and wintering waders; and the dune areas of Penhale Sands and Phillack Towans where the lime-rich sand supports fascinating plant communities. At Dizzard a strange stunted oak forest stretches down exposed landslip slopes almost to sea level. Below Beeny, Pentire Head and Godrevy seals breed, and gorse, thrift, spring squill, scurvygrass, kidney vetch, common bird's-foot-trefoil, rock samphire and wild carrot abound. There are countless nesting places for seabirds – auks, fulmar, kittiwake and other gulls – and one or two peregrine eyries. Stonechat, jackdaw, wheatear and pipits enliven the cliff tops. The coast itself is bare, but sheltered valleys inland are often wooded, two of the best examples being at Marsland on the Devon border (described under WELCOMBE AND MARSHLAND VALLEYS) and the Valency Valley at Boscastle, both of which contain reserves. And wherever the sea meets the land, there is the constantly varying scene of moving tides exposing and then covering again mussel beds, banks of seaweeds, and rock pools.

The south coast is different in character. Here the scenery is gentler, and the cliffs are lower and less abrupt. Most Cornish rivers flow towards the south and open out into estuaries bounded by woods and edged by saltmarsh where waders and wildfowl feed. All the river valleys are interesting to naturalists, and there are reserves proper in both the TAMAR and FAL-RUAN ESTUARIES.

Inland, deciduous woods are mostly dominated by oak and ash with hazel, hawthorn, holly and

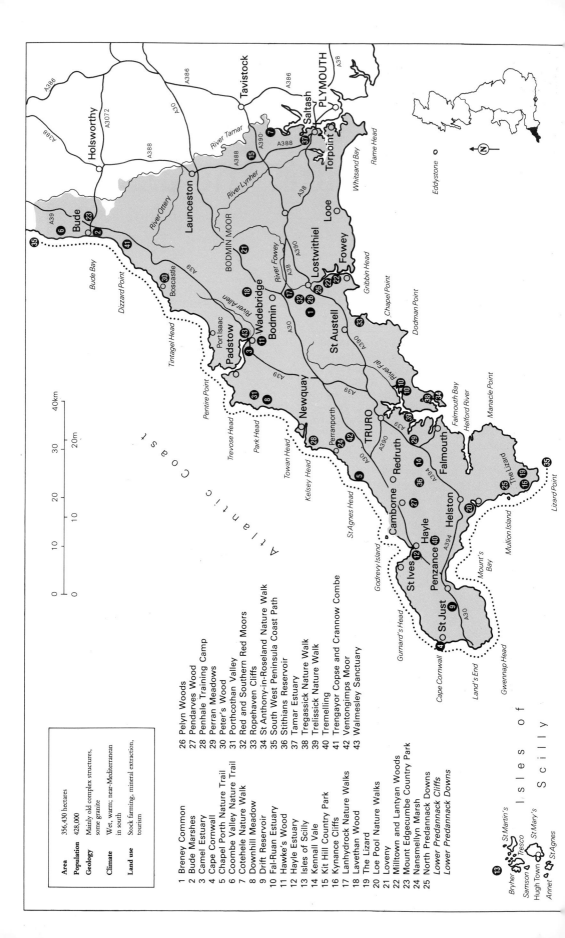

willows in the valley bottoms; a varied ground flora is seasonally ablaze with bluebells. Sadly many such ancient woods have been replanted with conifers.

Here visitors will find quarries rich with ferns; stone-wall Cornish hedges and sunken lanes bright with foxglove, honeysuckle, stonecrops and primrose. There are marshes, bogs, inland waters and scrubby hillsides. Mammals – notably badger, fox and even a few red deer – birds of the woods, countryside and coast, and countless invertebrates amount to an exceptional diversity of wildlife.

The pressures upon this rich natural heritage, particularly those of uncontrolled tourism, are severe; nature reserves protect only a very small part of it. But the National Trust is extremely active in Cornwall. Many of the best stretches of coast, some fine woods such as those of LANHY-DROCK, and the upper slopes of Rough Tor are safely in the ownership of the National Trust, and introduce a wide public to Cornwall's landscapes and wildlife.

RENNIE BERE

Anne's Wood

SW 547372; 0.6ha; WdT reserve
Mixed woodland
Spring, summer

A small wood on the banks of the HAYLE ESTUARY.

Antony Wood

SX 401547; 0.1ha; WdT reserve
Mixed woodland
Spring, early summer

A small area of land has been planted up with saplings to provide a broad-leaved woodland when the trees grow to maturity.

Benskins Wood

SX 409539; 1.1ha; WdT reserve
Mixed woodland
Spring, early summer

With views across Plymouth Sound and the Tamar, the site consists of both standing woodland and open areas that have been replanted with young trees.

Breney Common

SX 055610; 55ha; CTNC reserve
Heathland, ponds, scrub and grassland
Nature-trail guide available from CTNC
Spring, summer

There is a remarkable array of habitats of biological importance on this reserve. The wet heath area supports fine stands of royal fern, marsh cinquefoil and various sedges, with heath spotted-orchid in the drier areas. Nightjar and tree pipit are two of the 97 bird species recorded breeding, and there are good butterfly and moth populations. The emperor dragonfly frequents the ponds along with a number of other uncommon dragonflies and damselflies.

Bude Marshes

SS 207062; 3.2ha; North Cornwall DC reserve
Coastal marshland
All year

The hide offers views of winter snipe and autumn migrants. The marshland includes yellow iris and common reed, shelters breeding reed and sedge warbler, and is visited by heron and kestrel.

Camel Estuary

SW 980735; c.800ha; various bodies
Long tidal mudflats and saltmarsh
All year

A disused railway line has been established as a waterside walk from which the waders and wildfowl of the estuary may be seen. A small flock of white-fronted geese winter in the estuary.

Cape Cornwall

SW 350318; 31ha; NT
Rocky shore, cliffs, maritime grassland and scrub
Spring, summer

The cliffs rise to some 70 metres above the sea giving good views of Land's End, the Isles of Scilly and the rocky islets – the Brisons.

The most interesting part of the area for plants are the maritime grasslands which include stands of heather; less common species such as western clover, dyer's greenweed, autumn squill, lanceolate spleenwort and early meadow-grass also occur. The mild, moist climate provides ideal conditions for a wide range of mosses and lichens. The Kenidjack Valley is a particularly good place for migrant birds in the early spring and autumn; a number of rare vagrants, including American redstart, have been recorded.

Bell heather, thrift and a mosaic of lichens.

Carn Moor

SW 795538; 1ha; CTNC reserve
Wet heathland, bog and carr
Late spring, summer

A mosaic of black bog-rush, purple moor-grass, bog myrtle and ericaceous shrubs cover this small reserve, while the hollows support bog asphodel, sundews and the spectacular royal fern. Fringing scrub and willow carr encourage a variety of birds and mammals, including snipe and curlew which use the area in winter.

Cecil Stevens Memorial Hide

Permit only; RSPB
Hide overlooking the Fal-Ruan Estuary
All year

Described under FAL-RUAN ESTUARY.

Chapel Porth Nature Trail

SX 697495; 3.2km; CCC
Atlantic coast nature trail
Booklet from CCC
Spring, summer

A splendid range of features includes a stream-cut valley, typical coastal heathland and magnificent rocky cliffs. Stonechat, rock pipit, raven and buzzard may be seen, together with fulmar, kittiwake, guillemot and gannet.

Coombe Valley Nature Trail

SS 203116; up to 2.5km; CTNC
Wooded valley trail, much planted with conifers
Booklet from CTNC
Spring, early summer

The trail includes areas of broad-leaved trees and may reveal such interesting plants as winter heliotrope and autumn crocus, birds such as dipper and kingfisher, and the silver-washed fritillary butterfly.

Cotehele Nature Walk

SX 423681; 2.4km; NT
Riverside woodland
Spring, early summer

A circular trail has been laid out in the woodlands of Cotehele, a large estate on the western bank of the Tamar, which includes river and marshland as well as woods.

Downhill Meadow

SW 863689; 2ha; CTNC reserve
Grassland and wet heath
Summer

This small unimproved meadow contains a range of characteristic Cornish plants. The wetter heathland supports royal fern, black bog-rush and three types of heath. The dense blackthorn and gorse around the margins of the reserve provide valuable nesting sites.

Drift Reservoir

SW 435291; 36ha; Cornwall Bird-Watching and Preservation Soc. reserve
Reservoir and margins
All year

The reservoir is noted for rare and vagrant birds, due to its position as the most south westerly body of fresh water in mainland Britain, and provides a site for many migrant wintering and breeding species. The margins are variously woodland, wet woodland, scrub and herb-rich meadows, with a good range of plants including both heath spotted-orchid and southern marsh-orchid.

Fal-Ruan Estuary

SW 875405–886412; 100ha; CTNC reserve
Inland estuary
All year

Probably the most beautiful of the inland estuaries of Cornwall, the Fal-Ruan is a winding fingered spread of pale mudflats ringed by gently sloping hills, sheltered, quiet and inaccessible. The land around is privately owned, without rights of way, and the only access is to CTNC members or to key-holders of the CECIL STEVENS MEMORIAL HIDE (apply to RSPB).

The mudflats are unusually rich in suitable food for waders, particularly in ragworms. This is due to the high levels of mica-rich kaolin clays which have been washed down from china clay works higher up the river and which encourage a plentiful supply of tiny bacterial food.

When high tides cover the mudflats the estuary becomes a shallow saltwater lake, lapping the low cliffs below the woodland and washing across the narrow fringe of saltmarsh. This is a habitat of considerable local interest containing not only typical saltmarsh plants, but also three species uncommon in Cornwall: celery-leaved buttercup, lesser sea-spurrey and common saltmarsh-grass. One area of the estuary is of special fascination for its complete succession from mudflats to saltmarsh to alder–willow and to birch–oak woodland, a most uncommon occurrence in Britain, where most tidal areas have been altered by reclamation for grazing or for building.

A host of gulls may rest on the mudflats here, including such uncommon species as Mediterranean gull, and this is a site for winter birds. Mallard, shelduck, teal, wigeon and occasional shoveler may be seen with waders such as black-tailed godwit, dunlin, oystercatcher and lapwing, curlew, grey and golden plover, greenshank, ruff and spotted redshank and, perhaps, green, wood and curlew sandpiper. Uncommon birds recorded include osprey, spoonbill, glaucous gull and whiskered tern.

Hawke's Wood

SW 987709; 3.6ha; CTNC reserve
Mixed woodland
Spring, early summer

A small, plant-rich quarry adds to the variety of the wood which includes oak with ash, holly, sycamore, hazel and guelder-rose, with alder and birch along a stream. The upper slopes are more acidic with oak, originally coppiced, over hazel, hawthorn, holly and gorse. Many other species occur throughout the reserve which contains a typical range of woodland birds.

Hayle Estuary

SW 553373; c.100ha; various bodies
Sandflats, mudflats and saltmarsh
All year

Lying beside the busy A30, the Hayle Estuary has none of the quiet beauty of the FAL-RUAN yet still attracts good numbers of birds and, above all, is easily accessible. The estuary is formed by two arms of tidal waters lying north and west of the town and may be overlooked from various points on the roads which run beside them.

The western arm is probably the more important: some 70ha of sandy flats between the A30 and the single-track railway line on its western side. The sands become more muddy where the river drains into the basin, and here saltmarsh adds further variation. Below the head of the estuary a non-tidal embanked pool, the Carnsew Basin, forms a permanent deep-water area suitable both as a roost and as a fishing ground for divers. An additional range of habitat, and one which may be welcomed by smaller migrants, is provided by an area of scrub and woodland which lies beside the railway at the river end of the estuary.

The northern arm is even more easily studied since a trackway runs along its northern bank. It is a much smaller narrow strip of muddier flats which passes into a small reedmarsh by the river inflow. Low water provides a good feeding area for waders and, like RADIPOLE in Dorset, the fact that the area lies entirely within the edge of the town seems to make no difference to the birds. Summer numbers of birds will obviously be smallest but there may be much of interest to see here at any time. Winter wildfowl include wigeon, teal and shelduck, with occasional goldeneye, goosander and red-breasted merganser or less common species such as Slavonian grebe. Waders, in winter or on spring and autumn passage, include numbers of dunlin, lapwing and golden plover, together with birds such as curlew, bar-tailed godwit, knot, oystercatcher, grey and ringed plover, redshank, sanderling and turnstone.

The Hayman

SW 750498; 1.8ha; CTNC reserve
Steep wooded valley
Spring, early summer

The woodland is oak above a rather thin acid ground cover and sweet chestnut over a richer array of bluebell, enchanter's-nightshade and sanicle, with a show of ferns on the wet ground near the stream. Most of the commoner woodland mammals and birds are present.

Howard's Wood

SX 368803; 1.4ha; WdT reserve
Mixed woodland
Spring, summer

Overlooking the River Tamar and the well-known Greystone Bridge, this attractive area is partly covered with mature woodland and more native trees and shrubs are being planted.

Isles of Scilly

See map: 1600ha; Duchy of Cornwall–NCC
Small group of islands
Guides from local newsagents and
bookshops
Spring, summer

The Scillies group consists of five inhabited islands, with around 40 more which are large enough for land plants, and more than three times as many high-tide rocks too small or too exposed for vegetation. From several of the islands, old field walls run out into the central sea, showing how it was only won by the tides when a single granite island was drowned, long after the ice ages, and only a low-lying ring of hills was left above the water.

The sea life is as rich and attractive as the shores themselves. Where sand has been washed across the shallows, such beautiful sea snails as the common necklace shell and netted dog whelk may be found, together with strange-looking worm-like creatures such as *Glossobalanus* where the sand becomes slightly muddy. *Chaetopterus*, a weird three-part tube-dwelling worm, lives in the wet sand, and the wide variety of beach types contains a rich assortment of sea-anemones. Snakelocks, dahlia and beadlet anemone spread their tentacles, together with the beautiful coral-like organ-pipes of *Corynactis viridis* and the rare small Devonshire cup coral.

The common sea-urchin favours rocky shores and is strongly spined for protection, while the heart-urchin and rarer purple heart-urchin live buried under the sands and tend to be hairy rather than spined. An outstandingly beautiful member of this family, and one which is elsewhere only found in deeper waters, is the feather star, an elegant starfish with five pairs of feather-like arms.

The sands and dunes have a characteristic plant life: sea-rocket, sea sandwort and prickly salt-wort below spreads of marram and sand sedge, of yellow horned-poppy, sea bindweed and spiny sea-holly, sea spurge and Portland spurge, or a low cover of buck's-horn plantain and sea stork's-bill. The rocky cliffs carry plants such as sea beet, common scurvy-grass, rock sea-spurrey and thrift, with shore dock, rock samphire, navelwort, tree-mallow and the alien Hottentot-fig. Above are cliff tops decorated with spring squill and sea pearlwort, giving way to sweeps of wind-pruned heathland, occasional thickets of gorse and western gorse, or stands of bracken where the soils are deep enough.

Bracken performs an important function on the Scillies, sheltering woodland plants whose woodland cover has long since been removed. It forms a canopy where plants such as bramble, foxglove, balm-leaved figwort and wood spurge in turn shelter bluebell, lesser celandine, ground-ivy and common bird's-foot-trefoil. Marsh vegetation occurs occasionally by the freshwater pools, with plants such as bulrush and common reed, with yellow iris, ragged-Robin and royal fern, but in general plants must be acid-tolerant, due to the granite beneath, and are often fleshy or very tough-skinned to avoid drying out in the wind. Danish scurvy-grass and sea spleenwort, found on inland heaths, show how the salt blows across the islands.

A large number of alien species have been planted or have colonised the islands, but several native plants are of particular note. The dwarf pansy of the acid dunes is found only here on the Scillies and on the Channel Islands; the low cliffs have the best British populations of shore dock, small tree-mallow and orange bird's-foot. The heathlands, of heather and bell heather, are subjected to a wind-pruning so severe that they tend to resemble a sea where waves of plants, grey and dead on the windward side, break green in the lee of their own lower foliage. The relative freedom from frost, coupled with high humidity, makes the Scillies a wonderful early-growing site provided that plants can be sheltered from the high winds and the spray.

Characteristic animals include a subspecies of meadow brown butterfly, and an island race of common blue which is only known from Tean. Grey seal breed in small numbers and are plentiful in summer, but the mammal speciality is the tiny Scillies shrew, an attractive insectivore widespread on the heathlands and which frequently hunts among the rocks on the shore.

The islands are also important for bird life. The best time is probably May and June, when cushions of thrift and stands of rank weeds shelter varied colonies of seabirds. Annet, an important breeding island, is closed to visitors from mid-April to August to afford some privacy to birds such as storm petrel, Manx shearwater and puffin, together with raucous colonies of gulls. Puffin numbers unfortunately have fallen, part of a recognised national decline, but they may still be seen arrowing low across the waves or floating buoyantly on the water. Manx shearwater and storm petrel too are burrow or crevice nesters which only visit to breed, wintering in distant seas, but neither is commonly seen on the Scillies, being nocturnal at their breeding sites. Guillemot and razorbill nest here; whereas razorbill is the less common in mainland colonies, here it considerably outnumbers guillemot.

Other breeding birds include both common and roseate tern, fulmar, kittiwake, cormorant and shag, with waders such as ringed plover and oystercatcher, and a varied range of land birds, from duck such as gadwall, shoveler and teal to goldcrest, linnet, rock pipit and stonechat. Birds such as little stint and purple sandpiper may be seen at migration times, while the position of the islands encourages landfalls of many uncommon European and Transatlantic species. Pectoral sandpiper and Baltimore oriole from America have been recorded, together with alpine swift and golden oriole; other visitors include Lapland and ortolan bunting, Pallas's and yellow-browed warbler, tawny pipit and red-breasted flycatcher.

Marram, on the edge of Tresco, overlooks the intertidal flats.

Kemyel Crease

SW 460244; 2ha; CTNC reserve
Mainly coniferous coastal woodland
Permit only off right of way
Spring, early summer

The woodland has developed from shelter belts planted on a 2ha, steep, sloping sea cliff where 121 tiny fields were once cultivated. It is now so darkly shaded that ground cover is virtually confined to Italian lords-and-ladies and ferns such as hart's-tongue and male-fern. The South Cornwall Coast Path crosses the reserve.

Kennall Vale

SW 747370; 8ha; CTNC reserve
Broadleaved woodland, river, quarry and lake
All year

This fascinating reserve, which ranges from majestic limes planted along a track to small pockets of semi-natural oakwood, surrounds the remains of a nineteenth-century gunpowder works. Among the wood-sorrel and bluebells less common plants such as sweet woodruff and wood spurge may be seen. The lake formed from a disused quarry is reputed to contain carp, and dippers feed along the river. The area is also a favourite feeding ground for bats.

Kit Hill Country Park

SX 375713; 162ha; Cornwall CC
Grassland, heathland and scrub
Summer

The hill is a wild, windswept place 333m above sea level towering above the surrounding countryside. The flora is rich in lichens and the hill is well known for the abundance of bilberries. There are badger setts and the scrub provides an important habitat for a wide variety of birds.

Kynance Cliffs

SW 688132; 26ha; NT reserve
Coastal cliffs, grassland and heath
Spring, summer

The cliffs are formed from serpentine which supports a wonderful variety of typical LIZARD plants and provides nesting sites for birds.

Lanhydrock Nature Walks

SX 099635; various lengths; NT
Mixed woodland
Information boards at site
Spring, early summer

The Lanhydrock woodlands, straddling the River Fowey, are as important for their wealth of wildlife as for the beauty of their walks.

Lavethan Wood

SX 104730; 10ha; WdT reserve
Valley woodland
Spring, summer

Annet Head, above a spread of thrift.

The wood lies in a valley of a tributary of the River Camel on the slopes of Bodmin Moor. It consists of oak, beech and other broadleaved trees with attractive riverside walks.

The Lizard

SW 701140; 400ha; various bodies
Complex of coast and heath
Spring, summer

The incredibly complicated geology of the Lizard has given rise to rock formations which carry a very special range of plants. It provides a superb scenery of heathland, and of coastal cliffs.

Most of the West Lizard is formed of serpentine, a rock which occurs nowhere else in Britain except on Anglesey and in Scotland.

The coast provides a wide range of contrasts, from sheltered stream-cut valleys to very exposed cliff slopes. The NT's LOWER PREDANNACK CLIFFS (at SW 660163) are representative of the Lizard's unique geology and plantlife. Stunting is a characteristic of the area, and along the Lizard coast may be found distinct populations of dwarf varieties of betony, oxeye daisy, common knapweed, saw-wort and devil's-bit scabious. Prostrate varieties of wild asparagus, broom, dyer's greenweed, privet and juniper occur on the Lizard cliffs.

The area is known not only for these specialities but also for its rare or uncommon species such as twin-flowered, upright and long-headed clover, another clover, *Trifolium occidentale*, fringed rupturewort, spring sandwort, thyme broomrape and hairy greenweed.

The Downs, of which LOWER PREDANNACK DOWNS (SW 690145) are typical, support a unique variety of plants in dry to wet heathlands with stretches of mixed gorse and heather, damp tall heath, and contrasting dry short heathland away from the serpentine. Cornish heath, found only in Cornwall, is one of the main plants of the mixed heath, together with a variety of unusual species including dwarf rush, pigmy rush, Dorset heath and chives. Spring squill makes a wonderful April show with both pale and common dog-violet and their hybrids. The damper situations contain tall heath where sprays of black bog-rush are mixed with purple moor-grass and Cornish heath while, even on the serpentine, some areas are acid enough for bog asphodel and small spreads of peat where species such as round-leaved sundew grow.

The short heath grows on soils derived from Loessic drift. Cornish heath does not grow on these more acidic soils; here the cover is generally of bristle bent with spreads of heather, bell heather, cross-leaved heath, purple moor-grass and western gorse. Areas of peat are rich in *Sphagnum* mosses and many plants in common with the tall heath, but plants such as pale butterwort, common butterwort – uncommon in the country – tawny sedge and lesser butterfly-orchid may also occur.

Other plants of interest include the grass-like fern pillwort, yellow centaury, three-lobed crowfoot and the very rare heath *Erica williamsii*, a cross between Cornish heath and cross-leaved heath.

Loe Pool Nature Walks

SW 639259; various lengths; NT
Shingle bank, freshwater lake and surrounding woodland
Information boards at site
All year

An extensive system of footpaths demonstrates shingle, lake and woodland plants in an area renowned for its birds.

Loveny

SX 183744; 160ha; CTNC–Cornwall Bird-Watching and Preservation Soc. reserve
Open water, heathland and grassland
Western margin of reserve only
All year

Loveny reserve covers the northern limb of Collingford Reservoir, which lies in the St Neot river valley on Bodmin Moor. The reservoir is likely to become an important ornithological site and already mallard, wigeon, teal and tufted duck use the water. Lapwing, curlew, green sandpiper, redshank and dunlin feed at the edge, while golden plover, short-eared owls and hen harriers are occasionally seen in winter. Marsh fritillary is just one of the interesting range of butterflies recorded.

Lower Predannack Cliffs

See THE LIZARD.

Lower Predannack Downs

See THE LIZARD.

Lower Tamar Lake

Permit only; 20.4ha; SWWA
Bird Sanctuary
All year

A hide overlooks the lake where over 170 bird species have been recorded. Winter wildfowl include gadwall and goldeneye, and the marsh has become an important breeding site.

Maybrook Drive

SX 417589; 1ha; CTNC–Caradon DC reserve
Meadow and stream
Spring, summer

Wild flowers including angelica, meadowsweet and yellow iris find a haven in this urban nature reserve. There are great crested newts, frogs and toads, and many common garden birds in the area.

Milltown and Lantyan Woods

SX 110570 and SX 108578; 33ha; WdT reserve
Deciduous woodland
Spring, summer

These two woodlands, linked by a narrow belt of trees, lie on the western shore of the Upper Fowey Estuary. Clothing the side of the valley right down to the edge of the river, these oaks form an essential feature of this beautiful Cornish river.

Mount Edgecumbe Country Park

SX 245053; 350ha; CC–Plymouth City Council
Maritime cliffs, grassland woodland and scrub
Leaflets on site
Spring, autumn

The Country Park covers 16km of coastline from Cremyll to Treganhawke in Whitsand Bay. The rugged and windswept cliffs, Penlee Point and Rame Head support an interesting range of habitat from rocky shore, strandline community to maritime grassland, heath and scrub. Rame Head is particularly interesting for migrating birds. A wild herd of fallow deer is found in the deer park.

Nansmellyn Marsh

SW 762543; 3.4ha; CTNC reserve
Reedbed and willow carr
Spring, summer
The reedbed is of particular interest for birds, and where many species regularly breed.

North Predannack Downs

SW 688174; 42ha; CTNC reserve
Heathland and pools
Late summer, winter

The Downs support a mosaic of wet and dry heathland with three small pools which attract wintering wildfowl and abound with dragonflies and damselflies in summer. The reserve is dominated by Cornish heath with many interesting wetland plants such as royal fern, southern marsh-orchid and the delicate pale butterwort.

Pelyn Woods

SX 092586; 40.4ha; CTNC reserve
Old estate woodland
Spring, early summer

Beech, sweet chestnut and sycamore, rhododendron and laurel have been planted but oak and ash over hazel, holly, hawthorn and rowan are native. An attractive torrential stream adds wetland interest to a typical range of woodland plants and animals.

Pendarves Wood

SW 641377; 16ha; CTNC reserve
Old estate woodland and educational reserve
Spring, early summer

A nature trail runs through oak, ash, beech and sycamore woodland. Rhododendron and cherry laurel have been cleared providing space for young trees to be planted. An ornamental lake attracts winter wildfowl and is a breeding site for dragonflies and damselflies.

Penhale Training Camp, Perran Sands

SW 764585; 8km; MOD–NT
Coastal walk through large sand dunes with lime-loving plants
Visitors should read all notice boards carefully and keep to marked coastal footpath
All year

Penhale sand-dunes form part of a much larger sand-dune system extending along the North Cornwall coast from Perranporth to Holywell Bay. In places the dunes are over 60m high and represent some of the highest dunes in the British Isles with at least 12 to 30m of sand overlying bedrock. The coastal path from Holywell Bay gives spectacular views from the cliffs of Carters Rocks. Access to valley, stream and marsh area is by way of a bridlepath at Holywell Bay.

Perran Meadows

SW 774382; 3ha; CTNC reserve
Meadows and stream
Spring, summer

The meadows support a range of common wetland plants including angelica, figwort and water starwort, while bluebell, herb-Robert and enchanter's-nightshade may be seen along the hedgerows and woodland edge. Foxes and badgers regularly visit the reserve.

Peter's Wood

SX 113910; 10ha; CTNC reserve
Steep valley woodland
Spring, early summer

Peter's Wood has been much modified by planted trees, such as beech and sycamore, yet evidence seems to indicate that some, at least, is ancient woodland. Apart from the alien species, oak is the main tree cover, with birch, ash and wild cherry above an often sparse shrub layer including holly, hazel, rowan and guelder-rose. The wood is rather acid, with wide spreads of great wood-rush and hard fern, but damp flushes and the deeper soils of the valley floor, where hazel, hawthorn, alder and willow grow, contain nutrients enough for plants such as ramsons and opposite-leaved golden-saxifrage. Spring brings a typical show of woodland plants such as wood anemone, bluebell, primrose and wood-sorrel to contrast with hart's-tongue and lady-fern. Bilberry and common cow-wheat underline the acid nature of the wood but the richer valley floor adds marshland plants such as meadowsweet and hemlock water-dropwort. Among the interesting ferns of the reserve are the unusual royal fern and Tunbridge filmy-fern.

The river which once cut the valley is a feature of the reserve, a route by which animals such as mink might enter the area, a hunting ground for birds such as dipper and a breeding ground for insects which might feed the resident Leisler's, Daubenton's and long-eared bats. The rather sparse bird life is typical of these woodlands, with blackcap, whitethroat, willow warbler and chiffchaff, goldcrest, wren and buzzard.

Phillips's Point Cliffs

SS 200044; 0.5km; CTNC–North Cornwall DC reserve
Coastal clifftop grassland and heath
All year

In spring thrift, bladder campion and wild carrot add colour to the grassland, while the area of western maritime heath supports bell heather and western gorse with dodder. Wheatear, stonechat, and meadow and rock pipit breed along the clifftops, and gulls, raven and fulmars can often be seen. Seals also frequent the area.

Porthcothan Valley

Permit only; 7.2ha; CTNC reserve
Sheltered valley
Spring, early summer

The valley contains a range of habitats which include streamside meadowland, woodland and an old quarry. Badger breed on the reserve and birds to be seen include nesting sparrowhawk and buzzard.

Red and Southern Red Moors

SX 070615; 96ha; CTNC reserve
Wetland heath, scrub and woodland
Spring, summer

While man's activities have generally been so destructive in the modification of wild areas to fit the pattern of industry or farming, in a very few cases a wilderness has been created of benefit to wildlife. Red Moor is just such a case: working alluvial tin has left a marvellous complex of pools and wetlands, of hills and holes which are now a jungle, thick with wet woodland, scrub, reed-marsh, heath and bog.

One of the attractive features of the reserve is the mosaic nature of the site: an old bank, dry and thick with polypody, hard fern and gorse, may overlook a silted pool, wooded with willow like a rich dark mangrove swamp; a few metres away a screen of trees shelters the waters of the main pool, where it fills from a wide spread of bulrush reed-swamp, or where low coppiced oakwoods stand with every upper branch bunched with grey-green lichen. Clearings may be filled with tall gorse and leggy strands of heather, or with damp spreads of purple moor-grass and *Sphagnum* or dry heath invaded by birch.

Around 100 species of birds have been recorded here. Nightjar have bred on the heathland, an ideal site for typical birds such as stonechat, linnet and yellowhammer, while the wetlands attract water-birds and may be fished by birds such as heron. As one would expect from such a varied site, there is an excellent range of insects and spiders, and the wetlands of Red Moor encourage a variety of specialised animals including 11 recorded species of dragonfly.

Southern Red Moor is an extension to Red Moor. The wetlands are of special interest, supporting royal fern, marsh cinquefoil and several uncommon sedges. In drier areas hare's-tail and heath spotted-orchid carpet the heath, whilst the delicate ivy-leaved bellflower may be found in the more open grassland. The many silted-up ditches crossing the site are particularly good for dragonflies and damselflies.

Ropehaven Cliffs

SX 034490; 20ha; CTNC reserve
Cliffs, grassland and woodland
Access via South Cornwall Coast Path
All year

In spring the cliffs are carpeted with thrift, campion and vivid blue squill, contrasting sharply with the woodland flowers alongside the coast path where bluebells, primroses and violets peep from the hedgerows. Seabirds include fulmars and kittiwakes, while kestrels and peregrines may be seen hunting the cliffs. Ropehaven Bay is an important winter roosting site for seabirds including divers.

St Anthony-in-Roseland Nature Walk

SW 868329; 6.4km; NT
Coastal trail
Information board at site
Spring, summer

Circling part of the famous Roseland peninsula, the trail includes woodland and farmland, set beside a creek of the Percuil River or above the rocky cliffs of the open coast.

Shute Wood

SW 742522; 0.2ha; WdT reserve
Mixed woodland
Spring, early summer

The tiny copse, important for wildlife in an area where woods are sparse, has been doubled in size by the planting of a block of young oak saplings.

South West Peninsula Coast Path

SS 212174 SX 455534; 427km; CC
Part of coastal footpath
Spring, summer

Running around the spectacular coastline of Cornwall, the path passes through a superb range of coastal habitats from Plymouth, in the south, to the Marsland Valley, part of WELCOMBE AND MARSLAND VALLEYS reserve (Devon) in the north.

Stithians Reservoir

SW 715372 and SW 709373; 40ha; SWWA Cornwall Bird-Watching and Preservation Soc. reserve
Reservoir
Permit from Cornwall Bird-Watching and Preservation Soc., but can be viewed from the road
Summer, autumn, winter

There are two nature reserves on Stithians Reservoir – at Polighey Moor and at the 'cut off' opposite the Golden Lion Inn. The area is particularly important for its rare migrant wader and waterfowl, which are attracted from the Arctic, North America and the Mediterranean. In recent years solitary sandpiper, lesser yellowlegs, pectoral and semi-palmated sandpipers, blue-winged teal and white-winged black tern have all been recorded. There is also an annual passage of the more common waders, wildfowl and terns.

Ancient parkland at Trelissick, overlooking the Fal

Swan Vale

SX 800317; 1ha; CTNC reserve
Woodland and marsh
Keep to public footpath
All year

This wet wooded valley lies next to Swan Pool – an ideal birdwatching site – and many of the more sensitive species take refuge on the reserve.

Tamar Estuary

SX 430610; 400ha; CTNC reserve
Saltmarsh and mudflats
All year

The wide mudflats of the Tamar, fringed with saltmarsh, provide a suitable habitat for birds such as shelduck, curlew, oystercatcher and redshank, together with a small but regular wintering population of avocet outside the reserve area.

Tregassick Nature Walk

SW 857340; 3.2km; NT
Riverside trail
Spring, summer

From Percuil the walk follows the banks of the attractive tidal river and ends at Tregassick Farm, not far north of the ST ANTHONY-IN-ROSELAND NATURE WALK.

Estuary. Old parklands are often rich in fungi, lichens and uncommon insects.

Trelissick Nature Walk

SW 837396; 3.2km; NT
Woodland and parkland walk
Spring, summer

The circular trail includes the high-forest woodland on the slopes above the River Fal where cormorant and heron may be seen.

Tremelling

SW 550340; 2.8ha; CTNC reserve
Mixed woodland
Spring, early summer

The woodland contains willow, sycamore, holly, ash, blackthorn, hawthorn and hazel above a good show of woodland flowers and ferns.

Trengayor Copse and Crannow Combe

SX 180981; 17.4ha; WdT reserve
Deciduous woodland
Spring, summer

Part of one of the few remaining extensive areas of broadleaved woodland in this part of Cornwall, this fine wood contains oak, willow and ash with a rich understorey of shrub species. There is a colourful display of flowers in the spring and a wide range of mosses, liverworts and lichens.

Ventongimps Moor

SW 781513; 8ha; CTNC reserve
Wet and dry heath with pools
Spring, summer

The moor is slightly tilted, with streamlets draining through to the wet wooded brook at the boundary, but is varied by low, level plateaus which carry spreads of dry heath. These dry heaths contain common and western gorse, heather and bell heather and are filled with magnificent stands of Dorset heath. Below them, the wet heaths are a deep pattern of purple moor-grass, Dorset heath and black bog-rush, dissected by the streamlets where clumps of rushes, yellow iris and plants such as royal fern grow. Along the edges of the streams are groves of aromatic bog myrtle, while the wet willow woodland is floored with yellow iris, meadowsweet and water mint. This lower woodland is fringed with oak, birch and hazel while above the moor is a belt of coppiced woodland with a dense ground cover of bramble giving way to gorse as it grades into the heath.

Further variety is added by a number of pools varying from shallow, probably summer-dry, pits, through deeper pools rich in water plants, to a very deep, crystal-clear pond. Some of the pools provide breeding sites for frogs and for the 13 recorded species of dragonfly. Snipe and other wetland birds breed on the moor itself while the woodlands attract a typical range of nesting and visiting species.

Merely to list a few of the plants and animals of the reserve, however, is to do far less than justice to a quite exceptional heathland. Pale butterwort and yellow centaury are among the uncommon species here but the whole mosaic of colour, of richly scented plants and bright insects, in a valley bottom surrounded by formal farmland, combines to form a special wilderness.

Walmesley Sanctuary

No access; 17ha; Cornwall Bird-Watching and Preservation Soc. reserve
Wet grassland and foreshore
The sanctuary may be overlooked from SW 987744
Autumn, winter

White-fronted geese are fewer now than in former years, but duck include pintail and wigeon, and autumn brings waders such as wood and green sandpiper, greenshank and ruff.

Welcombe and Marsland Valleys

Described under Devon.

Woodland

Permit only; 3.6ha; CTNC reserve
Woodland, scrub and heath
Spring, early summer

Old coppiced oak with hazel, gorse scrub and herb-rich grassy heath contain plants such as common cow-wheat, bladderseed, bastard balm, heath spotted-orchid and lesser butterfly-orchid. The reserve is particularly rich in butterflies, including the attractive marsh fritillary.

Main Dale on the Lizard: short heath strewn with boulders formed from gabbro.

Sandymouth, North Cornwall, in winter sunshine, at low-tide.

Devon

From Atlantic-torn Hartland Point to the soft chalk of Beer in the south east, and from sea-level Dartmouth to the 666m summit of Dartmoor, Devon offers immense variety to the observer. Straddling the south west peninsula of England, with no higher ground to the west, it is bathed by the warm, moist air from over the Gulf Stream. Mildness is the climatic keynote, and softness the land's characteristic. Only on the most exposed western cliffs, and within Dartmoor's tor-ringed high plateau, do animals, plants and people have to struggle. In deep, narrow valleys sheltered even from the westerly wind, ferns and mosses give the oakwoods a sub-tropical luxuriance. Between the valleys massive Devon hedge banks shelter primroses, bluebells, marjoram and orchids. Copses support buzzard, raven and heron. Badgers trundle, and foxes dash, across lanes sunk below the fields by a thousand years of farming traffic.

Geologically Devon divides about the River Exe. West of it the bulk of the land is formed by slates and thin sandstones. They are old hard rocks, standing on end, interleaved in the south with the odd limestone, lava and volcanic ash. They lap around the great boss of the Dartmoor granite, which rises to high plateaus carrying peat up to 4m thick in places. The landscape thus formed is crossed from Dartmoor to the sea by a set of radiating rivers. The Taw flows north westwards to Barnstaple, the rest to the southern coast. The Teign and the Dart are largest; Avon, Erme, Yealm, Plym and Tavy have shorter runs to the sea. Tamar and Exe rise in Cornwall and Somerset respectively, both close to the north coast, but flow south either side of Dartmoor to the English Channel. East of the Exe, softer, younger rocks prevail. They run in procession from Exeter eastwards as new red sandstone with pebble beds, marls, greensand and chalk. This landscape is a succession of vales and flat-topped ridges capped by flint gravel, drained by the Otter, Axe, Sid and Yarty, smaller lowland streams meandering through water meadows with willows and alder.

Within this general pattern there are unique 'islands'. The lignites and clays of the Bovey Basin form a black-and-white sandwich well exposed in pits both new and abandoned. The china clay deposits of south west Dartmoor form a near-sterile landscape of their own, and the schists from Bolt Tail to Start Point are a southerly bastion protecting 96km of eastern coast from the Atlantic.

Devon is the only county in England with two separate coastlines. The north coast is entirely within the 'hard rock' landscape and all exposed to the Atlantic. Only the low entrance of the Taw–Torridge Estuary, with the great flat of BRAUNTON BURROWS across its entrance, relieves the continuous cliffline. LUNDY ISLAND is more exposed still, but houses the only puffins in the county. In contrast the southern and south eastern coast changes from hard to softer rock around the north end of Torquay, though the coastal character pivots about Start Point. To the west Atlantic attack means that rocky shores are narrow and exposed – only in the estuaries of Tamar, Plym, Yealm, Erme, Avon and Kingsbridge are sheltered shores found, and mud to support waders masks much of the bedrock within them. East of Start, beaches proliferate. The shingle of Start Bay supports its own flora, as do the remnant sand dunes at the mouth of the Exe. The Dart is the last narrow, steep-sided, oakwooded estuary. The Teign and the Exe are in wide shallow vales, with more mudbanks and sandbanks and hence bigger flocks of birds. The Otter and the Axe are now very small, much silted and contain saltmarsh. East of the Exe the cliffs are soft, crumbly and unstable. Landslips are common and the biggest – from Axmouth to Lyme Regis – forms a 14km-long reserve. The whole spectrum of seaboard habitat is within these 240km of coast. Kittiwake and rainbow limpet breed here, while gannet and basking shark are seen from the beach.

Warm but damp, the Devon year has a high number of rain days. Fog and mist are common at the sea's edge and on Dartmoor and Exmoor.

The other side of that same coin is that snow is rare, and lies only briefly even on the moors. Frost days are few and far between on the southern coast, and grass stops growing only for a very short time. Even a warm wind off the Atlantic blows strongly across plateau tops, and shelter is still sought by living things well inland.

All this adds up to a superior grass-growing landscape and for 3000 years Devonians have been graziers. South Devon and Red Devon cattle; South Devon, Devon Closewool, Dartmoor Greyface and Exmoor sheep; Dartmoor and Exmoor ponies are testimony to that. From Anglo-Saxon times the stock-rearing and dairying enterprise has been integrated into a mixed farming system for the self-sufficiency necessitated by remoteness from large towns. A pattern of small fields and woods separated by large earth and stone banks, all enmeshed in a dense network of deep narrow lanes, is the physical expression of that economy. Farmsteads and villages, with orchards, ponds and mills, seem to grow out of the hillsides and valley heads. This man-made landscape continues to support a rich plant and animal life, with gentle transitions to the seashore one way, and up on to stone-walled moors and blanket bogs the other.

IAN MERCER

Arlington Court Nature Walk

SS 611405; 2.4km; NT
Lakeside and river walk
Spring, early summer

The circular trail includes the lake, a wildfowl sanctuary overlooked by a heronry, and the riverside woodlands where raven and buzzard breed.

Ashculm Turbary

ST 147158; 6.4ha; DWT reserve
Wet heath
Spring, summer

A range of habitats from acid bog to birch scrub and wet alder–willow contains purple moor-grass, cross-leaved heath and round-leaved and oblong-leaved sundew. Some 40 bird species have been recorded here, along with a wide variety of other animals.

Avon Valley Woods

SX 736509; 40ha; WdT reserve
Mixed woodland
Spring, early summer

For roughly 3km the steep woodlands follow the valley of the Avon as old oak coppice with sweet chestnut, birch and alder at the riverside. The woods are rich in shrubs with splendid spring flowers and a good range of animal life including woodland and riverside birds.

Axmouth–Lyme Undercliffs

SY 268896 329916; 320ha; NCC reserve
Wooded cliffs and slopes
Permit only off right of way
Dangerous site with unstable cliffs
Leaflet from NCC
Spring, early summer

One winter's night in 1839, a huge chalk floe of cliff slid towards the sea, pushing in front of it the tumbled debris of many minor falls and opening up behind it a chasm into which an only slightly smaller section of cliff collapsed. Six broad hectares of chalk and sandstone had moved, unseen, in a single night to form an island of land in the loosely tumbled slopes below the fields. This and many smaller slips of rock make up the Undercliffs, which are altered every year by newer falls.

In places there are planted trees, conifers, everlasting and turkey oak, beech and ash, but much of the woodland has developed naturally, particularly the dense tangle which now fills the chasm behind Goat Island. The natural cover on these lime-rich rocks, where purple gromwell grows, is ash and field maple over blackthorn, dogwood, hazel and spindle, thickly tangled with traveller's-joy.

On the seaward slopes a wind-pruned scrub is contoured by exposure: dogwood, field maple, privet, spindle and wayfaring-tree with blackthorn and hawthorn, bramble, ivy, honeysuckle, traveller's-joy and wild madder. Shaded places are thick with hart's-tongue, male-fern, broad buckler-fern and soft shield-fern, while paths are edged with yellow archangel, dog's mercury, enchanter's-nightshade, herb-Robert, wood spurge and pendulous sedge. Water still drains down through the slopes to cause new falls, providing sites for common bird's-foot-trefoil, biting stonecrop, carline thistle and common rock-rose, with marshy sumps where a wet sandy porridge is filled with rushes, sedges and plants such as water mint, purple-loosestrife, great horsetail, bog pimpernel and the rare fen orchid.

The area is rich in animal life – adder and common lizard bask on the open slopes, badger and roe deer enjoy the secrecy of the thickets; sunlit glades and banks of flowers are alive with insect life: this is a key site for the wood white butterfly. The scrub provides food and shelter for many migrant birds; breeding species include herring gull, nightingale and long-tailed tit, goldcrest, stonechat and rock pipit, while buzzard, kestrel and sparrowhawk hunt across the reserve.

Aylesbeare Common

SY 057898; 180ha; RSPB reserve
Lowland heath
No access off footpaths
Extreme danger of fire; no smoking
Spring, early summer

While avocet, marsh harrier and peregrine may be spreading once more as British breeding species and recent colonisers such as collared dove

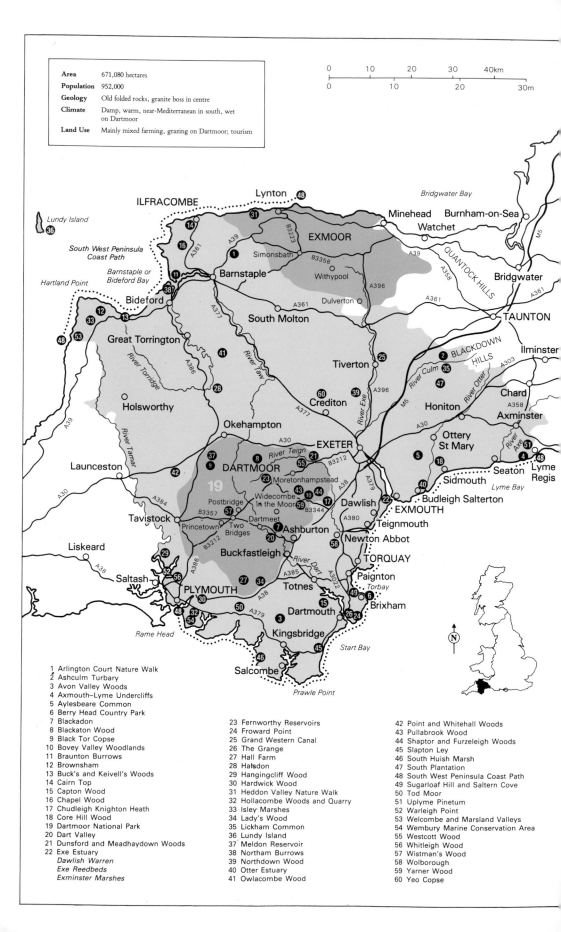

Area	671,080 hectares	
Population	952,000	
Geology	Old folded rocks, granite boss in centre	
Climate	Damp, warm, near-Mediterranean in south, wet on Dartmoor	
Land Use	Mainly mixed farming, grazing on Dartmoor; tourism	

1 Arlington Court Nature Walk
2 Ashculm Turbary
3 Avon Valley Woods
4 Axmouth–Lyme Undercliffs
5 Aylesbeare Common
6 Berry Head Country Park
7 Blackadon
8 Blackaton Wood
9 Black Tor Copse
10 Bovey Valley Woodlands
11 Braunton Burrows
12 Brownsham
13 Buck's and Keivell's Woods
14 Cairn Top
15 Capton Wood
16 Chapel Wood
17 Chudleigh Knighton Heath
18 Core Hill Wood
19 Dartmoor National Park
20 Dart Valley
21 Dunsford and Meadhaydown Woods
22 Exe Estuary
   Dawlish Warren
   Exe Reedbeds
   Exminster Marshes

23 Fernworthy Reservoirs
24 Froward Point
25 Grand Western Canal
26 The Grange
27 Hall Farm
28 Halsdon
29 Hangingcliff Wood
30 Hardwick Wood
31 Heddon Valley Nature Walk
32 Hollacombe Woods and Quarry
33 Isley Marshes
34 Lady's Wood
35 Lickham Common
36 Lundy Island
37 Meldon Reservoir
38 Northam Burrows
39 Northdown Wood
40 Otter Estuary
41 Owlacombe Wood

42 Point and Whitehall Woods
43 Pullabrook Wood
44 Shaptor and Furzeleigh Woods
45 Slapton Ley
46 South Huish Marsh
47 South Plantation
48 South West Peninsula Coast Path
49 Sugarloaf Hill and Saltern Cove
50 Tod Moor
51 Uplyme Pinetum
52 Warleigh Point
53 Welcombe and Marsland Valleys
54 Wembury Marine Conservation Area
55 Westcott Wood
56 Whitleigh Wood
57 Wistman's Wood
58 Wolborough
59 Yarner Wood
60 Yeo Copse

are extending their breeding range, the Dartford warbler seems doomed as a native species. Most British warblers are summer visitors but the Dartford is not a migrant species. Essentially it is a bird of the western Mediterranean where winters are mild enough; it has either never evolved, or has lost, the urge to move in autumn. These birds were once widespread in the south of England, but savage winters have cut their numbers down while forestry and farming have drastically reduced the lowland heaths. A national crash followed the winter of 1962–63, reducing the population to less than 100 pairs and wiping out the colony at Aylesbeare. By 1978 they had recolonised, only to vanish again that winter, but two pairs bred in 1986. Obviously Aylesbeare is close enough for juveniles from the Dorset strongholds, such as ARNE, to reach the heathland here but, if our climate grows colder, the Dartford warbler may become extinct in the British Isles.

Better-adapted species, though, still inhabit the heathland where curlew nest beside the valley bogs and nightjar breed in the dry heath. Linnet, stonechat and yellowhammer sing from the gorse, while the woodland fringe provides a habitat for tree pipit and green woodpecker, and buzzard and raven wheel above the reserve.

The heath is considered the finest of the Budleigh Salterton pebble heaths, a spread of heather, bell heather and western gorse which curves into shallow valleys and drains into small bogs. The change from dry to wet heath is marked by a change to cross-leaved heath and to a show of sedges, cottongrass and plants such as royal fern and bog asphodel, lifting between tussocks of purple moor-grass. The wettest places are rich in *Sphagnum* with white beak-sedge, round-leaved sundew, bog pimpernel and plants of western and south-western bogs – pale butterwort, oblong-leaved sundew and many-stalked spike-rush. Mineral-rich water seepages are marked by less acid-loving plants such as black bog-rush, devil's-bit scabious, marsh thistle, carnation and tawny sedge, while the green and russet *Sphagnum* mosses give way to brown moss species.

The reserve attracts a wide range of insects, with a variety of dragonfly species, with heathland moths such as emperor and fox, and an exceptional 32 species of butterflies recorded, including silver-studded blue and grayling, purple hairstreak and silver-washed fritillary.

Bailey Wood

SS 521275; 0.4ha; WdT reserve
Oak woodland
Spring, summer

A small area planted up to create an oak woodland.

Bantham Copse

SX 671439; 0.8ha; WdT reserve
Woodland
Spring, summer

The scrub and tree cover of this reserve make it particularly attractive to butterflies.

Bere Alston and Bere Ferrers Copses

SX 456670 and SX 452639; 0.4ha; WdT reserve
Mixed woodland
Spring, summer

These two small copses are conspicuous features of the very open landscape at the southern end of the high ridge between the Rivers Tamar and Tavy.

Berry Head Country Park

SX 943564; 43ha; Torbay BC
Limestone cliffs, grassland, heath and scrub
Restricted access to old quarry: apply to TBC
Booklet and nature trail leaflet from TBC or car park at site
Mid-May–mid-July

The country park consists of a headland capped with scrub and bracken–gorse–heather heathland. Its magnificent range of plants and birds is so important that the park is also scheduled as a nature reserve.

Below the heath a shallow turf curves to the sheer cliffs, filled with a colourful blend of lime-loving and coastal plants such as white and rock stonecrop, sea campion and thrift. Some of the special plants are uncommon and may represent a range of species which survived the ice ages here. White rock-rose, honewort, goldilocks aster, small hare's-ear and small restharrow grow together nowhere else in the country: small hare's-ear occurs in Sussex on chalk, the rest on western limestones. These plants seem unable to spread from their present small colonies and their strange distribution is a puzzle.

For the birdwatcher this is also a special site: Berry Head holds one of the very few south coast colonies of auks. Around 150 pairs of guillemot nest on the cliffs, together with small numbers of razorbill and other seabirds such as fulmar and kittiwake. Other cliff-breeders include jackdaw

The chalk and sandstone Axmouth–Lyme Undercliffs, above Charton Bay.

and rock dove x feral pigeon, while crevices in the sea cliffs and the quarry hold important gatherings of several bat species.

The heathland holds resident birds such as linnet and stonechat and affords a breeding or resting site for many small migrants, including black redstart, while buzzard and kestrel may often be seen hunting over the headland. The park also provides an ideal place for sea-watching: cormorant and gannet are frequent and passage birds may use the reserve as a staging post or be seen flying offshore.

Blackadon

SX 712732; 36.4ha; DWT reserve
Wooded valley slope and moorland
Spring, early summer

Oak woodland over bilberry rises from the River Webburn to an area of coppiced birch below slopes of grass–heather moorland invaded by bracken. Mosses, ferns and lichens are prolific.

Blackaton Wood

SX 677885; 4.8ha; WdT reserve
Deciduous woodland
Spring, summer

The typical oak woodland on the edge of DARTMOOR NATIONAL PARK lies in the valley of the Blackaton Brook and is rich in lichens.

Black Tor Copse

SX 567890; 28.9ha; Duchy of Cornwall NCC
reserve
Dwarf high-Dartmoor woodland
Spring, early summer

Set in a valley near Dartmoor's highest point, the dwarf oaks and the tumbled rocks are thick with lichens, mosses and ferns, a shelter for birds such as ring ouzel.

Bovey Valley Woodlands

SX 789801; 71.2ha; NCC reserve
Old coppiced woodland
Permit only off rights of way
Spring, early summer

Oak and hazel, with a variety of other tree species, fill the valley of the River Bovey with an abundance of lichens and riverside boulders thick with mosses, liverworts and ferns. The reserve varies from woodland to valley bog and has a typical bird life which includes pied flycatcher, redstart and wood warbler with dipper and grey wagtail.

Bradley Pond

Permit only; 4ha; DWT reserve
Disused claypit
Spring, summer

Birch, grey willow and oak woodland is developing around an old ball clay working, colonised by a fringe of wetland plants and supporting a wide range of aquatic invertebrates.

Braunton Burrows

SS 464326; 604ha; NCC reserve
Coastal dune system
No access to military zones when red flags are flying
Leaflet from NCC
Spring, summer

At low water the beach seems to reach as far as the horizon while the sand bars and ridges of the estuary form a foraging ground for shelduck and oystercatcher. The strand line tells of the life of the sands; empty shells of shore crab and masked crab mix with Baltic tellin, mussel and common whelk, with the egg cases of dogfish, the rounded tests of heart urchins, and the seaweed-like fronds of hornwrack.

Where the edge of the dunes meets the sea are special plants which can live in this sand-blown environment, including sea-holly, sea bindweed and the uncommon and beautiful sea stock.

At Braunton a wide range of conditions from the open sand of the beach to thick scrub may be seen in a full progression. The first small slacks are open spreads of lichens and mosses, rabbit-bitten turf and scatters of low plants such as biting stonecrop and common stork's-bill. Larger slacks further inland begin to show shrubby cushions of privet, patches of restharrow and plants such as Portland and sea spurge, viper's-bugloss, wild thyme and sprays of stinking iris.

Larger, wetter slacks, varied with shingle and pools of standing water, are a wonderful pattern of scrub and colourful plants – mounds of privet and dense tangles of bramble, clusters of willows and rushy herb-rich areas, wet places where marsh-orchids stand above tangles of creeping willow, fringed with clumps of sharp rush, contrasting with short-turfed sandy pockets of plants such as hound's-tongue. The reserve is also of great importance for its spreads of water germander and round-headed club-rush.

Further inland stunted hawthorn appears, with stands of bracken where the lime has been washed out of the topsoil. Damper areas are still amazingly rich, with the scrub becoming more varied and forming a mix of hawthorn, blackthorn, privet, willow and buckthorn, with birch in the drier sites, with yellow rattle and kidney vetch, common twayblade, hemp-agrimony, red campion and ragged-Robin and, everywhere, the flower spikes of the orchids.

The animal life of the dunes corresponds to their variation. The lime-richness encourages snails, the wealth of plant life draws insects, and many mammals and birds breed and hunt here.

Brownsham

SS 287257; 30ha; DWT-NT reserve
Heathy grassland and woodland
Summer

The wet heathy grassland on the reserve is very rich in meadow plants. Scrub covers large areas and there is some mixed deciduous woodland. A 'tree library' contains examples of all native tree and shrub species.

Buck's and Keivell's Woods

SS 357234; 13ha; WdT reserve
Coastal woodland
Spring, summer

The woodland lies along three cliffs and in a valley running down to the sea. The trees are mainly oak, which is suited to the exposed site. The North Devon Coast Path runs along the clifftops and through Buck's Wood.

Cairn Top

SS 515463; 7.6ha; DWT reserve
Hillside with mixed woodland
Spring, early summer

A small area of open hill top, surrounded by gorse and blackthorn, contrasts with steep slopes where mixed deciduous trees and conifers stand above a varied ground cover.

Capton Wood

SX 835539; 4.4ha; WdT reserve
Deciduous woodland
Spring, summer

The reserve is part of a larger area of woodland lying on the steep sides of a secluded tributary valley on the River Dart. It contains oak, ash, cherry, beech, birch and sweet chestnut, with shrubs such as hazel, hawthorn and elder. In spring the ground is covered with a carpet of bluebells.

Chapel Wood

SS 483415; 6ha; RSPB reserve
Mixed woodland
Spring, early summer

The woodland of oak, ash, birch, hazel, willow and alien species contains birds such as buzzard and raven which are limited to the west in southern Britain.

Chudleigh Knighton Heath

SX 838776; 74ha; DWT reserve
Lowland heath
Spring, early summer

Small ponds, containing such interesting plants as common bladderwort, occur in a wide spread of wet and dry heathland, scrub and woodland where nightingales breed and attractive small plants such as pale dog-violet may be found. This is the last extensive area of lowland heathland remaining in the Bovey Basin.

Clayton Wood

SY 068929; 1ha; WdT reserve
Mixed woodland
Spring, summer

A new woodland planted in 1980, which, as it matures, will provide a valuable haven for wildlife and fit in well in a landscape of scattered small woods.

Cleaveland Wood

SX 437651; 1.8ha; WdT reserve
Mixed woodland
Spring, summer

A mixed woodland in the Tamar Valley. An ivy-covered chimney near the edge of the wood is a reminder of the former mining industry for which the area is renowned.

Core Hill Wood

SY 115910; 9.7ha; WdT reserve
Mixed woodland
Spring, summer

This prominent wood overlooks the seaside town of Sidmouth, and contains some magnificent specimens of oak, beech and Scots pine.

Crowndale Wood

SX 474733; 1ha; WdT reserve
Mixed woodland
Spring, summer

A narrow wood of mature trees following the footpath of the Tavistock Canal.

Dartmoor National Park

See map; 94,500ha; DNPA
Moorland with granite tors and fringing valleys
Leaflets from DNPA and information caravans
No access to MOD ranges when in use
Spring, early summer

Dartmoor, the Cornish granites of Bodmin, St Austell, Carnmenellis and Land's End, the Scillies and the underwater outcrop of Haig Fras are all great masses which stand up from one huge buried reef of granite and represent bosses of rock which have been uncovered by erosion. When the Dartmoor granite was forced into the folded carboniferous crust many metres of layered rocks stood above the tors; time has now stripped these softer rocks away and the bare grey granite stands against wind and rain. Even this hard rock cannot hold for ever and one of the characteristic sights of the Moor is the clitters, the screes of huge boulders which frost has shattered from the tors.

The spreads of heather are varied with bright small plants such as tormentil, heath bedstraw and heath milkwort, together with bilberry and bell heather, with cross-leaved heath and purple moor-grass in damper situations. Bristle bent is one of the typical grasses, a fine-leaved, tufty grass which only grows in the south west and South Wales, often found with mat-grass and other grasses on the open moors which surround the central bogs.

The bogs vary from the eroded peats on some of the open hills to the dangerous quaking spread of Fox Tor Mires, from tiny wet hollows filled with vivid bog mosses to trembling bogs around the upland streams. Heather and cross-leaved heath grow on the blanket bogs, with common and hare's-tail cottongrass and occasional crowberry, while the valley mires have a richer vegetation

A colony of yellow iris at Braunton Burrows.

where round-leaved sundew grows on the *Sphagnum* mosses with plants such as bog asphodel, pale butterwort, marsh St John's-wort and ivy-leaved bellflower, bogbean and bog pimpernel.

While the open moors are heavily grazed by ponies, cattle and sheep the clitters are almost as hard to graze as the bogs and often support a luxuriant growth of plants. The crevices protect the plants from grazing and give shelter from the wind; this may be why some clitters carry the only native woods of the moor. BLACK TOR COPSE, Piles Copse and WISTMAN'S WOOD are strange small thickets of twisted oaks which cling close to the slopes of the moorland, dramatically gnarled and stunted. The lack of air pollution encourages splendid growths of lichens and mosses, so that these woods have long been famous for the species which clothe the trees.

At lower altitudes, the moorland edge is dissected by deep gorges where the granite meets the softer rocks around it. These valleys form a vital aspect of the wildlife interest of the park with oak woodland spreads on the steep sides and alders lining the river bank.

Although winter floods may sweep through them, scouring the narrow alluvial flats and the islands, the valleys are sheltered from storms and spring brings wild daffodil, primrose, wood anemone, bluebell and ramsons to flower under the trees.

The rivers which drain the moor are all torrential, for heavy rain on the uplands will gather to pour down the narrow valleys. Salmon come to breed in the shallow gravels, waiting for the spate to bring them enough depth of water to run. All the life of the river must be adapted to cope with flood, from the freshwater limpets to the mayfly nymphs, from the fish to the caddisfly larvae. The rivers, fishing sites for heron and kingfisher, are worked by dipper and grey wagtail, and provide hunting grounds and passage routes for otter and feral mink.

The valley woods beside the rivers are attractive sites for bird life. Truly moorland birds such as dunlin, red grouse and golden plover may occur in small numbers, and the high moor also provides nest sites for skylark and meadow pipit, ring ouzel, wren and wheatear, for stonechat and whinchat in rough moorland or snipe and common sandpiper in the bogs, but the valley woodlands are far more rich in birds. Buzzard and raven are frequent across the moor and often fly out from the surrounding woodlands but, while the raven is mainly a bird of the open sheep walks, the buzzard is an opportunist, just as much at home in farmland.

In the valleys, several of them nature reserves, all three British woodpeckers may be present, together with nuthatch and treecreeper and the western trio of pied flycatcher, redstart and wood warbler. Woodcock are uncommon in the south west peninsula but may be found in some of the woodlands where they nest, often in a sparse cover of bracken or tangle of bramble. The woods are frequently noisy with the raucous calls of jays, although magpies prefer more open situations, and provide nest sites for predators such as buzzard, kestrel, sparrowhawk and tawny owl. In winter they may shelter flocks of smaller birds: long-tailed and coal tits, finches, and gatherings of fieldfares and redwings which feed on the scrubland berries.

Several Dartmoor valleys have been flooded to form reservoirs and, while there is a loss of moorland habitat, there is some gain in wetland wildlife, in breeding and wintering wildfowl and in visitors such as osprey.

The open moors offer little shelter and are often too wet for small mammals and, while the moorland foxes may find sanctuary in the clitters, the valley slopes provide far more suitable homes. In valleys, too, fallow deer and badger make regular, well-worn pathways, and a good range of woodland mammals live in the shelter there.

Dart Valley

SX 672733 704704; 364ha; DNPA-DWT reserve
Valley woodland and heath
Spring, early summer

In one of the most attractive of the Dartmoor valleys, the reserve is a stretch of wooded riverside and steep-sloped open heath. The narrow steepness of the gorge has preserved the valley from agricultural improvement. The lower slopes are wooded, an oak woodland with hazel, birch, holly and beech, which grades through birch and bracken scrub to the open heathland above. The woods are very varied, a mosaic of coppiced areas with stands of almost pure birch, with alder at the water's edge, with taller trees in the deeper soils below and small, slow-growing copses on the arid steep scree slopes. Ground cover may be rich in mosses and ferns or be a more typical woodland spread of grasses and shade-loving plants.

The rapid flow of the torrential river is rich enough in oxygen for fish such as salmon and brown trout to breed, and for the insect larvae on which the dipper feeds. From dipper and grey wagtail to buzzard and raven high above, the valley is rich in bird life. Woodcock, green woodpecker and marsh tit, redstart, whinchat and ring ouzel, meadow pipit and skylark are among the breeding species, while winter may bring flocks of goldcrest, coal tit and long-tailed tit. Otter and mink may occur and the woods and scrub provide a habitat for fox and badger.

Dawlish Warren

SX 981787; 70ha; DWT-Teignbridge DC reserve
Sand dunes, scrub and marsh
No access to golf course
All year

Part of the EXE ESTUARY providing an important staging post for many immigrant birds.

Dendles Wood

Permit only; 29ha; NCC reserve
Oak-beech woodland
Spring, early summer

Beech trees, up to 300 years old, stand above a ground cover of little more than mosses but, where the trees become more mixed, holly, hazel and rowan, for instance, grow with bluebell, bracken, bramble, wood-sorrel and woodland grasses. Birds include buzzard, pied flycatcher, redstart, grey wagtail and wood warbler, with silver-washed fritillary and green hairstreak among the insects.

Dishcombe Wood

SX 660933; 1.8ha; WdT reserve
Mixed woodland
Spring, summer

A small field bounded by a line of fine hedgerow beech trees, this area has been planted up in order to provide a mixed broadleaved woodland.

Lydford Gorge: many of Devon's rivers flow off the moor and cut through the valley woods.

Dunsford and Meadhaydown Woods

SX 805883; 56ha; DWT–NT reserve
Mixed valley woodland
Booklet from DWT
Spring, early summer

The slopes are covered with an open woodland of old coppiced oak while blackthorn, hazel and spindle or level plains of grass and bracken spread across the valley floor. The reserve is noted for its wild daffodils and has a good range of woodland birds, including the locally uncommon lesser spotted woodpecker. There are large colonies of wood ant and some 23 butterfly species including pearl-bordered and silver-washed fritillaries.

Exe Estuary

SX 980785; 12sq.km; various owners
Large area of open water, mudflats, saltmarsh and sandy spit
No access to golf course at Dawlish Warren
All year

The great estuary, one of eleven in the county, forms the most important wetland in the whole south west peninsula. Sand, pushed into a long narrow spit by the eastward thrust of the longshore drift, almost closes the estuary mouth at DAWLISH WARREN, while wide sandflats spread from The Point at Exmouth, holding the river against the western shore. The estuary may be overlooked from footpaths along the shoreline, north from Powderham at SX 973845 and south from Lympstone at SX 992836, and from a hide.

The habitats include mudflats thick with the seaweed *Enteromorpha*, and with dwarf and narrow-leaved eelgrass; saltmarsh building around spreads of cord-grass with species such as glasswort; the dunes and scrub of Dawlish Warren, where the rare sand crocus grows; and areas of common reed together with grazing marshes at the northern head of the estuary.

Enormous numbers of wigeon winter here with flocks of dark-bellied Brent geese. Large flocks of mallard, shelduck and teal, with lesser numbers of eider, goldeneye, pintail and red-breasted merganser, are usually present along with mute swan and Canada goose, common scoter, pochard, scaup, shoveler and tufted duck. Dunlin and oystercatcher together will probably outnumber all the other waders but there are still good numbers of curlew, bar-tailed and black-tailed godwit, lapwing and redshank, with smaller numbers of golden, grey and ringed plover, turnstone, knot and sanderling. Avocet, greenshank, spotted redshank, ruff, curlew sandpiper, purple sandpiper and whimbrel may occur, while stormy weather may bring in many unexpected birds.

Exe Reedbeds

SX 955885; 25ha; DWT reserve
Reedbeds
Can be viewed from the banks of Exeter Canal
All year

These extensive reedbeds within the tidal reaches of the River Exe are important for birds. In winter jack snipe, black-tailed and bar-tailed godwits, and common and green sandpiper all frequent the area, while mute swan, reed and sedge warbler and reed bunting find the area ideal for nesting.

Exminster Marshes

SX 958875; 13.8ha; RSPB reserve
Estuary marshes
No parking facilities, visit on foot only
All year

A wild, flat landscape of low-lying meadows with reed-fringed ditches that is a haven for birds from the EXE ESTUARY during periods of high tide. On the estuary itself large concentrations of wildfowl and waders are found – especially during very cold weather when other estuaries in the country have frozen over. Wigeon, dark-bellied Brent geese and black-tailed godwits use the area in winter, along with red-breasted merganser, oystercatcher, grey and ringed plover, bar-tailed godwit, curlew and turnstone, all of which are present in nationally important numbers.

Both lapwing and redshank stay on to breed in the damp meadows of the reserve. Sedge, reed and Cetti's warblers nest in the reeds and scrub alongside the water-filled ditches. These in turn contain many water plants including flowering-rush and frogbit, and a wide variety of dragonflies such as the ruddy darter.

Fernworthy Reservoir

SX 665840; 30.8ha; SWWA
Reservoir
All year

Unlike most of the other Dartmoor reservoirs, Fernworthy has shallow, reedy banks which give excellent cover for water-birds. The nature reserve area is situated at the inlet of the reservoir and is surrounded by scrub and mature deciduous trees. Summer migrants include swift, redstart, siskin, redpoll and crossbill, while in winter goldeneye, teal, great crested grebe, goosander and heron frequent the reserve.

Fordy Park Wood

SS 818058; 0.7ha; WdT reserve
Woodland
Spring, summer

A small woodland that is a vital feature of the landscape.

Froward Point

SX 904496; 22.8ha; DWT NT reserve
Coastal woods and cliffs
Spring, early summer

Coniferous and mixed woodland, scrub and cliffs provide nesting sites for birds, while the cliff-top grassland contrasts with the wooded areas and provides a stand for sea-watching near the mouth of the River Dart.

Grand Western Canal

SS 963124–ST 074195; 17.6km; DCC
Linear park based on old canal
Leaflets from DCC
Spring, summer

Devon has very few slow waters but the old Tiverton Canal provides an example of a lowland waterway rich in plant and animal life.

The Grange

SX 895500; 11ha; DWT reserve
Coastal woods and cliffs
All year

Good views of the sea and the Dart Estuary can be obtained from the South Devon Coastal Footpath, which passes through pinewoods on this reserve.

Hall Farm

SX 631598; 97ha; WdT
Farmland
Summer

The farm was given to the Woodland Trust by its founder, Kenneth Watkins, who farmed the area for many years with conservation in mind. There are many areas of trees and hedges. One part of the reserve has been excluded from all agricultural activities for many years, and this has developed into attractive natural grassland and woodland as a result.

Halsdon

SS 554131; 57ha; DWT reserve
Woodland, grassland and river
Spring, summer

The large block of ancient woodland supports a wide range of birds and mammals, and slopes down the side of the Torridge Valley to marshes alongside the river, where kingfishers and sand martins may be seen.

Hangingcliff Wood

SX 425655; 3ha; DWT reserve
Mixed woodland
Spring, early summer

The mainly broad-leaved wood contains typical woodland birds such as pied flycatcher, redstart and wood warbler and is set on steep cliffs overlooking the TAMAR ESTUARY (Cornwall).

Hardwick Wood

SX 530555; 21ha; NT WdT reserve
Mixed woodland
All year

High on a hill on the eastern edge of Plymouth, the wood is an important feature of the city's landscape. There are many rides and paths through the wood, giving excellent views over Saltram House and Plymouth to the south, and over the lower slopes of DARTMOOR to the north.

Heddon Valley Nature Walk

SS 655483; 3.2km; NT
Coastal valley walk
Spring, summer

The circular walk follows the valley through fine oak woodlands and damp rich meadows to the sea at Heddon Mouth.

Hemborough Beeches

SX 828522; 0.7ha; WdT reserve
Beech wood
Spring, summer

These beeches on the Totnes to Dartmouth road are a well-known landmark.

Higher Kiln Quarry

Permit only; 1.2ha; DWT reserve
Disused quarry
Cave system and study centre–museum let to William Pengelly Cave Studies Trust
Access to caves and museum: Mr D. Curry, Plymouth Museum (tel. Plymouth 668000, ext. 4376)
Spring, early summer

The main interest of this reserve is an extensive Devonian limestone cave system containing colonies of bats at certain times of year. Fossil remains of straight-tusked elephants, narrow-nosed rhinoceros, hippopotamus and bison can be seen where they fell about 10,000 years ago.

Hollacombe Woods and Quarry

SX 527506; 6.6ha; WdT reserve
Deciduous woodland
Spring, summer

A varied broadleaf woodland that contains a worked-out quarry and a profusion of wildlife.

Isley Marshes

SS 283322; 39ha; RSPB reserve
Saltmarsh
All year

The saltmarsh lies on the southern shore of the River Taw, and BRAUNTON BURROWS is just across the river. The area is nationally important for wintering waders including oystercatcher, ringed and golden plover, sanderling and curlew, as well as there being good numbers of wigeon, shelduck, lapwing and redshank. Other species such as ruff, greenshank, green sandpiper and spotted redshank pass through on migration; lapwing, redshank and shelduck breed. The marsh also contains a good range of associated plants.

Lady's Wood

SX 687591; 3.2ha; DWT reserve
Coppiced woodland
Spring, early summer

Active coppicing maintains oak and ash standards over ash and hazel, with some grey willow. There is a good show of springtime flowers.

A feeder stream at Burrator: moss-covered rocks in low oak woodlands watered by rushing streams typify the change from open moorland.

Lickham Common

ST 126122; 4ha; DWT reserve
Heath and carr
Spring, early summer

Open areas are dominated by purple moor-grass, with bracken in drier parts and bog myrtle in wetter places; alder and alder buckthorn occur in the wet woodland, with old coppiced birch and willow, while standard oak trees prefer the drier sites. Roe deer and fox are present.

Littlewood

SX 539684; 0.4ha; WdT reserve
Mixed woodland
Spring, summer

The wood is an important feature of Dousland.

Liverton Copse

SY 025823; 2.8ha; WdT reserve
Mixed woodland
Spring, summer

A copse in the centre of Exmouth which was once planted with conifers. These have now been felled, except for a shelter belt on the seaward side, and the wood replanted with oak, ash and lime trees.

Longlands Brake

SX 502492; 0.7ha; WdT reserve
Broadleaf wood
Spring, summer

The reserve on a steep slope with the village of Heybrook Bay is a haven for birdlife.

Longstone Wood

SX 467753; 1ha; WdT reserve
Mixed woodland
No public access

This clump of mature beech and ash trees is a well-known landmark between Tavistock and Launceston.

Lundy Island

SS 143437; 450ha; Landmark Trust-NT reserve
Granite island
Passage bookings from the Administrator, Lundy via Ilfracombe, Devon
Booklet from site or LT
Spring, summer

The granite of Lundy is later than that of Dartmoor, perhaps as young as 50 million years old, and forms a sea-washed island about 5km long and less than 1km wide. Not only is Lundy a nature reserve above sea level, it has also been designated a marine nature reserve. The rocky foreshores and tidal zones are rich in seashore life and, some 17km from the mainland, provide a site where oceanic species may occur.

Above, the slopes and cliff ledges are filled with cushions of thrift and of sea-coast plants which give way to the heather, bracken and acid grasses of the peat. Here and there, pools provide water for grazing stock and a habitat for wetland plants, reinforced by small patches of bog.

The island is of special interest to botanists and coleopterists as the site for Lundy cabbage, which grows nowhere else in the world, and for two species of beetle which live on it.

Some 40 species of breeding birds nest around the island, taking advantage of the habitat range which includes, with the cliffs and moorland, woodlands of sycamore, rhododendron scrub, derelict quarries and tumbledown buildings, stone walls, grassland and gardens. The island's emblem, the puffin, is sadly diminished but still occurs with guillemot and razorbill while other seabirds include fulmar, kittiwake and shag with lesser black-backed and great black-backed gulls and herring gull. A few Manx shearwater still breed on the island and raven nest on the rocky crags of the cliffs, with wheatear and rock pipit flitting among cliff-top boulders and with small songbirds in the woods and the pockets of scrub. Over 400 different birds have been recorded, with the chance of sighting some rare or unusual species.

Martyn's Wood

SS 336031; 0.8ha; WdT reserve
Scrub and hedgerow
Spring, summer

A field of bracken and brambles adjacent to a hedge with tall trees forms a valuable wildlife habitat.

Meldon Reservoir

Permit only; 5.6ha; DWT reserve
Sanctuary area in moorland reservoir
May be overlooked from slopes around e.g. SX 563915
All year

In winter the reservoir may contain waterfowl, such as goldeneye and goosander, while early summer shows breeding stonechat, whinchat and wheatear. The banks contain both wet and dry heath with bog asphodel and heath spotted-orchid. The contrast between the ungrazed area of the reserve and the moor beyond is impressive.

New Bridge

Permit only; 2.2ha; DWT reserve
Mixed woodland
Spring, early summer

The woodland, mainly oak, is bounded in part by the River Teign, in part by a large tip of clay waste; the range of habitats includes those suitable for colonising species and for water plants.

New Cross Pond

Permit only; 11ha; DWT reserve
Clay pond, scrub and woodland
Winter

The disused clay pond is an important refuge for wintering wildfowl. It is surrounded by a mixture of other habitat types.

Northam Burrows

SS 444298; 263ha; DCC reserve
Coastal sand dunes and saltmarsh
Booklet from DCC
All year

The fascinations of the seashore, of rock pool and sandy beach, of saltmarsh, sand dune and estuary are all here, set in the mouth of the Taw and the Torridge. Plants such as glasswort, sea spurge and sea-holly colonise the mud and sand, common stork's-bill and wild thyme attract butterflies such as common blue and brown Argus. The birds that may be seen from this reserve include skylark, wheatear, ringed plover and shelduck, curlew and oystercatcher.

Northdown Wood

SS 923062; 9ha; WdT reserve
Mixed woodland
Spring, summer

This wood has a great variety of tree species and a rich flora. It has a long tradition of management as a nature reserve, for the Fursdon family who owned it for over 150 years also looked after it with conservation in mind.

Old Sludge Beds

SX 952888; 5.2ha; DWT reserve
Reedswamp and open water
All year

Common reed, bulrush, hemlock and willows provide a habitat attractive to birds, particularly small migrants.

Otter Estuary

SY 075825; 18ha; DWT reserve
Saltmarsh
Winter

The saltmarsh, a rare habitat in the south west, shows characteristic zonation from glasswort and sea-blight through sea club-rush to patches of common reed. In winter several hundred snipe are often present, along with little grebe, heron, Brent goose and shelduck. Meadow and rock pipits and stonechats breed on the fields adjacent to the estuary.

Dark-bellied Brent geese on the Exe Estuary.

Owlacombe Wood

SS 567166; 3.6ha; WdT reserve
Woodland and stream
Spring, summer

A stream running down the entire length of the reserve increases the variety of associated wildlife and plants in this attractive broadleaved woodland.

Page Wood

SY 137879; 0.4ha; WdT reserve
Mixed woodland
Spring, summer

The prominent small wood is situated on the west side of Salcombe Hill.

The Plantation

SX 734385; 0.8ha; WdT reserve
Mixed woodland
Spring, summer

This small area of mature mixed broadleaved trees forms part of the background to the town of Salcombe when seen from the estuary.

Point and Whitehall Woods

SX 483879; 9.4ha; WdT reserve
Mixed woodland
No public access
Spring, summer

An important wildlife and amenity woodland that is situated just outside the DARTMOOR NATIONAL PARK.

Pullabrook Wood

SY 787800; 20.6ha; WdT reserve
Mixed woodland
Spring, summer

At present sixty per cent of the wood is covered with conifers, but the Woodland Trust intends to replace most of these with broadleaved species in the coming years.

Rectory Field

SX 842696; 2.2ha; WdT reserve
Meadow and scattered trees
Spring, summer

A field with several groups of young trees, and mature trees in the hedgerow, the reserve is being managed by grazing to create an area of pasture woodland.

Scanniclift Copse

SX 841865; 11ha; DWT reserve
Broadleaved woodland
Spring

The copse is a small block of ancient woodland lying in the Teign Valley which exhibits a range of different woodland types and has a rich ground flora.

Shaptor and Furzeleigh Woods

SX 819797; 78ha; WdT reserve
Mixed woodland
Spring, early summer

Considerably varied, containing both dwarfed oaks and areas of coppice with planted beech and invading birch, the woods contain an excellent range of characteristic plants and animals including a good variety of birds.

Shears Copse

SS 614097; 1.2ha; WdT reserve
Scrub woodland
Spring, summer

A coppice of naturally regenerated scrub woodland on the edge of the old Winkleigh aerodrome. It has an especially plentiful and varied bird population.

Slapton Ley

SC 826431; 190ha; FSC reserve
Freshwater lagoon, reedbeds, mixed woodlands and shingle
Permit only to woodlands and Higher Ley, from South Hams Countryside Unit, Slapton Ley Field Centre, Slapton
Leaflets from South Hams Countryside Unit
All year

The beach carries a fine variety of plants. Ray's knotgrass, shore dock, sea radish and yellow horned-poppy grow on the long stretch of shingle while, beyond the road, the back slope of the ridge is thick with a cover of bramble and gorse and a mixed low tangle of scrub. Behind the ridge is the Ley, 100ha in area and up to 3m deep: a rich lake, full of plant and animal life. The Higher Ley is an almost continuous reedbed, a fen, invaded by willow, with quiet pools where mink and otter survive – a sanctuary for shyer birds.

Over 230 birds have been recorded here: the curve of the bay is such that the Ley offers shelter from south western winds. Spring and autumn offer passages of migrants while winter brings its regular seasonal flocks and storms at sea or bitter cold inland will bring birds here for shelter.

Shingle-breeding birds are gone, the visitor pressures are probably too high, and the same stress may deflect the breeding wildfowl, but great crested grebe, mallard and water rail, Cetti's and occasional grasshopper warbler, stonechat, grey wagtail and goldcrest all breed on the reserve. Nesting nearby, cormorant, fulmar and great black-backed gull declare the closeness of the sea and, in winter, gulls gather here in huge flocks – perhaps 10,000 birds roosting on the shingle beach and the Ley.

Snakey Copse

SX 874675; 0.4ha; WdT reserve
Mixed woodland
Spring, summer

The small woodland is mainly of local interest.

South Huish Marsh

No access; 1.5ha; DBWPS reserve
Wet pasture
May be overlooked from SX 677414
Autumn, winter

Migration times and winter are probably best here, when waders and wildfowl may be seen in the marshy grassland.

South Milton Ley

Permit only; 16.2ha; DBWPS reserve
Coastal reedbed
All year

A hide may be used by permit holders but the main importance of the reserve is as a ringing station. Reed and sedge warbler, occasional grasshopper and Cetti's warbler are among the breeding species while autumn brings a large roost of yellow wagtail and, in recent years, gatherings of bearded tit.

South Plantation

ST 114094; 12ha; WdT reserve
Mixed woodland
Spring, early summer

A mixed wood of conifers and broadleaves which will gradually be converted to a pure deciduous wood by felling the conifers as they reach maturity and replanting with native broadleaved trees.

South West Peninsula Coast Path

North Devon: SS 213174 793487; South Devon:
SX 493531 SY 332916; 256km; CC
Part of long-distance way
Leaflet from CC or booklet from HMSO bookshops
Spring, summer

Both the North and South Devon coastlines form part of this famous and well-walked long-distance path. This includes a wide spectrum of coastal scenery and habitat.

Sugarloaf Hill and Saltern Cove

SX 895583; 51.5ha; Torbay BC reserve
Small cove and coastal grassland
Spring, summer

Part of the reserve includes the active railway line and is out of bounds to visitors. The open-access grasslands and shallow cliffs are rich in flowers and typical scrub plants and the rocky shore is important for the wildlife of its tidal zones.

Tod Moor

SX 624540; 6.8ha; DWT reserve
Wet heath
Spring, summer

Wet, heathy grassland supports marsh plants such as bogbean and marsh-marigold. Oak–hazel coppice, hedgerows and gorse scrub add variety and encourage a good population of birds in spring and summer.

Uplyme Pinetum

SY 316936; 28ha; WdT reserve
Woodland and arboretum
Spring, summer

The pinetum is partly a deciduous wood of fine oaks and beeches and partly an arboretum of specimen conifers. It contains the country's tallest Prince Albert's yew and Japanese red cedar. There are also fine specimens of Caucasian fir and Wellingtonia.

Warleigh Point

SX 446610; 31ha; DWT reserve
Woodland and mudflats
Spring, summer

Wild service-tree, an ancient woodland indicator species, grows alongside the estuarine fringe. Much of the wood was clear-felled in the early 1960s and is now being re-coppiced in rotation. The reserve also includes mudflats and part of the fundus of the River Tavy.

Wedd's Copse and Tanglewood

SX 484745; 1.2ha; WdI reserve
Mixed woodland
No public access
Spring, summer

The area contains a disused railway line and associated woodland.

Welcombe and Marsland Valleys

SX 214174; 208ha; RSNC reserve
Coastal valley woodlands, scrub and grassland
Permit only off rights of way
Spring, summer

Including land in both the valleys and straddling the border between Devon and Cornwall, the reserve contains a magnificent range of habitat, from the weirdly folded rocks at Welcombe Mouth, through streamside valley woodland, to once-farmed fields high up in the valleys which are tending to revert to forest.

Much of the reserve is tall high-forest woodland, damp and sheltered in the deep valleys, with alder and willow along the marshy stream sides and with oak and mixed woodland in the valley bottoms and clothing the drier slopes. The oakwoods stand over hazel and holly above a ground cover of bramble varied with bluebell, hard fern and male-fern, honeysuckle and creeping softgrass. Spindle and privet mark areas of richer ground where dog's mercury, primrose, sanicle and hart's-tongue grow on the woodland floor, and higher slopes may be acid enough to support bilberry, common cow-wheat, heather and tormentil.

Mixed woodland of ash and sycamore tends to contain oak in the drier sites but, in damper situations, contains much alder over plants such as wild daffodil and yellow pimpernel or marsh plants including common valerian, marsh-marigold and meadowsweet. Beech in places reduces

The South West Peninsula Coast Path includes dramatic scenery such as this near Hartland.

ground cover to a spread of ferns, while other areas are wet enough for alder–willow carr. A full range from grassland to woodland may be seen: the old fields are invaded by bracken and bramble, then by a scrub of gorse and thorn trees, then by a secondary woodland which stands over hawthorn and blackthorn. These fields seen from the opposite slope, make a wonderful pattern on the hillside.

Other major habitats are the gorse heath, which holds acid plants such as lousewort, heath milkwort and trailing St John's-wort, and the short-tufted coastal grassland. The coastal turf is rabbit-grazed, trodden by visitors and exposed to bitter winds and salt spray, yet it carries a vivid range of such plants as spring squill, sea campion, thrift, restharrow, wild carrot and kidney vetch with a host of other small herbs.

There is a rich diversity of animals, with a good range of cliff-breeding, grassland, scrub and woodland birds. Mammals include badger and, among the insects, the reserve is particularly rich in butterflies with five species of fritillary.

Wembury Marine Conservation Area

SX 507484; 6km; WMCA Advisory Group reserve
Rocky foreshore and adjacent shallow water zone
Spring, summer

Comprising a length of rocky coast from Gara Point to Fort Bovisand at the mouth of Plymouth Sound, the reserve was set up in 1981 by voluntary agreement between landowners and users of the area, including the DWT. The inter-tidal reefs at Wembury are regularly visited by educational parties, while the rocky sublittoral areas are of great interest to divers. Wembury Point (SX 502482) is important for waders and migratory birds.

Westcott Wood

SX 785873; 5.6ha; WdT reserve
Coniferous woodland
Spring, summer

The conifer wood lies in the valley of a small tributary of the River Teign within the DARTMOOR NATIONAL PARK. The conifers will eventually be replaced by broadleaved trees.

Weston Mouth

SY 163879; 1ha; DWT reserve
Coastal scrub and grassland
Spring, summer

From the footpath through the reserve can be seen its speciality – purple gromwell – growing among the scrub.

Whitleigh Wood

SX 482599; 15.3ha; WdT reserve
Deciduous woodland
Spring, summer

The mixed broadleaved woodland has a series of attractive walks. The opening up of a glade and ride has increased the variety of habitats much enjoyed by the people of Plymouth.

The wood lies on a hillside in the centre of Tamerton Foliot and is an important landscape feature of the area.

Wistlandpound Reservoir

Permit only; 2ha; DBWPS–SWWA reserve
Wooded reservoir
Permit from SWWA
All year

The DBWPS manage a section of the reservoir where two hides overlook the coniferous woodland and a bay with a small artificial island. Birds include typical winter wildfowl species and woodland species such as buzzard and sparrowhawk.

Wistman's Wood

SX 612772; 24ha; Duchy of Cornwall–NCC reserve
Dwarfed moorland oakwood
Leaflet from NCC
Spring, early summer

The stunted oak woodland grows on a boulder-strewn slope, thick with mosses and lichens in conditions of harsh exposure, exceptionally high rainfall and frequent mists.

Badgers frequently inhabit the woodlands of south western England.

Small pearl-bordered fritillary can be seen in Welcombe and Marsland Valleys.

Wolborough

SX 866703; 5.2ha; DWT reserve
Small fen area
Spring, summer

The reserve is mainly wet birch and willow carr over *Sphagnum* moss, but also includes areas of fen and reed, which are uncommon in the county.

Woodcot Wood

SX 734384; 2.8ha; WdT reserve
Woodland
Spring, summer

The prominent woodland is situated on the west side of the Salcombe Estuary.

Yarner Wood

SX 785788; 150ha; NCC reserve
Oak–birch woodland
Permit only off marked trails
Leaflets from site or NCC
Spring, early summer

A mainly oak woodland, with birch colonising disused farmland, and with areas of moorland and planted conifers, the reserve contains wood warbler and pied flycatcher with holly blue and white admiral butterflies.

Yeo Copse

SS 801151; 5.6ha; WdT reserve
Oak woodland, river
Spring, summer

This attractive area of oak woodland lies on the south side of the valley of the River Sturcombe. An old mill leat is situated by the public footpath.

Dorset

Enter Dorset from almost any direction and you feel that here is a county that has survived into the late twentieth century relatively unscathed by modern development, with most its wild, rugged coast unspoiled and unpopulated, and its hinterland little changed from the countryside of Hardy's novels. Only at Dorset's eastern limits is this illusion completely shattered. Here Bournemouth, Christchurch and Poole form an extensive built-up area. It has obliterated a vast expanse of heath and subjugated most of its shoreline, but protection has been given to the wild beauty of Christchurch Harbour and HENGISTBURY HEAD, where the imposing eminence of Warren Hill broods over the bird-haunted levels of STANPIT MARSH.

West Dorset is quite another world. Its soft countryside melts imperceptibly into that of Devon, with deep lanes and sleepy villages, the rich pastures of the Marshwood Vale, and the oddly isolated hills capped with upper greensand. Different again are the chalk uplands which make a broad sweep over central Dorset and stretch a slender arm across the so-called ISLE OF PURBECK, which forms its south eastern corner. Chalk downland is Dorset's main scenic feature, but little now remains of its characteristic grassland. Some remnants which have escaped the modern plough are now enshrined in reserves like FONTMELL DOWN, but survival of the chalk plant life and its invertebrates often depends on the steepness of the hill slope and the legal protection afforded to the county's rich legacy of archaeological sites. It is indeed fortunate for present-day naturalists that these hills were cleared, grazed, settled, cultivated and defended in prehistoric times. The Neolithic and Bronze Age barrows which break the skyline, the Iron Age ramparts which crown the summits of the higher hills, the linear earthworks, circles, trackways and field systems now offer sanctuary, in an age of intensive farming, to such threatened species as chalkhill blue and marsh fritillary, fragrant orchid, clustered bellflower and knapweed broomrape.

In the south east of the county chalk hills enclose the tertiary sands and clays of the Poole Basin, once covered with heathland and bog that developed after Bronze Age man had stripped the woodland and scrub. For centuries the heaths survived virtually unchanged, providing fuel for humans and fodder for their livestock. Grazing, browsing and heather-burning ensured their treelessness and created a great wilderness of melancholy beauty, the fictional Egdon Heath of Thomas Hardy and Gustav Holst. Now the heathland mantle lies in shreds. The disintegration process began slowly but by 1900 much had already been ploughed into oblivion or sealed beneath the streets of Bournemouth, and now the expansion of Poole is taking its toll. Other areas have been ripped apart for their sand and clay, probed for oil, used by the military, smothered in domestic rubbish, swamped by conifers or converted into grassland. It is unfortunate that these southern heaths are the principal habitat of rare species such as Dartford warbler, sand lizard, smooth snake, marsh gentian and Dorset heath. Other species, especially among the invertebrates, are equally vulnerable but much less publicised. Their fate depends on the retention of a few large heathland reserves, which must be scientifically managed to prevent their reversion to woodland.

Recent conifer plantations account for much of the woodland on the tertiary deposits, and self-sown birches and pines are well established on those parts of the heath which have escaped fire. Oakwood with hazel is characteristic of the vales – the hazel is no longer coppiced to a great extent – with ash and beech on the lime-rich soils. Quite small deciduous woods can sometimes retain such treasures as lungwort, heath lobelia, greater butterfly-orchid, broad-leaved helleborine, white admiral and silver-washed fritillary, and the much-maligned conifer plantations are not without interest. The forests of Purbeck and Wareham are the daytime retreat of sika deer, and the BROWNSEA ISLAND pinewoods accommodate a heronry and a population of red squirrel.

Dorset has four main rivers: the Avon (shared with Hampshire) and the Stour drain into Christchurch Harbour, while the Piddle and Frome are received into vast Poole Harbour, which, with its saltings, mudflats, creeks and islands is Dorset's most impressive wetland. It is the haunt of migrating waders and summering terns, and the winter quarters of several thousand wildfowl, some of which move to the freshwater lake of STUDLAND's Little Sea.

One of Britain's long-distance footpaths begins on the Studland side of the narrow harbour entrance. Legions of students have descended upon Lulworth to examine its Cove and to look at the sea-carved arches of Stair Hole and Durdle Door and the places which gave their names to Kimmeridge clay and Purbeck marble, studied the development of Studland's acid dunes, followed the ghost of Mary Anning across the fossil-bearing lias of Lyme Regis, and stood upon the quarried heights of Portland to gaze upon the great westward sweep of Chesil Bank and the shingle-shielded waters of THE FLEET.

The ISLE OF PORTLAND holds itself aloof from the rest of Dorset, its back to Weymouth and its lowered head pointed at the unseen coast of France, somewhere beyond the tide race and the plunging gannets. First impressions may be unfavourable – it is bleak, grey and practically treeless – but Portland has character, and even without its bird observatory, rare plants, raised beach and ancient fields it would still exert a strange fascination on the visitor.

Further east, beyond Lulworth, lie the shores of Purbeck; the restless cliffs of Kimmeridge clay, the spray-lashed headlands of Portland stone, and the tilted, faulted Purbeck Beds, which dip beneath the waves at Peveril Point. Along this coast fulmar glide past jostling guillemot, the weary Channel-crossing migrants find rest in scrub-filled gullies, and downland butterflies and orchids still decorate the cliff-top fields of limestone grassland.

Dorset provides an embarrassment of riches for the naturalist, in its towns as well as in its countryside. Where else, save at Weymouth's reedy wilderness of RADIPOLE, can the sounds of water rail and bearded tit mingle with those of motor traffic and diesel trains?

W.G. TEAGLE

Allington Hill

SY 456935; 12.8ha; WdT
Woodland and grassland
Spring, summer

The reserve consists of rough grazing land and attractive hedgerows with woodland on its eastern edge. It affords excellent views over the surrounding countryside and coastline.

Arne

SY 984885; 531ha; RSPB reserve
Rich heathland and estuary margin
Leaflet from RSPB
All year

The mudflats, saltmarsh and reedbeds, the birch, oak and coniferous woodlands and the small old fields and roadside verges add to the variation of the reserve, but the main importance of Arne is the splendid heathland. Heather, bell heather and dwarf gorse are spread across the thin acid peats, with cross-leaved heath where the soil is damper and with fine stands of Dorset heath. Wetter sites are also rich in bog species, such as *Sphagnum* mosses, white beak-sedge and all three British sundews and, with open pools formed from old bomb craters, provide an important habitat for some of the special insects of the reserve, such as small red damselfly, downy emerald, scarce ischnura, scarce and southern aeshna.

A special feature of the Dorset heathlands is their colonies of reptiles and, here at Arne, all six British species may be found.

Considerable spreads of gorse grow in the coombs and around the heathlands, providing suitable nest sites for another Arne speciality, the tiny Dartford warbler, a rare non-migratory bird always threatened because, at the limit of its range, it cannot survive hard winters. Over 170 species of birds have been noted here, with impressive winter flocks of the larger waders, with a good range of wildfowl in winter and a fine variety of passage birds, including several hundred black-tailed godwit on spring migration. Breeding birds include species of heathland, woodland and marsh, such as stonechat, nightjar, sparrowhawk and redshank, while the reedbeds provide a nesting site which has attracted bearded tit.

A nature trail is laid out during the summer months and Shipstal Point provides a bird-watching site from which summer terns and winter wildfowl may be seen.

Avon Forest Park

SU 128023; 600ha; DCC
Heathland and plantations
Spring, summer

A relict area of the Dorset heathlands, the park includes a spread of grassland and heath within coniferous woodlands. Dartford warbler occur on the heath which is also a site for smooth snake and sand lizard.

Black Ven and the Spittles

SY 353931; 64.4ha; DTNC NT reserve
Undercliff, landslip, grassland and circular walk
This site is dangerous
Spring, early summer

Continual slipping opens a wide range of habitat from scrub woodland, on stable areas, to open sloping faces and puddingy mires where slips are frequent. Unimproved meadows form the western section of the reserve and contain a rich grassland flora. Cowslips flower on steeper banks, while the wet flushes support orchids and other wetland plants and harbour snipe in winter. Insects include great green bush cricket, while among the mammals are roe deer, fox and badger.

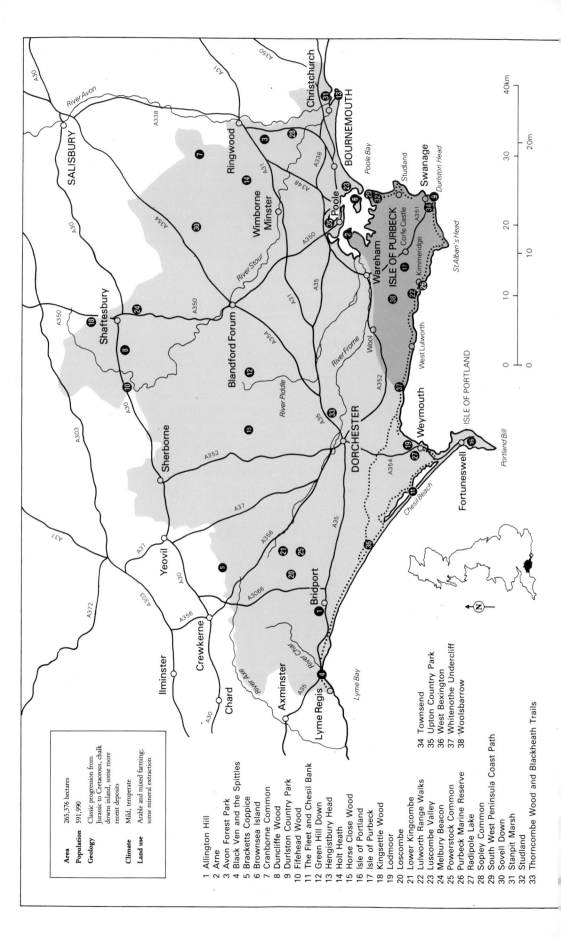

Area 265,376 hectares

Population 591,990

Geology Classic progression from Jurassic to Cretaceous, chalk downs inland, some more recent deposits

Climate Mild, temperate

Land use Arable and mixed farming; some mineral extraction

1 Allington Hill
2 Arne
3 Avon Forest Park
4 Black Ven and the Spittles
5 Bracketts Coppice
6 Brownsea Island
7 Cranborne Common
8 Duncliffe Wood
9 Durlston Country Park
10 Fifehead Wood
11 The Fleet and Chesil Bank
12 Green Hill Down
13 Hengistbury Head
14 Holt Heath
15 Horse Close Wood
16 Isle of Portland
17 Isle of Purbeck
18 Kingsettle Wood
19 Lodmoor
20 Loscombe
21 Lower Kingcombe
22 Lulworth Range Walks
23 Luscombe Valley
24 Melbury Beacon
25 Powerstock Common
26 Purbeck Marine Reserve
27 Radipole Lake
28 Sopley Common
29 South West Peninsula Coast Path
30 Sovell Down
31 Stanpit Marsh
32 Studland
33 Thorncombe Wood and Blackheath Trails
34 Townsend
35 Upton Country Park
36 West Bexington
37 Whitenothe Undercliff
38 Woolsbarrow

Boyden Wood

ST 404026; 0.8ha; WdT reserve
Young broad-leaved woodland
Spring, early summer

An area of farmland, now returned to woodland by planting with deciduous trees, will form a haven for many types of wildlife as it matures.

Bracketts Coppice

ST 517072; 21.6ha; DTNC reserve
Woodland and scrub grassland
Permit only off right of way
Spring, early summer

The wood is mainly of oak standards over a mixture of ash, birch, holly and old hazel coppice with shrub species such as wild rose, guelder-rose and privet. Generally the ground cover is fairly thin but there is a great deal of variation; areas of woodland grasses alternate with splays of fern, with woodland flowers such as bugle, primrose and violet or with spreads of enchanter's-nightshade or carpets of ivy. The reserve has a spectacular show of pendulous sedge, in some places covering the entire woodland floor.

Bramble, hawthorn and honeysuckle grow among the other shrubs and, in places, the ground is thick with young blackthorn seedlings, while an area of denser woodland is filled with ash saplings beneath the coppiced hazel. The natural climax on these lime-rich clays of fuller's earth is probably oak–ash woodland, but above the stream it is acid enough for bracken. The stream itself is edged with ferns and rich-wood plants such as dog's mercury and wood spurge.

The grasslands are also damp, with tussocks of purple moor-grass, rushes, sedges, and plants such as devil's-bit scabious, fleabane, tormentil, sawwort and common spotted-orchid. Scrub, spreading from the woodland, varies these clearings with birch, blackthorn, dogwood, gorse, hazel, hawthorn and wild rose. The damp-meadow plants, scrub and woodland edge make these grassland areas most attractive to a good range of butterflies and birds and they probably harbour the deer whose tracks may be seen in the wood.

Brounlie Wood

ST 601118; 1.5ha; WdT reserve
New woodland and wetland
Spring, early summer

A mixture of tree species has been planted in a small area which includes three ponds.

Brownsea Island

SZ 032877; 100ha; DTNC–NT reserve
Estuary island
Regular guided visits; no dogs
Boat service from Poole Quay or Sandbanks Ferry
Leaflet from DTNC
April–September

The reserve occupies slightly less than half of the island and contains red squirrel, sika deer and the heronry. The North Ridge is wooded with pine trees, varied with several exotic species, which stand over an often dense scrub of rhodo-dendron. The ridge slopes down to the central valley, where two lakes provide freshwater pools for waterfowl, and falls in a steep short scarp to the reedmarsh and the lagoon. A further range of habitat is added by a wet woodland of willow and alder between the lakes and the reedmarsh and by spreads of grassland, heath and mixed woodland in the southern half of the island.

Common and Sandwich tern breed on the islands in the lagoon, little grebe, mallard, teal and tufted duck may nest by the lakes, and the reedbed and marsh provide sites for birds such as reed and sedge warbler, reed bunting and, probably, water rail. Other breeding species include great and lesser black-backed, black-headed and herring gull and shelduck.

In late summer, 100 or more cormorants rest on the sea wall or spread their wings on islets while herons, which nest in the pines on the North Ridge in the second largest heronry in Britain, regularly visit the lagoon.

Charlton Beeches

ST 897041; 1.2ha; WdT reserve
Narrow roadside woodland
Spring, early summer

The small stand of large trees provides a refuge for woodland wildlife in an area comprising mainly arable farmland.

Cranborne Common

ST 103112; 42.8ha; DTNC reserve
Typical Dorset heathland
Access by public footpath
All year

The habitats range from dry heath, with gorse and heather, through wet heath and bog, with bog asphodel and good populations of dragonflies and crickets. The reserve is notable for reptiles and breeding birds, including nightjar and Dartford warbler.

One of Arne's special plants is Dorset heath.

Duncliffe Wood

ST 825225; 88ha; WdT reserve
Mixed woodland
Spring, summer

The reserve forms one of the largest areas of woodland in north Dorset, set like a saddle on top of two hills overlooking the Blackmoor Vale. This ancient wood was once all oak and hazel coppice but has now been substantially replanted. The woodbank is surmounted by huge pollards, one of which is thought to be the oldest living thing in Dorset.

Durlston Country Park

SZ 032773; 104.4ha; DCC
Coastal limestone grassland, scrub, old quarry workings and part of long-distance way
Leaflets from information centre or DCC Planning Dept
Spring, summer

Although not strictly a nature reserve, Durlston Country Park is managed as a wildlife sanctuary. The cliff-top walk, part of the SOUTH WEST PENINSULA COAST PATH, provides dramatic views of seabirds and their nesting colonies. The importance of shelter is shown by the scrub on these slopes: the lower stands of blackthorn are spectacularly pruned while higher up, although still showing signs of wind sculpting, the scrub is more variable with hawthorn, gorse and bramble and, above and behind the crest of the headland, a belt of taller scrub is thick with traveller's-joy.

A great variety of lime-loving plants may be seen on the grassland slopes where deeper soils carry gorse, bramble and wild rose over coarse grasses, clovers and thistles, and shallow soils are filled with bright small herbs.

Above the grassland is a broken plateau, an area of the hills and holes of old quarry workings and of slabby limestone walling. The steep thin sunny slopes are ideal sites for such plants as pyramidal orchid while deeper, sheltered soils show taller plants such as greater knapweed, wild parsnip and woolly thistle, or bracken where rain has washed the lime from the soil.

The scrub provides shelter and feeding for migrant birds while the plants attract a great range of butterflies including Adonis, chalkhill and small blue, and dark green fritillary.

Fifehead Wood

ST 778218; 20ha; WdT reserve
Oak-ash woodland
Spring, early summer

Dry and wet woodland with oak and ash standards over old hazel coppice; part of the wood was once wet enough to support an osier bed.

The Fleet and Chesil Bank

SY 568840-668754; 800ha; Strangways Estate
Large tidal lagoon and shingle beach
No access to part of Chesil Bank in nesting season, and no access at any time to sanctuary
All year

The huge storm beach is one of the five largest shingle ridges in Europe and the sheltered lagoon behind it , the Fleet, is open to the sea in Portland Harbour and lies behind the eastern half of the shingle bank which extends for over 25km from the ISLE OF PORTLAND.

The western part of the Fleet is a sanctuary and contains the famous Abbotsbury Swannery where mute swan have bred for centuries; winter numbers of these birds may approach 1000. They feed on the richest beds of brackish-water plants remaining in Britain, for the lagoon holds good amounts of eelgrass, with both narrow-leaved and dwarf eelgrass and beaked tasselweed. Wigeon, too, are attracted here and several thousand may be present in winter, together with very large numbers of coot, Brent goose, gadwall, goldeneye, pintail and pochard. Shelduck, shoveler, teal and tufted duck also winter on the Fleet, with red-breasted merganser here and in Portland Harbour.

Small numbers of waders may feed on the muddy shingle edges or on the clay beaches of the Fleet, including species such as dunlin, bar-tailed godwit, lapwing, oystercatcher, ringed and grey plover and redshank. The shingle is an important breeding site for common and little tern and is wardened in summer to protect them from disturbance; no access is permitted then.

Westwards, beyond the Fleet, the shingle lies against the land, backed by arable slopes, small lagoons, and an interesting area of reedbed at WEST BEXINGTON where reed-nesting birds and migrants may be seen. The shingle has developed a good range of typical plants such as sea-kale and yellow horned-poppy. Within its length the Chesil Bank contains populations of rough clover, shrubby sea-blite and sea pea, and is also the only known British site for *Mogoplistes squamiger*, a species of wingless cricket.

Fontmell Down

ST 884176; 57.2ha; DTNC NT reserve
Chalk downland, scrub and woodland
Leaflet from DTNC
Spring, summer

Fontmell Down overlooks the Vale of the Stour and the other great chalk banks which thrust out into the plain.

The reserve itself is a dry valley patterned with scrub, with woodland along one side. The slopes are steep, full of chalkland flowers and butterflies and scattered clumps and thickets of lime-loving scrub. Blackthorn, hawthorn, bramble, gorse and wild rose, dogwood, wayfaring-tree, whitebeam, privet, holly and yew are tangled with traveller's-joy and honeysuckle. The woodland proper is chiefly of planted conifers which the DTNC intend to replace with native hardwoods, but it also contains beech, ash and whitebeam, with birch and with spectacular spreads of traveller's-joy, in places covering entire trees.

The grassland plants are exceptionally rich and grow in great profusion on the thin chalk soils or on the mounded ant hills which cover the slopes. Quaking-grass, harebell, carline and dwarf thistle, lady's bedstraw and common bird's-foot-trefoil, with restharrow, small scabious, wild thyme and salad burnet are among the typical plants. Other less common species include early gentian, clustered bellflower, bastard-toadflax and autumn lady's-tresses while, to the south of the reserve, is an additional small plot which is managed for an interesting population of greater knapweed parasitised by knapweed broomrape.

Green Hill Down

ST 792037; 12ha; DTNC reserve
Chalk downland, clay-with-flints capping
Access by public footpath; no dogs
Spring, summer

Scrub and scattered oak, ash and beech add variety to an area of grassland which, with a small pond, contains a wide range of habitat and includes a strong population of marbled white butterfly.

Hartland Moor

Permit only; 258ha; NCC NT reserve
Fine example of Dorset heath
Leaflet from NCC
Spring, early summer

See ISLE OF PURBECK

Hengistbury Head

SZ 175907; 100ha; Bournemouth BC reserve
Low coastal promontory
Leaflet from BBC
Spring, autumn

A circular trail demonstrates the promontory which includes heathland, woodland, grassland, ponds, dunes, saltmarsh and seashore, important as a staging post for spring and autumn migrants.

Higher Hyde Heath

Permit only; 40ha; DTNC reserve
Heathland, acid bog and carr woodland
Summer, early autumn

The dry heath is home for both the smooth snake and the sand lizard, while the attractive marsh gentian occurs locally in the wetter areas. The acid bog is scattered with small pools, which, together with nearby streams, have given rise to a particularly rich and interesting dragonfly and damselfly fauna.

Hod Hill

Permit only; 2.6ha; NT reserve
Chalk downland
Spring, summer

The two small blocks of fine unimproved grassland contain chalkland plants and butterflies.

Holt Heath

SZ 060040; 450ha; NCC reserve
Heath and oak woodland
Spring, early summer

Dry, damp and wet heath occur widely on the reserve, together with valley bogs that merge into a flat mire at the southern end. To the north the land rises to its highest point at Bulbarrow and from here, looking south, it is possible to obtain an impression of wild Dorset as it must have appeared for many years. The heath's large size and diversity allow a rich fauna with good populations of characteristic heathland birds and insects.

In Holt Forest the massive pollarded oaks, standing over a dense understorey of holly, support many lichens and invertebrates.

Holton Heath

Permit only; 80ha; NCC reserve
Heathland and woodland
Spring, summer

A belt of saltmarsh and reedbed adds a further range of habitat to a varied area of dry heathland with stands of birch and Scots pine. The heathland is rich in animal species such as spiders, wasps and butterflies, including both grayling and silver-studded blue. Smooth snake and sand lizard are present and breeding birds include stonechat and, possibly, Dartford warbler.

Horse Close Wood

ST 715045; 16.4ha; WdT reserve
Mixed woodland
Spring, early summer

Under oak standards the wood is a mix of alder, ash, oak and hazel coppice and contains one of the very few Dorset populations of meadow saffron. There is a typical range of woodland birds and a large and active badger sett.

Isle of Portland

SY 682738; c.1050ha; various bodies
Massive limestone outcrop
All year

Connected with the mainland by the pebble ridge of the Chesil Bank, the island provides a site for formal wildlife studies in the presence of a ringing station and bird observatory. Cliffs and quarries demonstrate the geology and fossils of the limestone, supporting an exciting range of plant and insect life, while the island is a staging post for migrant birds and a superb site for sea-watching.

Isle of Purbeck

See map; c.22,000ha; various bodies
Chalk and limestone hills set between heathland and sea
Spring, summer

Purbeck's seaward defences are the cliffs, where layered and buckled rocks provide ideal nesting sites for birds and shallow ledges on which plants can grow above the reach of the sea. The sea continually carves and whittles the rocks away, forming complex and spectacular bays, such as Lulworth Cove. The 'Isle', once joined to the Isle

The Chesil Bank protects the Fleet from the sea.

of Wight, is built of an extraordinary geological mix unique in Britain and draws geologists from all over the world to visit the Purbeck coast.

The cliffs themselves may be sheer towers of hard rock or steep crumbling faces, ranging from dazzling chalk to dark shales; green slopes and jungled spreads of scrub show where landslips have broken the rock face, while the pale limestone may be marked by caves, old quarry workings cut in the face of the cliffs. These caves are important sites for bats and hold colonies of greater horseshoe, Bechstein's and grey long-eared bat, while the cliffs provide nesting sites for birds such as fulmar and kittiwake, shag and cormorant, guillemot, razorbill and perhaps a few pairs of puffin. The cliff tops are rich in plants, with notable species such as wild cabbage, Italian lords-and-ladies and early spider-orchid growing among a host of colourful flowers. A fine variety of insects includes Adonis, chalkhill, little and common blue with marbled white and dark green fritillary butterflies, together with wart-biter cricket and long-winged cone-head. The landslip jumbles provide cover for breeding buzzard and larger mammals such as fallow deer and badger.

Inland, where soft rocks separate the limestone from the chalk, a spread of agricultural land gives a scenery of fields and hedges, of farmsteads and small villages protected by the chalk ridge to the north. Except where the slopes are steep, farming has modified the grassland and most of the chalkland flowers have been lost but, on these steeper slopes, some characteristic downland remains. Some of the scarps are wooded and

oak and hazel coppice contrasts with the wide plantations on the plain below.

The heaths beyond the chalk ridge have formed on coarse sands, laid down in tertiary times, where clays prevent free drainage and assist the development of the mires. These wet and dry heaths include STUDLAND, HARTLAND MOOR and ARNE and form a striking contrast with the higher land of Purbeck; where the hills are rich in lime-loving plants, the heathlands are far more acid; where all but the steepest upland slopes are farmed, the heaths form an open wilderness. These heaths once stretched from here almost to Dorchester, Thomas Hardy's inspiration for the daunting Egdon Heath, but they have been ploughed, planted with conifers and buried under houses and industry. Now only a broken scatter of heathland remains, a last small refuge for plants and animals unique in the British Isles.

Adder and grass-snake, slow worm and common lizard slither or scuttle among stands of Dorset heath and here, but nowhere else in Britain, they share their hunting grounds with smooth snake and sand lizard. The smooth snake only occurs in southern England and the Dorset heaths are the stronghold of both these species. For the Dartford warbler, also, Dorset is a key area, and other typical heathland birds include linnet, stonechat and yellowhammer with nightjar and hobby.

To these special animals of the heaths might be added insects such as feathered footman moth, dragonflies from the pools and mires such as scarce coenagrion, scarce blue darter, scarce aeshna and small red damselfly, and other interesting species such as heath and large marsh grasshoppers. The wetter areas, too, contain a splendid range of plants which includes brown beak-sedge, intermediate bladderwort, marsh clubmoss, royal fern, great sundew, marsh gentian and the delicate small bog orchid. The heathlands provide a wide diversity of interest and, coloured with Dorset heath, filled with the scent of bog myrtle, are an irreplaceable part of our national heritage.

Kingsettle Wood

ST 865255; 21ha; WdT reserve
Mixed woodland
Spring, summer

The reserve sits on top of a ridge overlooking Blackmoor Vale, straddling the Dorset–Wiltshire county boundary. In the last 35 years much of the wood has been felled and replanted, mainly with conifers and some beech. The Trust plans to restore the site to native broadleaves but in the meantime it provides a wonderful place to enjoy the views over the River Stour.

Lodmoor

SY 686807; 61ha; RSPB reserve
Damp pasture, reedbeds, dykes and scrub
All year

Behind Weymouth's seafront lies a wetland area with an outstanding variety of birds. By following the footpath from the Sea Life Centre, the reserve can be viewed from three different hides. In the breeding season bearded tits, water rails and sedge warblers can be heard, and sometimes seen, in the reedbeds, and Cetti's warblers lurk in the scrubby areas. On the wet pasture yellow wagtails and redshank nest, while stonechats, linnets and whitethroats are found in the drier grassland with scrub. In autumn passage waders use the reserve and there is always the chance of seeing North American rarities, such as grey phalaropes and pectoral sandpipers. Winter visitors to the reserve are large flocks of lapwing and snipe, with smaller numbers of jack snipe and water pipits, while floods bring shoveler, wigeon, teal, pintail, gadwall and Brent geese.

Loscombe

ST 506982; 10ha; DTNC reserve
Grassland and wetland
Access on public foothpath only
Leaflet from DTNC
Spring, summer

Lying in a narrow valley tucked away in a remote and relatively unchanged part of west Dorset, the reserve consists of species-rich pasture and hay meadow, a marshy field, a stream, wet woodland and many ancient hedgerows. The grassland is full of ant hills of the yellow meadow ant, and in the wet areas there are good populations of southern marsh-orchid. A wide range of interesting butterflies can be seen and buzzards often circle overhead.

Lower Kingcombe

SY 545983; 133ha; DTNC reserve
Grassland and hedgerows
Access via public footpaths
Ownership map from DTNC
Spring, summer, autumn

When Lower Kingcombe estate came up for sale in 1987, it was dubbed 'a farm held in a rural time-warp'. The area had been managed on traditional lines for generations, hedges had been cut and laid by hand, the fields bordering the River Hooke were undrained and as wet and lush as they had always been and the use of modern pesticides and fertilisers had been kept to a minimum.

The wildlife of Kingcombe is therefore Dorset at its best. There are fallow, roe and sika deer in the woods; buzzards and sparrowhawks wheel overhead, and butterflies abound, including the local and declining marsh and small pearl-bordered fritillaries.

But the real jewel in Kingcombe's crown must be the unimproved lowland meadows. They are a haven of colour and scent with devil's-bit scabious, cowslips, rough hawkbit, yellow rattle and oxeye daisy.

What makes the reserve special is the sheer abundance of flowers, not its rarities. However, there are marsh orchids, adder's-tongue, dyer's greenweed, lady's-mantle, pepper saxifrage, wood horsetail and the local corky-fruited water-dropwort.

The chalkland of Fontmell Down overlooking the Vale of the Stour.

Lulworth Range Walks

SY 882804; various lengths; MOD
Coastal downland
The range is still used: visitors must keep to marked
footpaths
Open most weekends but check local press or tel.
Bindon Abbey 462721, ext. 859
Leaflets from exhibition centre, DCC or DTNC
Spring, summer, on open days only

Several walks have been laid out in an area rich
in lime-loving plants and animals. Over 2000ha
of downland with around 10.5km of coast make
up the range. Large numbers of butterflies occur
in sheltered areas including dark green fritillary,
marbled white and Lulworth skipper. The wild
flowers include wild cabbage, gentians and squinancywort. The village church of Tyneham has
been converted into an interpretative centre open
to the public.

Luscombe Valley

SZ 045891; 4.5ha; Poole BC reserve
Grassland, heathland and scrub
All year

The valley supports a wide variety of flowering
plants and grasses indigenous to this low-lying
land. The area is interspersed with trees, predominantly pine and silver birch, with heather and
other heathland flora. There is a good variety of
wildlife, particularly birds.

Melbury Beacon

ST 874197; 80ha; NT
Grassland
Summer

This very attractive, large area of chalk grassland
adjoins FONTMELL DOWN, and has a similar
profusion of downland plants which attract a very
good selection of butterflies.

Morden Bog

Permit only; 149ha; NCC reserve
Dry heath, bog and old decoy ponds
Spring, early summer

An exceptionally rich heathland holds a very
varied insect population. The surrounding FC
woodland encourages a good variety of bird life
and supports a large deer population.

Powerstock Common

SY 540963; 115ha; DTNC reserve
Oak woodland, scrub, grassland and disused railway
Permit only off bridleway and tracks
Leaflet and nature trail from DTNC
Spring, early summer

The reserve is made up of several areas within
the FC plantations which cover much of the
common. Where the bridleway passes through
one of the oakwoods, the ground is damp and
heavy, a slope of clay with an understorey of
hazel, varied with stands of dense blackthorn or

with shrubs such as spindle, privet and dogwood.
Ash standards occur with the oaks and the less
dense areas are floored with rich-wood species
such as primrose, violet and dog's mercury.
Bracken grows in well-lit drier parts, with bramble
and red currant, and gives way in damper shade
to broad buckler-fern or male-fern; the wettest
clays are marked by clumps of pendulous sedge
and occasional grey willow.

The open grassland field is also damp, a spread
of purple moor-grass, filled with wetland plants
and ringed with trees. Cross-leaved heath and
heather, devil's-bit scabious, tormentil, fleabane
and betony contrast with rushes, sedges and
horsetails, and a small pond at the edge of the
meadow has a variety of water plants including
lesser spearwort and bogbean.

The forest tracks provide another very varied
habitat, fringed with drainage ditches and marshy
places thick with meadowsweet and yellow iris,
with rushes and pendulous sedge, edged with
stands of common spotted-orchid, with vetches,
clovers, knapweeds and carpets of creeping
cinquefoil. Heather and gorse spread beside the
tracks beneath young plantations of conifers which
form an open scrub, highly suitable for hunting
birds such as sparrowhawk. Taller plantations,
with their dark forest floors, have little undergrowth but the many animal tracks which cross
the rides indicate that they probably shelter some
of the larger mammals here. Another habitat is
provided by the bracken-covered slopes which
run up to the crest of the old common. The
bracken is dense and laced with bramble, some
of it planted with conifers, but a variety of saplings
have become established and show how the native
woodland would easily spread, if it were given
the opportunity to do so.

The disused railway line adds a cutting suitable
for lime-loving species and noted for butterflies.
The area as a whole is rich in insects and supports
a wide range of birds and other animals, including
fallow, sika and roe deer.

Purbeck Marine Reserve

SY 909788; *c*.650ha; DTNC reserve
Cliff top to as far as 1km offshore
Leaflets from information centre or DTNC
Spring, summer

Although marine nature reserves have been established at LUNDY ISLAND (Devon) and SKOMER ISLAND
(Dyfed), Purbeck is the first reserve of its kind to
be set up on the mainland. It has an excellent
interpretative centre at Kimmeridge Bay, a deep
curve dominated by the great shaly cliffs which
fall to the Kimmeridge Ledges.

The difference in height between high and low
tides is relatively small, less than 2m, but the
shallow slope of the beaches means that a wide
area is exposed at low water, ideal for seashore
studies. The pools at various stages down the
beach will hold the plants and animals which are
typical of that zone.

Channelled wrack marks the top zone, followed
by bladder wrack, with knotted wrack in sheltered

areas, and then serrated wrack. Below this, and in the deeper pools, sea-lettuce and kelp mark the margin of the tides. Throughout the zones the animals move or live cemented to the rocks or seaweeds, a wonderful variety of colour, shape and size.

The reserve is mid-way between the western and eastern basins of the Channel and contains several species at or near the limits of their normal distribution. These include cushion starfish, wartlet anemone, and a range of algae and of molluscs including Pandora shell.

Radipole Lake

SY 677796; 78ha; RSPB—Weymouth and Portland BC reserve
Reedbeds and lakes
Leaflet available on site
All year

This unique reserve is situated in the heart of the seaside town of Weymouth, and yet 250 species of birds have been recorded here. The extensive reedbeds provide ideal breeding areas for reed, sedge and grasshopper warblers, while in the area of scrub one of the site specialities, Cetti's warbler, can be heard. Gadwall also nest, and in autumn many migrants use the area as a staging post. The reedbeds provide a safe roosting site for large numbers of swallows and yellow and pied wagtails. Butterflies such as red admiral, painted lady and clouded yellow come from over the sea, too, as do convolvulus and striped hawk moths.

The lake is an important wintering area for wildfowl with mallard, teal, shoveler, tufted duck and pochard present in good numbers, and gadwall and shelduck sometimes numerous. Among the more interesting plants are sea aster, sea milkwort and sea club-rush which indicate the site's estuarine past. Southern marsh and pyramidal orchids and the uncommon summer snowflake also grow on the reserve.

Sopley Common

SZ 135975; 34ha; DTNC reserve
Wet and dry heath and woodland
Spring, summer

Both wet and dry heath and a small area of woodland are found on this interesting old common. Many typical heathland species occur including smooth snake, sand lizard, nightjar, silver-studded blue and the rare heath grasshopper.

South West Peninsula Coast Path

SY 344928 SZ 042860; 116km; CC
Very varied section of long-distance way
Leaflet from CC or DCC, or booklet from HMSO bookshops
Spring, summer

The Dorset stretch of the pathway begins at Lyme Regis and ends at Poole Harbour. On its way it passes through or by a variety of areas of wildlife interest from BLACK VEN AND THE SPITTLES in the west to STUDLAND in the east.

Sovell Down

ST 992108; 1.6ha; DTNC reserve
Chalk grassland and scrub
Access by public footpaths
Spring, summer

The reserve is rich in chalkland plants, with over 135 species recorded. It contains a good range of butterflies while the scrub provides feeding and nesting sites for small birds.

Stanpit Marsh

SZ 169920; 48.7ha; Christchurch BC reserve
Estuary marshland
No access off rights of way
Information caravan
All year

The reserve ranges from grazing marsh to freshwater marsh and saltmarsh, and from estuary waters to ditches and pools. Waders, together with birds such as shelduck and heron, are attracted to the site.

Stonecrop Wood

SY 988955; 0.8ha; WdT reserve
Mixed woodland
Spring, early summer

Mainly a birch woodland, Stonecrop Wood is situated on the urban outskirts of Broadstone and provides a valuable retreat and shelter for wildlife in that area.

Studland

SZ 034836; 631ha; NCC–NT reserve
Dry and wet heathland, lagoon and woodland
Observation hut open Sun or by appointment
There is severe danger of fire: do not drop matches or cigarettes
Leaflets from NCC
Spring, early summer

Some of the specialities of the reserve are hidden within the heathland which makes up most of the area, but two nature trails have been set up to show the general wildlife interest.

The Sand Dune Nature Trail includes a stretch of foreshore, outside the reserve, which demonstrates a good variety of shells together with birds such as oystercatcher, ringed plover, common and Sandwich tern and perhaps, in winter, red-breasted merganser, common scoter and eider. The trail proper begins in the dunes which are stabilised by sand couch, lyme-grass and marram, decorated with sheep's-bit, common centaury and sea bindweed. Behind the first ridge a damp gully, a slack, has developed and in the damper areas characteristic plants are found. Cross-leaved heath and round-leaved sundew, bog myrtle, purple moor-grass and common cottongrass occur while similar sites hold royal fern, great sundew and marsh gentian. Grey willow, birch and gorse form clumps of scrub, and occasional pools, old bomb craters, may contain greater bladderwort. The drier levels and intervening ridges are thick with

Stair Hole and Lulworth Cove demonstrate the astonishing geology of the Isle of Purbeck.

heather, here and there laced with lesser dodder, a parasite which grows on heather and gorse.

The Woodland Trail, open from April to September, leads through birch, grey willow and aspen, gladed with bluebell and bramble, with blackthorn, hawthorn and elder scrub. Part of the trail overlooks the Little Sea, a site for the rare spring quillwort. The woodland contains typical bird life and roe deer may be frequent. The reserve is home to all six British reptiles and is rich in insects, with a fine range of dragonflies.

Tadnoll Meadows

Permit only; 44ha; DTNC reserve
Heathland, damp meadowland and bog
Spring, summer

Heathland, of heather, bell heather and cross-leaved heath, and species-rich meadowland with plants such as water avens, great burnet and common spotted-orchid, grade into a spread of purple moor-grass and *Sphagnum*, with abundant stands of bog myrtle. The reserve is noted for smooth snake and for good numbers of roe deer and resident badger.

Thorncombe Wood and Black Heath Trails

SY 726922; 3.5km; DCC
Woodland and heathland trails
Leaflet from DCC
Spring, early summer

The trail passes through mixed woodland and scrub-covered heath with the added interest of two old ponds. A good variety of birds may be seen together with characteristic butterflies.

Townsend

SZ 025783; 12.8ha; DTNC reserve
Limestone grassland and scrub
Leaflet from DTNC or DCC
Spring, summer

The area has been extensively quarried, giving scrub-filled hollows, good for small birds such as nightingale, to contrast with herb-rich stony banks. Plants such as kidney vetch, horseshoe vetch and sainfoin attract a good range of butterflies including Lulworth skipper and little blue.

Troublefield

Permit only; 6ha; DTNC reserve
Grassland and woodland
Leaflet from DTNC
Summer

This reserve is of particular importance for dragonflies and eighteen species have been recorded. The area consists of species-rich wet grassland and deciduous woodland in the flood plain. Snipe, kingfisher and woodland birds such as lesser spotted woodpecker may be seen.

Upton Country Park

SY 995930; 22.3ha; Poole BC
Formal gardens, farmland, woodland, saltmarsh and mudflats
9 a.m. until dusk. Nature trail leaflet available from Upton House
All year

The hide overlooking Poole Harbour allows good views of the waders and wildfowl. There is also an interesting selection of woodland birds.

West Bexington

SY 525870; 16ha; DTNC reserve
Shingle beach and reedbed
No access to reedbed
Spring, early summer, autumn

Forms an integral part of THE FLEET complex.

Whitenothe Undercliff

SY 765813; 46ha; NT DTNC
Scrub, clay and chalk grasslands, wetland and crags
Some sections may be dangerous, particularly after rain
Leaflet from DTNC or DCC
Spring, early summer

This is a superbly varied area, backed by cliffs up to 140m high, which overlooks the great sweep of Weymouth Bay and the humpbacked ISLE OF PORTLAND. The landslips have formed a series of slopes, terraces and gullies, a complex of wet and dry situations filled with a wide range of plants. There is a contrast not only between the wet and dry areas but also in exposure: because of the hummocked and tilted slopes, some places lie completely open to the strong sea winds while elsewhere hidden pockets are sheltered by banks and scrub, warm and windless on all but the stormiest days.

The thickets of scrub on the more stable slopes and filling the drier gullies are very varied – perhaps a tangle of blackthorn, hawthorn, wayfaring-tree, privet, elder, bramble and wild rose. Ivy, honeysuckle, traveller's-joy and wild madder climb around the edges of the paths or up the shrubs, and this riot of vegetation is mirrored in the damper areas where groves of great horsetail, hart's-tongue and stinking iris grow. Some of the gullies are wet enough for common reed and fleabane, rushes and stands of great willowherb, and damp washes from the soft collapsing cliffs are colonised by colt's-foot and plants such as yellow-wort, restharrow and viper's-bugloss. Less disturbed or stable areas are grassed and filled with lime-loving plants, including a number of orchids.

The animal life, too, is rich, and the population of small mammals may be hunted by kestrel or buzzard. Small birds nest in the thickets, which also provide shelter for migrants, and the grasslands are nesting sites for meadow pipit and skylark. The scrub also gives cover to other animals – roe deer lie up in the daytime – while warm banks are sunning sites for adder. Among the insects, a good range of species includes Lulworth skipper and great green bush-cricket.

Woolsbarrow

SY 892925; 7.6ha; DTNC reserve
Dry heathland and Iron Age hill fort
No access away from tracks
Leaflet from DTNC
Summer

A fine heathland area, an oasis among FC plantations, the reserve contains classic heathland species. It is a focal point for birds such as nightjar, as well as reptiles and insects, including wood tiger beetle.

Kimmeridge Bay: the sea-cut ledges form an important feature of the marine reserve.

Cannop Ponds in the Forest of Dean.

Gloucestershire

Though lacking wild coast and mountain, this is a county of great richness and diversity. Eastward, from the limestone cliffs of the Wye Gorge, the land bears a forest shading traces of the working of coal, iron and sandstone. Beyond, a rich red rolling landscape of orchards, farms and copses borders the wide plain of the lower Severn. The heavy pastures of the Gloucester and Berkeley Vales were once golden with cowslips. Above the vale runs the long rampart of the Cotswolds, hung with beechwoods where the rock is harder, and humpy fields where sand and clay have slumped. The beech reaches back into the Stroudwater Valley, but is succeeded by ash to the north and south.

The Cotswolds, whose golden stone has been used for centuries to build fair towns and pretty villages, slope gently eastward again, in arable farms and coverts, down to the long, well-watered valleys leading to the young Thames. Salt water laps the Severn saltings and mudflats, the winter base for wildfowl and waders. Only in the far north west of the county is there a small corner of true hill land, the southern tip of the Malverns, where a bone of granite and schist shows through the gentler contours of less old rocks.

There is no wild heath, no acid wilderness: the hand of man shows everywhere in the landscape. Management has rarely been unsympathetic, and up to the 1940s the rich countryside had evolved from medieval sheepwalks and eighteenth-century remodelling of agriculture and of the whole landscape, producing a web of fields and copse, hedged and walled, between the remaining great woods. These woods of oak and ash, in the FOREST OF DEAN, in Over Severn, in the vales and on the clayey upper levels of the Cotswolds, were still managed very much on traditional lines, though plantation of oak, fir and larch was succeeding the smallwood producing coppices. Where the limestone surfaced beechwoods thrived, some stored up from coppice, others planted in the last two centuries on the great estates. Some commons still remained among all this good husbandry of field and wood: on the high Cotswolds at Cleeve at 350m, on lower ground in the Stroudwater Hills, in the vales beside the Severn and the Stratford Avon, on the Malverns and within the Royal Forest of Dean, where only a limited area was enclosed.

As farming practice has intensified with the introduction of fertilisers and herbicides, traditional land management has been superseded, and semi-natural wood and grassland and its associated wildlife have disappeared. Much of what remains has been surveyed and noted for conservation by establishing reserves and by consultation with and advice to owners and managers. The list shows great diversity: among woodlands there are ancient beech, oak associated with small-leaved lime, elm, field maple, crab apple, wild cherry, whitebeam and wild service-tree beyond the Severn and beside the Wye; a plainer oakwood with birch and rowan in the Forest of Dean; one of ash, field maple, elm and whitebeam on the Wold; with willow and alder in the wet vale. A few meadows remain rich in flowers, bearing cowslips and orchids in the vale, wild daffodils in the west and an astonishing variety of spring and summer flowers in the Wold.

The gorge of the Wye contains nationally important woodland sites, some contained in reserves which conserve the native limes and whitebeams. At LANCAUT there is an unusual transition from salting to oakwood; within the Forest of Dean oaks two herds of fallow deer wander; pied flycatcher nest in the remaining oakwoods now being conserved; and there are wet places kept for their insects. Many trails are laid out to show people these wilder areas. Wild daffodil are reasonably safe in the pure sessile oakwoods of Over Severn, complementing the drifts of bluebells, and are succeeded in clearings by campion and foxglove. The great lime coppice of COLLIN PARK WOOD is still managed on traditional lines. In these sandstone woods wild cherry flowers plentifully on the margins. On the level fields and saltings beside the Severn, the wildfowl gather and find special shelter and exotic cousins under the protection of the Wildfowl Trust at SLIMBRIDGE; from here Bewick's swan and other wildfowl flight out to flooded fields and wet pastures. In summer warblers sing in the osiers of former claypits by the river.

In the Cotswolds the hanging beechwoods shelter a special flora; some continental orchids reach their northern limit here and are watched over carefully. The interspersed commons carry many orchids of varying rarity and occasional juniper, and locally pasqueflower and meadow

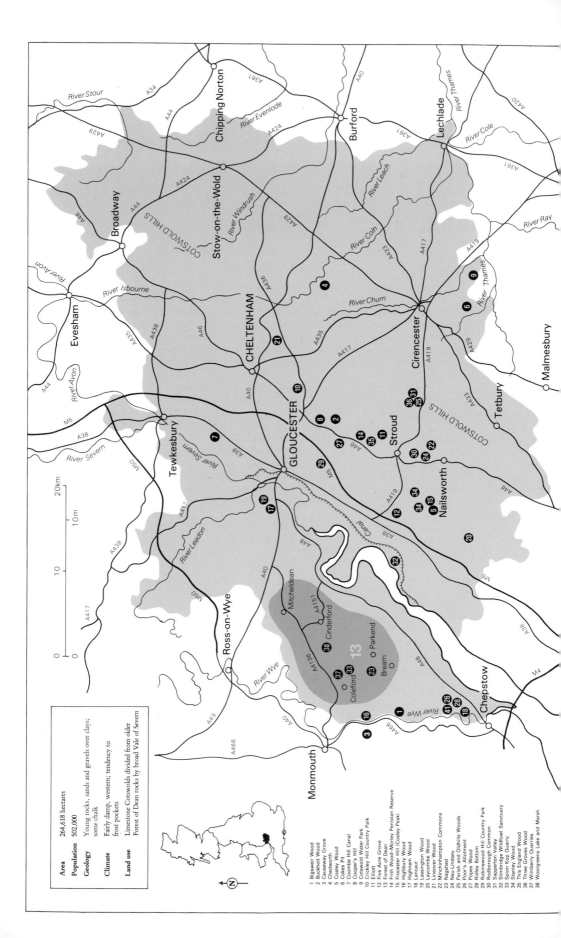

Area	264,618 hectares
Population	502,000
Geology	Young rocks, sands and gravels over clays; some chalk
Climate	Fairly damp, western; tendency to frost pockets
Land use	Limestone Cotswolds divided from older Forest of Dean rocks by broad Vale of Severn

1 Bigsweir Wood
2 Buckholt Wood
3 Causeway Grove
4 Chedworth
5 Coaley Wood
6 Cokes Pit
7 Coombe Hill Canal
8 Cooper's Hill
9 Cotswold Water Park
10 Crickley Hill Country Park
11 Elliott
12 Five Acre Grove
13 Forest of Dean
14 Frith Wood–Morley Penistan Reserve
15 Frocester Hill (Coaley Peak)
16 Highbury Wood
17 Highnam Wood
18 Lancaut
19 Lassington Wood
20 Leyscombe Wood
21 Linesover Wood
22 Minchinhampton Commons
23 Nagshead
24 Neu-Lindsey
25 Parish and Oldhills Woods
26 Poor's Allotment
27 Popes Wood
28 Ridley Bottom
29 Robinswood Hill Country Park
30 Rodborough Common
31 Sapperton Valley
32 Slimbridge Wildfowl Sanctuary
33 Spion Kop Quarry
34 Stanley Wood
35 This England Wood
36 Three Groves Wood
37 Wimberry Quarries
38 Woorgreens Lake and Marsh

clary. Elsewhere much of the ancient grassland has gone, but some samples are managed well in the old way, to the benefit of many butterflies as well as an abundance of flowers. In one place an ancient boxwood still survives.

Nightingale visit the dense thorns of the vale and upland on the edge of their northern range, and hobby hawk for flying quarry over the tall woods. There are curlew in the river meadows; dipper and kingfisher work many streams; but sadly the barn owl, symbol of the Gloucestershire Trust for Nature Conservation, is now rare. In the flooded gravelpits of the upper Thames and on Severnside many waterfowl share water space with sailors and fishermen, and some pits reserved for wildlife are densely populated by human visitors at winter weekends.

Most streams are clear and hold trout; salmon are still caught in the wicker putchers made from wands cut in lowland woods; and there is still a rich harvest of elvers in season. Seals can be seen in the Severn mouth. Gloucestershire hopes to claim the otter as a resident again, though it regrets its mink, descended from fur-farm escapes and now a pest. Roe deer are spreading up from Wiltshire to share the woods with fallow deer, a few muntjac deer and many foxes. Some of the plentiful badgers have unhappily caught tuberculosis and reinfect cattle.

Like many more in the Midlands, the elms have survived only as swarms of hedgerow suckers. But Gloucestershire still has a good mixture of woods, fields, hedges, streams, pools and some marsh, the home of many plants and animals, and some 50 reserves help conserve examples of most of them.

MORLEY PENISTAN

Ashleworth Ham

No access; 40.9ha; GTNC reserve
Flood meadows and woodland
Can be viewed from hides adjacent to public road
All year

The chief interest must be the wildfowl in winter, when thousands of duck may be observed from the hides, but there is also a varied population of breeding birds and a good range of wetland plants: meadowsweet, great burnet and golden dock.

Badgeworth

Permit only; 394sq m; GTNC reserve
Tiny wetland and pond
June

The reserve is established to protect a rare buttercup, adder's-tongue spearwort.

Baunhill Quarry

Permit only; 0.02ha; GTNC reserve
Geological site
All year

This seabed exposure of the middle Jurassic period contains fossil oysters with marine worm and mollusc workings.

Betty Daws Wood

Permit only; 8.8ha; GTNC reserve
Fragment of ancient woodland
Spring, early summer

The mainly oak woodland, including small-leaved lime and wild service-tree, has a good show of spring flowers with abundant wild daffodil.

Bigsweir Wood

SO 544056; 44ha; WdT reserve
Deciduous woodland
Spring, summer

The wood is a part of the LOWER WYE VALLEY woodlands, which are some of the richest in the country. The wood is an excellent example of the acid woodlands of this complex. Lying on sandstone, the wood is dominated by sessile oak and beech high forest; ash occurs in areas of

The Severn Vale, looking across the lowlands and into Wales.

slightly less acid soils. There are areas of coppice, including both beech and small-leaved lime. The ground flora includes great woodrush, cow-wheat, hard fern and honeysuckle.

Offa's Dyke, marking the old Welsh border, runs through the wood, as does the long distance footpath OFFA'S DYKE PATH.

Bourton Wood Nature Trail

Permit only; 5km; Batsford Estate
Commercially managed and ancient woodland
Access generally restricted to GTNC members and school parties
Trail guide and permit form from Batsford Estate Office, Moreton-in-Marsh
May–September

The woodland has a good range of flowers and is rich in birds and mammals.

Buckholt Wood

See COTSWOLD COMMONS AND BEECHWOODS.

Causeway Grove

SO 089536; 5ha; WdT reserve
Deciduous woodland
Access from road difficult due to steep bank
Spring, summer

The woodland lies on a steep valley side overlooking the River Wye and is an excellent example of the ancient woodland of this area. It is dominated by ash, small-leaved lime and wild cherry. The flowers are varied, with drifts of the strongly scented ramsons.

Chedworth

SP 051138; 1.5km; GTNC reserve
Disused railway line
Car park for members only
Spring, early summer

The reserve runs either through cuttings, rich in lime-loving plants such as large thyme, basil thyme and blue fleabane, or raised on an embankment with good views over the surrounding woodlands. The cuttings show important exposures of middle Jurassic inferior oolitic limestone.

Coaley Wood

ST 788999; 23ha; WdT
Deciduous woodland
Spring, summer

The ancient woodland contains mature beech and ash trees as well as some areas of derelict coppice. In spring there is a fine display of woodland flowers.

Cokes Pit

SU 026953; 3.2ha; GTNC–GCC reserve
Flooded gravelpit in Cotswold Water Park
Access restricted
All year

The islanded lake is easily viewed from the roads around it and often contains a good range of wildfowl including less usual species such as red-crested pochard.

Collin Park Wood

Permit only; 14ha; GTNC reserve
Coppiced small-leaved lime woodland
Spring, early summer

A superb damp woodland of coppiced small-leaved lime and oak stands over a dense, rather acid ground cover with much bramble and bracken but also species such as bluebell, primrose and yellow archangel.

Coombe Hill Canal

SO 887270; 13ha; GTNC reserve
Disused canal
Public footpaths along tow-paths
Summer

Strawberry clover, fine-leaved water-dropwort, great yellow-cress, bladder sedge, greater dodder and flowering-rush grow alongside the 3.8 kilometres of disused canal. In summer there is a good population of warblers in the scrub, and the adjoining washland attracts Bewick swans, shoveler, pochard, gadwall, garganey and shelduck during the winter.

Cooper's Hill

SO 886142; 54.8ha; GCC reserve
Woodland, scrub and limestone grassland
Leaflet from GCC or GTNC
Spring, early summer

Spectacular views across Gloucestershire and over the Severn Vale into Wales give extra interest to a reserve which demonstrates some of the characteristic Cotswold woodland plants, together with scrub and grassland.

Cotswold Commons and Beechwoods

SO 894131 (Buckholt Wood); 270ha; NCC reserves
Beech high forest
Spring, summer

These reserves consist of several more or less contiguous woodlands which, collectively, form a superb example of beechwoods on the Cotswold limestone. One of these, Buckholt Wood, is described here.

Tall beech trees stand throughout the wood over younger beech with a scatter of other species such as common whitebeam, oak and wych elm or ash, alder and willow where the soils are deep and damp. The wood is often steeply tilted, sloping down in flinted folds, a cover to the hillside which probably dates from the last ice age. Although animals are not grazed there now, the woods are unenclosed and rights of common apply.

Below the high-forest beech the understorey contains a variety of shrub or sapling species such as ash, hawthorn, hazel, holly, wayfaring-tree, wild cherry and yew, with a considerable invasion of young sycamore. This shrub layer stands over a ground cover of bramble and wild rose with carpets of gleaming ivy and such rich-wood plants as dog's mercury and enchanter's-nightshade, sanicle, primrose and violet, woodruff and wood spurge. Climbing tangles of traveller's-joy and dark clumps of the strange green hellebore underline the lime-rich nature of the soil, and where a ride is edged by a grassy bank this is confirmed by a limestone grassland with salad burnet, small scabious and the tall ploughman's-spikenard.

Although at least part of the wood was once coppiced, present management involves removal of timber trees, achieved by thinning rather than clear-felling, and the former coppice areas have virtually disappeared. The heavy thinning opens out the woodland but leaves the essential beech cover and does not destroy the character of the wood. Bramble tends to spring up and fill the open clearings but this is later replaced by sapling trees and a good woodland structure. In places the soil becomes less lime-rich and stands of bracken and bluebell appear with honeysuckle, replacing traveller's-joy, while deeper, damper soils are shown by sprays of pendulous sedge.

These Cotswold beechwoods are important not only as fine examples of the natural woods which once covered all these hills, and as havens for woodland wildlife, but also for the unusual plants which still survive because they have been undisturbed for thousands of years.

Among these important Cotswold beechwood species are common wintergreen, generally a northern species but found here on the limestone and also in some East Anglian fens, narrow-lipped and green-flowered helleborine, and both bird's-nest orchid and yellow bird's-nest, two saprophytes that are characteristic of old beech woodland.

Cotswold Water Park

SU 026597; 5666ha; GCC Wilts CC
Flooded gravel workings
Leaflets from GCC or WCC
All year

Not many kilometres from Cricklade the River Thames is a young stream risen from the plain below the Cotswold Hills. Vast shallow diggings to remove the gravels of the plain, an older river bed, leave lakes of lime-rich water which, when all the extraction ends, will total around 1600ha.

Although there are obvious dangers in encouraging the destruction of one form of habitat to replace it with another, this enormous new wetland must make some slight recompense for loss of others. The eventual spread of waters will form the largest body of marl lakes in the country, which will encourage a richness of plant and invertebrate life to feed great numbers of fish and birds.

Many of the large flooded pits will be used for recreation which will keep wildlife away, but some, as with the GTNC reserves of COKES PIT, EDWARD RICHARDSON AND PHYLLIS AMEY and

WHELFORD POOLS, will provide oases of peace among the disturbance. Already over 120 species have been recorded including Bewick's swan, garganey, water rail, grasshopper warbler, little ringed plover, spotted redshank, terns, gulls and a host of smaller birds. Osprey on passage have inspected the waters and, as the scars of digging fade beneath spreads of vegetation, the lakes should acquire increasing attraction for other predators. Apart from the interest of the growing list of uncommon species such as marsh warbler and white-winged black tern, the Water Park is of great importance for the study of the plant colonisation of these waters and of the developing animal life within them.

Crickley Hill Country Park

SO 936163; 60ha; GCC
Woodland, scrub and limestone grassland
Leaflets from information centre or GCC
Spring, summer

The first impression of the scrubland area leading to the woodland is that of a great mix of species, one of the features of lime-rich scrub. Ash, elder, blackthorn, hawthorn, hazel, holly and wayfaring-tree are tangled together with wild rose and traveller's-joy; beech and field maple stand over banks of bramble; grassy path edges are decorated with small herbs such as salad burnet or tall betony.

A nature trail demonstrates the good range of characteristic Cotswold plants.

The woodland itself is typically beech with some very large old trees, a number of ancient oaks and some ash. Old coppiced hazel and holly form the understorey with a ground cover which varies with the amount of shade; under a dense canopy the woodland floor is virtually bare, except for a brief show of bluebells before the leaves cut out the light; where light can get in, bramble tends to take over but elsewhere typical rich-wood plants such as dog's mercury, violets and sanicle may be found. An area of recent coppicing is thick with rosebay willowherb, a blaze of colour compared to the rather sombre show in the shaded wood. Trampled pathways crossing old limestone workings indicate heavy use but this adds to the variety of the site since it keeps open areas which can be colonised by tiny plants.

Beyond the wood is scrub and grassland, again the mixed scrub species, clumped in and around glades of herb-rich grass. Harebell, eyebright, wild thyme and small scabious fill the clearings, together with more uncommon species such as clustered bellflower and autumn gentian, flourishing on the limestone.

The grassland in the more busy areas is heavily trampled but is still rich in species such as yellowwort and ploughman's-spikenard, or viper's-bugloss, carline and dwarf thistle and common rock-rose. Where the grassland is deeper many of the smaller species disappear but harebell and salad burnet persist and taller plants such as greater knapweed show with musk mallow and woolly thistle.

Daneway Banks

Permit only; 17ha; GTNC reserve
Limestone scrub and grassland
Spring, early summer

A superb range of lime-loving flowers such as columbine, clustered bellflower and meadow saffron are complemented by a good range of insects and scrubland birds.

Edward Richardson and Phyllis Amey

Permit only; 10ha; GTNC reserve
Scrub and flooded gravelpits
Spring, early summer

The ponds are too small to attract regular visits from the most unusual bird species but king-fishers, for instance, are frequently seen here and the variety of plant and insect life is extremely good.

Elliott

SO 877067; 9.6ha; GTNC reserve
Limestone grassland
Spring, summer

This small area of grazed common land is rich in lime-loving species, such as kidney vetch, autumn gentian and several orchids and in associated insects. A good variety of butterfly species is recorded.

Fairplay Ponds

Permit only; 1.6ha; GTNC reserve
Ponds and wet heathland
Spring, early summer

A mixture of acid and lime-rich areas add interest to a wetland showing purple moor-grass with western gorse, and a good display of iemon-scented fern.

Five Acre Grove

SO 791042; 5ha; GTNC reserve
Mixed woodland
Spring, early summer

Some 34 woodland bird species breed in the oak and ash woodland which stands over a good mix of species including wild service-tree, spindle and field maple.

Forest of Dean

See map; 10,935ha; FC
Mixed woodland
Leaflets from FC
Spring, early summer

The importance of the Dean is underlined by the fact that it contains several nature reserves, managed jointly by the FC and such bodies as the NCC, RSPB and GTNC.

Much of the Dean has been wooded for thousands of years but has suffered sweeping changes since man began to modify his environment so widely. The forest spreads across a tract of land

Longhorn beetle on bramble in the Forest of Dean.

which has been warped by great earth movements and this mix of tilted rocks provides hills, plateaus and valleys of a widely varying nature, reflected in the forest trees. Sessile oak, the oak of the western woodlands, with wych elm, small-leaved lime, hazel, holly and rowan would have been mixed with trees such as ash, wild cherry, field maple, whitebeam and yew on richer sites, with alder and species of willow in wetter places.

The forest, now, can tell a history of man in Britain. The open lands between the spreads of woodland in the Dean began with the forest-clearer, Neolithic man, and were enlarged and confirmed by farmers since, by Romans and Saxons, by Englishmen who resented the Norman deer and by men who also worked in the woods to find timber for their wars. Areas of coppice are reminders of the medieval management when wood was needed for charcoal and bark for tanning, and large quantities of poles were used for baskets, hurdles and building materials. Massive clearances fed wood to the two world wars and, even now, quarries and mines are worked to extract stone and coal from the forest.

Despite all the felling, clearing and planting, mining, quarrying, drainage and general alterations to the Dean, the forest still holds a splendid mix of ancient plantations and new.

The broad-leaved woodland is mainly pedunculate oak with beech, sweet chestnut, rowan, holly and sessile oak, standing above a ground cover of bracken, bramble or grasses. The predominantly high-forest structure possesses little understorey since sheep-grazing severely inhibits new growth – the woods are often composed of equal-aged tall trees. Other types of woodland contribute variety, with alder in the wetter sites and with ash, beech, large-leaved lime and wych elm. Birch will invade wherever it can while there are also areas of young plantation, grassland, heathland, bogs, pools, streams and rivers.

Unmanaged areas on the limestone outcrops have the richest plant life, perhaps where abandoned quarries leave slopes too steep to be worth replanting. Beech and wych elm are mixed with ash, birch, sweet chestnut, oak, rowan and sycamore above a shrub layer of holly and yew with dogwood, elder, guelder-rose, hawthorn, hazel, field maple, willow and wild rose. The ground cover may be equally rich and may contain such uncommon species as autumn crocus, herb-Paris and bird's-nest orchid.

Together with the variation provided by the managed woodlands there is a range of heath and bog habitats where plants such as purple moorgrass, bilberry, heather, bell-heather, cross-leaved heath, bog asphodel and bog pimpernel may be found.

Sheep are not the only grazing animals in the Dean – there are also two herds of fallow deer, one based on High Meadows Woods, the other around Speech House. Small mammals such as shrews, voles and mice are quarry for stoat, weasel and fox, and several species of bat may be recorded. Very occasionally otter or polecat may occur.

The bird life varies according to the habitat. New plantations may encourage shrub and heathland species such as tree pipit, whinchat, linnet and nightjar; the range in taller woodland includes goldcrest, redstart, warblers and all three native woodpeckers. Among the more interesting birds of the Dean are pied flycatcher and raven, around their eastern limit in southern Britain, and breeding populations of hawfinch and crossbill. Water adds an important range of habitat to the forest – dipper, kingfisher and visiting heron may be seen. The ponds and marshy areas draw winter migrants such as snipe, jack snipe, teal and whooper swan.

Water, too, provides a habitat for a range of dragonflies and damselflies while the grasslands, heath and woodlands are rich in other insects. Over 30 species of butterfly have been recorded including both grassland and woodland species. Brown argus, grayling, holly blue and white admiral have been recorded together with dark green, high brown, pearl-bordered, small pearl-bordered and silver-washed fritillary.

Among the specialities of the Dean are spectacular colonies of the exotic Martagon lily and a number of outstanding ancient woodland lichens, in particular those growing on the oaks around Speech House. Declared in 1938 as England's first National Forest Park, the Dean remains a wonderfully varied wildlife sanctuary – a place of fascination at any season.

Foxes Bridge Bog

Permit only; 5.3ha; GTNC reserve
Ancient marshland
Spring, early summer

Sphagnum mosses and plants such as marsh St John's-wort and marsh violet, a possible food plant for small pearl-bordered fritillary, characterise this area of bog.

The mixed woodlands of the Forest of Dean.

Frith Wood – Morley Penistan Reserve

SO 877086; 22ha; GTNC reserve
High-forest beech woodland
No access off cleared tracks
Spring, early summer

Frith Wood is an even-aged woodland. Slender, straight, very tall beech trees stand above the woodland floor, so tall that the canopy resembles a vaulted cathedral roof. The reserve lies on both sides of a narrow limestone ridge and this enables light to enter horizontally, to encourage a dense understorey of saplings and shrubs. An area of high-forest oak and ash lies near the plateau top of the ridge, standing over bare rubbly slopes with spreads of bramble and dog's mercury.

Thinning in the northern wing has opened some of the woodland, although many tall beech trees still stand, and this area is notable for old quarries filled with ash, whitebeam and yew, with steep ivy-covered slopes and spreads of rich green hart's-tongue, topped with lesser periwinkle. The southern wing is far more densely dressed, fringed at its lower edge with birch and oak saplings mixing with the lime-loving ash, yew, whitebeam and field maple. Strong young saplings of beech, hawthorn, hazel, holly and elder also occur, together with traveller's-joy and wild rose.

The ground cover is similarly varied with more acid areas showing stands of bracken and rides lined with rosebay willowherb and raspberry, with pendulous sedge and great willowherb in wetter places. The woodland grasses include wood melick, a lime-loving decorative grass which often grows on sunny banks or pathways, while the understorey may stand over carpets of woodruff or enchanter's-nightshade. Wood spurge and spurge-laurel may both be found with sanicle. Orchid species include broad-leaved helleborine.

The understorey offers both ideal nest sites for many woodland birds and also cover for small animals, the limestone providing a source of shell-building material for a good variety of snails while the woodland edge and clearings caused by tree-felling make attractive areas for butterflies.

Frocester Hill (Coaley Peak)

SO 794009; 5.6ha; GTNC reserve
Limestone grassland and scrub
Leaflet from GTNC or GCC
Spring, summer

Superb views across the River Severn to Wales add to the interest of the ungrazed grassland, scrub and wooded quarry. A good range of species is found including both nettle-leaved and clustered bellflower, with insects such as marbled white and holly blue butterflies and scarlet tiger and ghost moths.

Highbury Wood

SO 540085; 47ha; NCC reserve
Woodland
Via public footpaths only
Spring, summer, autumn

A fine example of ancient, semi-natural woodland which commands panoramic views of the surrounding countryside and is crossed by the OFFA'S DYKE PATH. In spring there is a fine display of flowers including bluebell, primrose, wood barley, greater butterfly-orchid and toothwort. There are also silver-washed fritillary butterflies and badger and fallow deer.

Highnam Wood

SO 787198; 119ha; RSPB reserve
Mixed woodland
Spring, summer

Wild service-tree, as well as a mixture of ash, wych elm, oak and beech, is found in this attractive ancient woodland. In spring it shimmers with bluebells and the melodious song of the nightingale can be heard. All three species of woodpecker are present, and other birds to look out for are nuthatch, pied flycatcher, and tawny and long-eared owls. There is a good population of dormice in the wood.

Hobbs Quarry

Permit only; 1ha; GTNC reserve
Geological reserve
All year

The chief importance of the quarry is an exposure of slump strata of Wenlock series limestone, although there is also an interesting small area of woodland with a ground cover which includes primrose and spurge-laurel.

Lancaut

ST 539967; 24ha; GTNC reserve
Woodland and quarry above the tidal River Wye
Permit only off public rights of way
Spring, early summer

The waters of the Wye are deep and muddy with an enormous tidal range, either exposing steep banks of glutinous mud or lapping the narrow saltmarsh zone below the woodland which thickly clothes the northern side of the gorge. The edge of the mud is thick with English scurvygrass, a fleshy plant with sprays of small white flowers, and sea aster, lifting its small flower clusters above all but the highest tides. Above this narrow lower zone is the saltmarsh proper with spear-leaved orache and buck's-horn plantain, common sea-blite, sea-plantain, sea-milkwort and sea-spurrey.

The river terrace is grassed and often quarried below the wooded slopes; in the stony banks a profusion of lime-loving plants take advantage of the open sunny position. Common rock-rose and yellow-wort vie with varieties of St John's-wort in the brightness of their colour, contrasting with the subtler shades of the tiny hairy violet or the rare lesser calamint. On the open limestone ledges oxeye daisy, red valerian and naturalised wallflower give the effect of window boxes.

In the cooler, deeper soils of the woodland a variety of species grow together. Small-leaved lime and wild service-tree, with varieties of whitebeam, grow with yew, field maple, oak and ash above luxuriant stands of woodland ferns. Bright spring flowers such as bluebell, primrose and violet make an attractive show before the leaf canopy closes over, a strategy also employed by wood spurge and spurge-laurel, while the climbing wild madder ensures its sunlight by growing on the woodland fringes and pathway edges.

The woodland contains a typical range of mammals and birds, while the cliffs provide nesting sites for a variety of species. On the river below are cormorant, heron and shelduck, though the muddiness of the water conceals elvers and salmon.

Lassington Wood

SO 803203; 6ha; Tewkesbury BC GTNC reserve
Mixed woodland
Spring, early summer

Lime-rich clays encourage a good variety of woodland species, with much ash over spurge-laurel and goldilocks buttercup. Nightingale nest, together with a good range of woodland birds.

Laycombe Wood

ST 764953; 49ha; WdT reserve
Mixed woodland
Spring, summer

A typical beech woodland of the Cotswold scarp which overlooks the picturesque valley known as Waterley Bottom. Parts of the wood were replanted with larch in the 1970s but there is still a rich ground flora.

Laymoor Quag

Permit only; 3.5ha; GTNC reserve
Wet heathland
Spring, early summer

The reserve contains a rich variety of heather, purple moor-grass and *Sphagnum* mosses and is also notable for petty whin, uncommon in the county.

Lineover Wood

SO 987190; 44ha; WdT reserve
Mixed woodland
Spring, summer

The rare large-leaved lime is found in this ancient wood, and ash, maple and hazel coppice grow on the upper slopes. Lower down the maturing conifer plantations will eventually be removed and replaced with native species. There is a rich ground flora including some unusual species.

Littleton Wood

Permit only; 0.5ha; AWT–NT reserve
Woodland
Spring

The reserve was established to protect a colony of the very local yellow star-of-Bethlehem.

Lower Lodge Wood

Permit only; 4.45ha; GTNC reserve
Mixed woodland
Spring, early summer

Since the scourge of Dutch elm disease the woods mainly consist of oak and ash over a hazel understorey. The ground cover includes spurge-laurel, and bird's-nest orchid and earth star fungus can be found where beech trees grow.

Merring Meend

Permit only; 1.6ha; GTNC reserve
Pools and wetland
Spring, early summer

Probably the last of the natural pools remaining in the FOREST OF DEAN, Merring Meend is the only site still to contain that beautiful pink-flowered wetland species, bogbean. Nodding bur-marigold also occurs on the reserve and there is a good range of wetland insects to complement the plants.

Minchinhampton Commons

SO 858013; 232ha; NT
Limestone grassland
Spring, summer

The commons contain a characteristic variety of lime-loving plants such as clustered bellflower and several orchid species.

Mythe Railway

Permit only; 2.8ha; GTNC reserve
Disused railway line
Spring, early summer

Wetland plants such as common comfrey, together with lime-loving species such as wild liquorice and spindle, add to the interest of this small reserve which also contains a good variety of butterflies and birds.

Nagshead

SO 606080; 308ha; RSPB reserve
Mixed woodland
Leaflet from RSPB
Spring, early summer

Part of the great FOREST OF DEAN, the reserve consists of a varied range of woodland types including recent Forestry Commission plantations with both enclosed and open woodland. The classic birds of mature western woodland are present, with goldcrest and sparrowhawk attracted by the conifers. Fallow deer graze the clearings.

Neu-Lindsey

SO 845014; 0.4ha; GTNC reserve
Unimproved grassland
Spring, summer

In early summer the grassland is a riot of colour with oxeye daisy, yellow rattle, sainfoin, horseshoe vetch and chalk milkwort, as well as bee and pyramidal orchid, attracting a host of butterflies.

Over Ponds

Permit only; 4ha; GTNC reserve
Ponds and marshland
Spring, early summer

The ponds contain interesting plants such as nodding bur-marigold, narrow-leaved water-plantain and frogbit, while flowering-rush occurs in the marsh. Water rail have been recorded.

Parish and Oldhills Woods

SO 906027; 14ha; WdT reserve
Deciduous woodland
Spring, summer

These woods lie on the banks of the River Frome in an area called the Golden Valley. In autumn this is a very apt name, as the woods are dominated by beech trees. Oldhills Wood has a large proportion of elm, most of which has died and is being replaced by other mature trees.

Pit House Pond and Bog

Permit only; 0.2ha; GTNC reserve
Acid wetland
Spring, early summer

The tiny wetland, contrasting with the forest around it, contains western gorse with delicate bog plants such as cross-leaved heath, marsh violet and bog asphodel.

Plump Hill Dolomite Quarry

SO 661172; 1ha; GTNC reserve
Disused quarry
Spring, summer

The quarry face is unstable and should be avoided, although the reserve may be visited for its interesting range of plants, among which are white horehound and autumn lady's-tresses.

Poor's Allotment

ST 559995; 28.3ha; Poor's Allotment Trustees reserve
Heathland and limestone grassland
Spring, summer

Acid soils over sandstone faulted against limestone give a most unusual mix of heathland with western gorse, all three common heathers and bilberry. In the limestone grassland flourish species such as carline thistle, common rock-rose and wild thyme. A small pond adds further interest to the reserve.

Popes Wood

SO 875128; 26ha; GTNC-NCC reserve
Beech woodland
Visitors must keep to paths and tracks
Spring, early summer

The fine high-forest beech woodland with a rich lime-loving ground cover is part of an NNR established to protect its wealth of interest. Characteristic plants include green hellebore, spurge-laurel and several orchid species.

Ridley Bottom

ST 564985; 1ha; GTNC reserve
Grassland and coppice
Spring, summer

The coppice contains small-leaved lime with maple, gean and yew, and the groundcover includes herb-Paris and hard and hart's-tongue ferns. There is a rich birdlife, and brimstone butterflies are common.

Robinswood Hill Country Park

SO 835157; 97ha; Gloucester City Council
Cotswold outcrop
Spring, summer

Robinswood Hill gives a taste of wildlife close to the city. A nature trail leads to the summit viewpoint, demonstrating the variation as the marlstones and sands give way to limestone and plants such as greater knapweed and small scabious appear.

Rodborough Common

SO 852035; 96.8ha; NT
Limestone grassland
Spring, summer

The Common's plateau has generally deeper soils than the steep, soft limestone slopes and is a mosaic of short and deeper grassland according to the grazing and the depth of soil. Even in the areas of coarser grasses, yellow rattle and common spotted-orchid, kidney vetch and greater knapweed are found. Where the grasses are shorter,

small scabious, harebell, common bird's-foot-trefoil and common rock-rose, cowslip and eyebright, common milkwort and lady's bedstraw, wild thyme and autumn gentian, salad burnet, quaking-grass and the lime-loving hoary plantain hint at the variety these limestone grasslands can carry. Much of the interest of the area lies in determining why some plants are on the slopes but not the plateau – why some prefer shallow turf while others shun it.

A shallow quarry-like depression at the top of the slope demonstrates the plants which can survive on the almost scree-like soft limestone. Yellow-wort and carline thistle grow on the very thin soils, with herb-Robert on the rocks themselves; scrublike bramble, wild rose and hawthorn throw up a protective screen which may have helped ash saplings avoid grazing animals. The ubiquitous wood sage has established a foothold here although, like the scrub, it does not generally appear upon the slopes. More characteristic lime-loving plants include the delicate pink common restharrow with bee and pyramidal orchid.

The pyramidal orchid also appears in coarser grassland lower down, together with common spotted-orchid and yellow rattle, so it cannot prefer thin soils. For yellow-wort and carline thistle, though, it seems to be true: wherever the slope is only thinly grassed, the two appear together. The slopes are faintly terraced, either by soil creep or grazing animals or both, and the small banks so formed are crowded with bright

small flowers such as horseshoe vetch and marjoram, oxeye daisy and clustered bellflower, in addition to the species found in the short grass of the plateau. To complement the common restharrow above, spiny restharrow occurs on the slopes, while tiny saplings of birch and oak appear, pointers to the natural progression of grassland, through scrub, to woodland.

Of special interest here are two species of local distribution, pasqueflower and wild liquorice, together with a good range of orchids including a particularly good show of early-purple, green-winged, fragrant and pyramidal.

The rich variety of limestone plants attracts an appropriate range of insects, including blues and marbled white among the butterflies with six-spot burnet among the moths.

Sandhurst

Permit only; 7.5ha; GTNC reserve
Flooded brickpits
Spring, summer

Two areas of old brickpit workings, one of them converted to an osier bed, form an interesting wetland reserve with a good variety of plants and animals. The osier willow is allowed to grow until it has established itself, and then the crown is cut out so that growth is concentrated into producing finger-thick flexible straight shoots which are harvested to stimulate a further crop.

The most important osier beds were planted in the northern section, a complex of pools and banks

The Cotswold beechwoods, such as Popes Wood, are a special feature of Gloucestershire.

where the willows are still maintained to preserve nesting sites. Hemlock water-dropwort and fine-leaved water-dropwort fringe the pools while the alder and willow woodland shading them contains damp-loving species such as guelder-rose, remote and swamp meadow-grass, bladder-sedge, cyperus sedge and wood club-rush. Great bellflower raises its tall blue-purple flowered stem and orange balsam shows a jewel-like delicacy compared with the large-flowered Indian balsam which lines many river banks. The pools themselves contain whorled water-milfoil together with the beautiful rose-pink flowering-rush, white-flowered frogbit and the speciality of the reserve, greater bladderwort, which had disappeared from the area before the reserve was established.

The southern area is more unkempt. A scrub of willow, hawthorn and blackthorn, backed by a colourful jungle of nettle, meadowsweet and meadow crane's-bill, bright yellow tansy and common toadflax, common comfrey and great willowherb which, with a variety of vetches, shelters a sizeable open pool. The pool contains stands of arrowhead, water-plantain and flowering-rush, with rigid hornwort hidden beneath.

Mallard, shoveler and teal have been recorded together with heron, kingfisher and water rail and with sedge and reed warbler in the osiers or surrounding scrub. Siskin and redpoll may feed in the alder stands of the northern pool when winter brings them down from colder latitudes. Numerous insects include a good range of dragonflies and damselflies, the spectacular musk beetle and a rare water beetle, *Agabus undulatus*.

Sapperton Valley

SO 939034; 3.7ha; GTNC reserve
Disused canal
Spring, summer

Parts of the canal are thick with marsh-marigold, yellow water-lily and plants such as purple-loosestrife, while the towpath shows woodland influence, with yellow archangel and wood melick. Typical woodland and some wetland birds may be seen.

Siccaridge Wood

Permit only; 27ha; GTNC reserve
Mixed woodland
Spring, summer

Lily-of-the-valley and angular Solomon's-seal occur in this interesting woodland.

Silk Wood

Permit only; 8.5ha; GTNC reserve
Remnant of ancient woodland
Spring, early summer

Oak over coppiced hazel is the main pattern throughout, but other species include field maple and wild cherry, with a rich ground cover including herb-Paris and meadow saffron. White admiral and silver-washed fritillary are among the butterflies and there is a good range of woodland birds.

Slimbridge Wildfowl Sanctuary

SO 723048; 800ha; WT
Mudflats, saltmarsh, grazing meadows and lagoons
Leaflets from reception centre
Winter

The world's largest wildfowl collection is here, and beyond is the Severn Estuary and natural salt grassland, together with the great open levels of reclaimed saltmarsh, the New Grounds, where winter weather brings thousands of wild birds to rest and feed. A series of carefully designed hides along the south and west overlook these meadows where up to 20,000 wildfowl may be seen.

White-fronted geese fly in from Europe every winter to form the largest flock in the country, and up to 600 Bewick's swan also winter here from the cold north west, to gather in the lagoons to wait for feeding time. They can be seen at close quarters and, since the beak marking is different in every bird, be individually recognised.

Whooper swan are occasionally seen, while mingling with the huge flocks of white-fronted geese are numbers of feral greylag and Canada geese, with regular barnacle, bean, Brent, pink-footed and lesser white-fronted geese. The rare lesser white-fronted goose is seen at Slimbridge nearly every winter: this is the only site in the country where birdwatchers may hope to see it.

Thousands of wigeon and mallard, perhaps a thousand pochard and teal, hundreds of tufted duck, pintail, gadwall and shelduck, with smaller numbers of shoveler, may be present. Several hundred coot winter, while the cold, short days are busy with the movement of wader flocks, of large gatherings of curlew and huge congregations of dunlin and lapwing.

In times of passage, the lagoons may be visited by small but regular numbers of migrant waders. Bar-tailed and black-tailed godwit, ruff, ringed, little ringed, grey and golden plover, green and wood sandpiper, curlew sandpiper and whimbrel are regular visitors while merlin may prey on the smaller passage migrants. Spring also brings swallow and house martin and, while they feed on insects above the lagoons and meadows, a hobby can sometimes be seen harrying them.

Snows Farm

Permit only; 21.3ha; GTNC reserve
Limestone grassland and woodland
Spring, summer

Bee and fly orchid and greater butterfly-orchid are among the great variety of attractive plants here which draw many species of butterfly. A brook increases the habitat range.

Spion Kop Quarry

SO 598102; 0.7ha; FC-GTNC reserve
Disused quarry
All year

The quarry contains probably the best example of coal measures in the FOREST OF DEAN. Jackdaw and redstart breed on the reserve.

Stanley Wood

SO 895015–817022; 38ha; WdT reserve
Mixed woodland
Spring, summer

The wood stretches for 1½ miles along the scarp slope of the Cotswolds above the villages of Kings Stanley and Leonard Stanley. It forms part of the wooded edge of the Cotswolds that can be seen from much of the Severn Valley. From the wood itself there are superb views across the valley to the FOREST OF DEAN and the MALVERN HILLS. Much of the wood was felled in the 1950s and parts were replanted with conifers. However, there was considerable natural regeneration of beech and ash and the Woodland Trust's management involves a programme of thinning to promote the broad-leaved trees. This will not only improve the wood from a landscape point of view but will help to conserve the rich ground flora so characteristic of ancient woodland on limestone in this area. The Cotswold Way runs through the wood and the Coaley Park Picnic Site is next to the wood.

Stenders Quarry

Permit only; 2.8ha; GTNC reserve
Disused quarry
Spring, early summer

The quarry is geologically important, with exposures of carboniferous limestone shales, lower dolomite and the junction with the old red sandstone. It also carries limestone woodland and grassland with cowslip, primrose and autumn gentian.

Stuart Fawkes

Permit only; 8.3ha; GTNC reserve
Limestone grassland
June, July

Cowslip and common restharrow are among approximately 70 plants recorded here, but the reserve was established to protect a fine colony of the very local meadow clary.

This England Wood

SO 875083; 2ha; WdT reserve
New plantation
Spring, early summer

Recently planted up with some 1400 young broad-leaved trees it will, in time, grow on to maturity colonised by woodland plants and animals.

Three Groves Wood

SO 911030; 3.3ha; GTNC reserve
Deciduous woodland
Spring

The mainly beech woodland lies in a steep-sided valley, and other trees and shrubs include ash, oak and whitebeam, field maple, wayfaring-tree and guelder-rose. The ground is carpeted with woodland flowers such as bluebell, primrose, sweet woodruff, and later in the year broad-leaved helleborine and nettle-leaved bellflower.

Westbury Brook Mine Pond

Permit only; 0.2ha; GTNC reserve
Small pond
Spring, summer

The pond, hidden within a plantation, is lined with rushes and bulrush, contains bog pondweed and supports both common and palmate newt.

Whelford Pools

Permit only; 20ha; GTNC reserve
Flooded gravelpits
All year

Two large pits with sheltering high hedges and well-vegetated margins provide ideal breeding and wintering sites for waterbirds. There is a hide.

Wigpool

Permit only; 1.6ha; GTNC reserve
Small wetland
Spring, early summer

The pool has lost much interest through drying out but still contains *Sphagnum* mosses, fringed with tufted hair-grass and purple moor-grass.

Wimberry Quarries

SO 594121; 2ha; GTNC reserve
Disused quarries
Spring, summer

The complex of four disused quarries has been colonised by a rich flora of ferns and mosses, including oak fern. There is an area of mixed woodland with beech, ash, oak and sweet chest-nut. Above the quarries there is a small area of heathland with ling and bilberry.

Witcombe Reservoirs

No access; 28ha; STWA–GTNC reserve
Reservoir and surrounds
Can be viewed from public right of way at SO 904149
Winter

The open water areas contain wintering wildfowl and the muddy edges occasional waders. Black tern visit at migration times, and great crested grebe breed.

Woorgreens Lake and Marsh

SO 630129; 9ha; GTNC reserve
Lake and marsh
All year

In winter the lake supports dabbling ducks, including teal, while the marsh attracts large numbers of snipe; other waders that can be seen on passage are spotted redshank, greenshank and green sandpiper. In drier areas among recent plantations there are good breeding populations of whinchats and tree pipits. Seventeen species of dragonfly and damselfly have been recorded. The reserve is the best site in the FOREST OF DEAN for brown argus and grayling butterflies.

1 Abney Park Cemetery
2 Ainslie Wood
3 Alexandra Park
4 Barnes Common
5 Battersea Park
6 Bayhurst Wood Country Park
7 Beckenham Place Park
8 Belmont Nature Walk
9 Benhill Road Nature Garden
10 Bramley Bank
11 Brent Reservoir
12 Bully Point
13 Camley Street Natural Park
14 Cannon Hill Common Nature Reserve
15 The Chase
16 Claybury Hospital Woods
17 Coppetts Wood
18 Covert Way Field
19 Crane Park Island
20 Darlands Lake
21 Devonshire Road
22 Duck Wood Community Nature Reserve
23 Epping Forest
24 Fox Wood
25 Fryent Country Park
26 Gillespie Road
27 Gunnersbury Triangle
28 Hainault Forest Country Park
29 Ham Lands
30 Hampstead Heath
31 Hither Green
32 Hutchinson's Bank
33 Isleworth Ait
34 Lavender Pond
35 Litten
36 North Cray Woods
37 Nunhead Cemetery
38 Oak Hill Woods
39 Old Park Wood
40 Parkland Walk
41 Scadbury Park
42 Selsdon Wood
43 Staines Reservoirs, North and South
44 Stanmore and Harrow Weald Commons and Bentley Priory
45 Stave Hill Ecological Park
46 Sydenham Hill Wood
47 Ten Acre Wood
48 Thamesside Community Farm Park
49 Tower Hamlets Cemetery
50 Upper Wood
51 Walthamstow Marsh
52 West Kent Golf Course
53 Wilderness Island
54 Wimbledon Common

Area	157,949 hectares
Population	6,713,000
Geology	London clay over chalk, with sand capping high points and gravel deposits along Thames
Climate	Mild; built-up area noticeably warmer than surrounding countryside
Land use	Urban and suburban, farmland on periphery. Chain of reservoirs to west and east, gravel extraction in Lea and Colne valleys

Greater London

Despite the mass of buildings in the central areas, the suburban sprawl of the 1920s and 1930s, and the motorways and high-rise estates of the last three decades, London's 7 million inhabitants co-exist with a surprising variety of wildlife. Birds in vast numbers visit its reservoirs and gravel pits. Fish are returning to the tidal Thames as it reverts to the purity of centuries ago. Animals such as foxes flourish within the sound of Big Ben. The plant life of the region is so varied it includes species found nowhere else in Britain.

The capital's formal wildlife sites range from ancient woodlands to wastelands and wholly artificial nature gardens. In the rural fringe surrounding the built-up area, large woods such as High Elms are plentiful on the slopes of the North Downs where there are also extensive chalk grasslands. Encapsulated countryside survives within the suburbs, whether as huge areas such as Richmond Park and WIMBLEDON COMMON or smaller woodlands such as SYDENHAM HILL WOOD or PERIVALE WOOD in Ealing.

Largely as a result of nineteenth century open space campaigns, commons were widely protected against the incursions of the Victorian developers, as at Riddlesdown and Farthing Downs in Croydon, Keston Common in Bromley and, towards the centre of the connurbation, Wandsworth Common. Most famous of these battles saved EPPING FOREST and HAMPSTEAD HEATH where Ken Wood provides one of the innermost stands of mature woodland. Private estates also withstood the building tide, securing areas such as Holland Park and SCADBURY PARK which are now valued for their wildlife.

Nature sites arising from former or continuing industrial uses form oases within London's middle ring – literally so in the case of reservoirs such as RUISLIP and BRENT in the west, BARN ELMS and LONSDALE ROAD at Barnes, Stoke Newington in the north and the WALTHAMSTOW RESERVOIRS east of the Lea. Superfluous sewage works at Beddington, South Norwood and the Wandle offer the prospect of future reserves as part of their redevelopment, while redundant water treatment plants in the Lea valley, the MIDDLESEX AND ESSEX FILTER BEDS are already being managed for their nature interest.

Canals, lamentably filled in in south London, form a 'blue chain' through the most densely populated neighbourhoods of north London, as does the astonishing New River, constructed as early as 1613 to bring drinking water to Sadlers

Wells from the Lea in Hertfordshire. The Regent's Canal now links bankside reserves such as the CAMLEY STREET NATURE PARK and Wenlock Basin. The railways which put the canals out of business, and at one time covered no less that 10 per cent of London's area, constitute a network of green corridors throughout the metropolis. Sometimes reserves spread over their larger cuttings, as at DEVONSHIRE ROAD, or surplus sidings as at Bricklayers Arms, GILLESPIE ROAD, AND HITHER GREEN. Disused lines have been transformed into linear nature parks at *Parkland* and *Belmont Nature Walks*.

In the last century large cemeteries were landscaped as arboreta to attract visits from the quick as well as the dead. Since the war lack of management in ABNEY PARK, NUNHEAD and TOWER HAMLETS has allowed them to develop as atmospheric secondary woodlands with plentiful unmown grassland which are now run as nature reserves. Also designed for recreation, Victorian parks such as BATTERSEA and ALEXANDRA now contain recognised wildspace.

As the pace of technological progress increased so industrial sites became more quickly obsolete. Bankside power station, commissioned as recently as the 1960s, is already an empty eyrie for kestrels, and Barking power station ash tip has become the THAMESIDE COMMUNITY FARM PARK. In the innermost city districts, artificial nature gardens have been created in neighbourhoods otherwise lacking natural greenspace. The Surrey Docks, closed in 1970 and subsequently mostly infilled, are location for London's best new park, Russia Dock Wood, and two ambitious habitat creation reserves – LAVENDER POND and the STAVE HILL ECOLOGICAL PARK.

Since geography shapes any city's form, it is London's rivers and their valleys which are the most permanent and resilient skeleton for the capital's wildlife sanctuaries. The Thames, its reason for being, retains some of its pre-industrialised character at Syon Park meadows and at the Rainham and Crayford grazing marshes.

Despite intensive exploitation since mediaeval times, the Thames tributaries are the location of diverse important reserves.

In the west the Colne sustains a chain of reserves from HAREFIELD PLACE to OLD PARK WOOD and Frays Island. In the middle of the River Crane is CRANE PARK ISLAND, built in the 1770s to provide water power for Hounslow Heath's gunpowder industry and now an important educational reserve. Where it debouches into the Thames, other man-made islands such as ISLEWORTH AIT are valuable wildlife refuges. To the south the Wandle is coming back into its own with reserves near its headwaters in the form of ST PHILOMENA'S LAKE and, further down, WILDERNESS ISLAND and the National Trust's properties around Morden Hall Park. Eastwards, the Ravensbourne supports several wildlife areas along its course, including BECKENHAM PLACE PARK. More or less the boundary with Kent, the River Cray nurtures in its valley various reserves such as THE WARREN.

In the north-east the Lea is a linear park but lacks a protected link with the Thames along the last mile or so of Bow Creek where the London Wildlife Trust is attempting to preserve the Limmo peninsula as a downstream complement to the WALTHAMSTOW MARSHES and BULLY POINT. The River Roding is a major waterway on its own account, with CLAYBURY WOODS overlooking its higher reaches. Lower down it passes through Wanstead Park before reaching the Thames at Barking Creek. Beyond the giant Ford Works at Dagenham the Beam River passes a large new reserve at THE CHASE, Eastbrookend. Towards the Essex countryside one of the Beam's tributaries rises in the CRANHAM MARSH WOOD.

As London approaches the 1990s it is gratifying that its greenspace is recognised as an important ingredient of its future. The successive editions of the Macmillan Guide are not only a practical handbook for the public but also, in the case of London, a historic record of the increasing number of important sites protected.

BOB SMYTH

Abney Park Cemetery

Stoke Newington High Street. N16; 13ha; LB Hackney reserve
Overgrown cemetery
All year

The area is a semi-wild woodland dominated by sycamore, ash and poplar. The trees and undergrowth are home for a variety of birdlife and small mammals. Grassland alongside pathways includes many herb species which attract butterflies. The cemetery is lightly managed by the council parks department as an educational reserve.

Ainslie Wood

Royston Avenue, Walthamstow, E4; 2ha; LWT reserve
Woodland
All year

This oak woodland includes abundant wild service-trees as well as hornbeam, hawthorn and crab apple. Bluebell, bramble and ivy dominate the ground flora but there are scattered areas of dog's mercury, wood anemone and Solomon's-seal. As well as common woodland birds, tawny owl, treecreeper and spotted flycatcher have been observed. A pond has recently been cleared out.

Alexandra Park

Wood Green, N22; 4ha; Haringey Wildlife Group
Alexandra Palace Dev. Team reserve
Woodland, scrub, grassland and pond
Information centre
All year

The former racecourse is managed as meadow grassland, and a new pond sustains plant and insect species as well as wildfowl.

Barn Elms Reservoirs

Permit only 34ha; TWA
Open water
All year

A favourite spot for birdwatchers: its regulars include great crested grebe, grey heron, gadwall and Canada goose. Among migrants are common sandpiper, sand martin and yellow wagtail with occasional wheatear and whinchat. Large numbers of gulls and wildfowl visit in winter, while summer visitors include swift and meadow pipit.

Barnes Common

Rocks Lane, Barnes, SW13; 50ha; LB Richmond
Grassland and scrub
May July

The common supports a workaday stock of plants, mammals, insects and birds, with burnet rose a speciality. With changes in management, oak woodland and scrub have encroached over a large part of the common and provide a contrast to relic areas of acid grassland which, still contain characteristic herbs such as heath-bed straw.

Battersea Park

Queenstown Road, SW8; 1ha, LB Wandsworth-LWT reserve
Grassland, shrub and woodland
All year

Mist's Pitch just inside the Chelsea Bridge entrance, established in 1985, is the first reserve inside the former GLC inner-city parks since the setting up of the Hampstead Heath Conservation Unit in 1968. There is a leaf dump covered by cinders from the nearby power station and former miniature railway; its variety of habitats attracts 65 bird species and 18 types of butterfly. The informally maintained fringe of trees and understorey along the eastern edge of the park also provides a complementary contrast to the attractions of the rest of the park.

Bayhurst Wood Country Park

TQ 068889; 39.5ha; LB Hillingdon
Woodland and lake
Nature trail leaflet available on site
All year

A woodland, linked by paths to RUISLIP, which once formed part of the ancient Middlesex Forest, it contains interesting standard and coppiced hornbeam, as well as fine standards of oak and beech. There is a good diversity of woodland plants and animals.

Beckenham Place Park

Beckenham Hill Road, SE6; 120ha; LB Lewisham
reserve
Woodland
Leaflets from nature centre in park
All year

The park includes 30ha of ancient woodland, plus a swamp, pond and a stretch of the River Ravensbourne. The woodland consists of oak, sweet chestnut, sycamore and ash, with shrubs including hawthorn, elder, holly, hazel and black-thorn. The ground flora in undisturbed areas includes bluebell, dog's mercury, wood millet, remote sedge and male-fern. While the river bed and edges have been concreted in places, parts are pleasingly rural in appearance with bankside plants including marsh thistle, reed canary-grass and bistort.

Belmont Nature Walk

Vernon Drive, Belmont, Harrow; 3km; LWT reserve
Disused railway line
All year

This middle section of the former Harrow to Stanmore railway, the name 'The Rattler' survives its closure, has developed tree and bramble cover and matching birdlife. The site is being managed to continue its use as an informal walkway and to enhance the variety of fauna and flora.

Benhill Road Nature Garden

Camberwell, SE5; 0.5ha; local management association reserve
Grass and trees
May–July

Over 40 wild plant species have already estab-lished themselves on this former prefab site. Small tortoiseshell butterfly and garden tiger moth are among the insect life already flourishing, while increased variety will result from tree planting and a new pond.

Bramley Bank

Riesco Drive, Croydon; 10ha; LWT reserve
Woodland, acid grassland and ponds
Access for disabled. Leaflet from LWT
All year

Oak, ash, hazel and sycamore are the main constituents of this woodland left to the people of Croydon by the Riesco bequest. A good understorey of hawthorn and rowan, together with the bramble-dominated ground layer provide a good habitat for birds such as treecreeper, nuthatch, great spotted woodpecker and tits. Bluebells, dog's mercury, sanicle and wood-sedge are found. A large pond supports all three species of newt.

Brent Reservoir

Welsh Harp, West Hendon, NW9; 47.2ha; BWB and Welsh Harp Conservation Group
Open water, fen and woodland
All year

A reservoir since 1835, its sloping banks and silted areas at the entry of the River Brent and Silk Stream exhibit the succession from open water to willow carr with beds of common reed and bulrush. Of particular interest is the variety of waterfowl to be seen here especially during the breeding season. Access is limited in wildfowl refuge areas.

Bully Point

Temple Mill Lane, E15; 2.4ha; Lea Valley Regional Park Authority reserve
Grassland and scrub
Spring, summer

Alongside the River Lea, the site was once marsh but was infilled after the last war. With little management in past years, it has developed a diverse flora with large areas of scrub and grass-land. Species discovered during a recent LWT survey included weasel, rabbit and cuckoo, reed warbler and blackcap, and Essex skipper and comma butterfly. An area which is subject to flooding by the Channelsea River branch of the Lea supports crack willow and a small stand of common reed and kingfishers can be seen here.

Camley Street Natural Park

ST Pancras, NW1; 1ha; LWT reserve
Scrub, grassland, pond and canalside marsh
Leaflet from LWT
May–July

Britain's finest example of an artificially created wildlife park, it has been established on a former canalside coal depot.

The existing goat willow scrub and grassland support a variety of birds and common blue butterflies. An interpretive centre and pond attracts hundreds of schoolchildren and adult visitors to the reserve each year.

Cannon Hill Common Nature Reserve

Cannon Hill Lane, Raynes Park, SW20; 0.75ha;
LWT reserve
Woodland, scrub and pond
Spring, summer

Although small, the reserve is interesting as a rare example of a local Wildlife Trust-run reserve in the middle of a public park (LB Merton). The Common, whose name probably derives from its former ownership by the canons of Merton Priory, covers a low hill with grassland sloping down towards a lake. Wildfowl shooting here led to the creation of a bird sanctuary shortly after its opening to the public in 1927. The plantation and pond that lie within the sanctuary are important as nesting and breeding sites for birds and amphibians.

The Chase

Dagenham Road, Romford; 45ha; LWT reserve
Grassland, scrub, reed bed, ponds and river
All year

Though currently restricted on this new reserve, access will be possible once facilities are installed. An area of flooded gravel diggings alongside the River Rom at the point where, at its confluence with the River Ingrebourne, the two form the Beam River, the site surrounds Eastbrookend Farm. The local boroughs, Barking and Dagenham, and Havering, recently handed this major area of wildlife importance to LWT and plans include the creation of a riverbank nature trail and construction of bird hides. The pools also support a rich aquatic flora and fauna; while the grasslands contain several uncommon and rare plants including spiny restharrow and marsh cudweed.

Claybury Hospital Woods

Tomswood Hill, Woodford Bridge; 17ha; LWT reserve
Woodland
Spring, summer

Within the grounds of Claybury Hospital, this large area of ancient woodland of mostly oak and hornbeam also has adjoining scrub, meadowland and ponds. The wooded areas include fine specimens of wild service-tree, and although the ground flora is sparse, active management will increase diversity in coming years. The pond has been restored as an improved habitat for its surviving population of frogs, toads and newts.

Coppetts Wood

Colney Hatch Lane, North Finchley, N12; 8ha;
LWT reserve
Ancient woodland
All year

This is an oak-dominated woodland with an understorey of derelict hazel with hornbeam and sweet chestnut coppice which is a remnant of the former Finchley Common. A variety of scrub and trees is colonising the grassland, where plants such as harebell and perforate and imperforate St John's-wort are found. The adjacent glebeland has unrestricted access.

Covert Way Field

Hadley Wood, Enfield; 6.5ha; Enfield Nat. Hist. Soc.
reserve
Scrub, tall grassland and coppice
April–July

Tree cover of ash, oak, hawthorn and various willows supplementing the Hadley Common woodland accompanies tall grassland, an area of which is mown to produce a herb-rich pasture.

Crane Park Island

Ellerman Avenue, Hounslow Road, Twickenham; 1.8ha;
LWT reserve
Wooded river island
All year

Buddleia, an introduced species, has nectar-rich flowers that attract butterflies such as peacock.

Formerly the site of a gunpowder factory, this island in the River Crane has become overgrown since then. At its eastern end is a mixed woodland containing ash, horse chestnut and sycamore together with a large variety of fungi; no less than 45 species have been found. All three British woodpeckers, tawny owls, voles and a family of foxes breed here. In the middle of the island the former millpond attracts birds including kingfisher, goldfinch, reed warbler, blackcap and even sparrowhawk and green sandpiper. Scrubland covers the western end, and the river around it supports numerous invertebrates such as caddis flies, leeches, swan mussels, small fishes and edible frogs.

Darlands Lake

TQ 244934; 5.1ha; H and MWT reserve
Lake and marsh
April, June, September

A former duck refuge; around the lake are marshy areas, mature alder woodland and damp grassland. Breeding birds include a variety of warblers, mandarin duck and goldcrest.

Devonshire Road

Devonshire Road, Forest Hill, SE23; 2.8ha; LB Lewisham
reserve
Railway cutting
Saturday afternoons, educational access at other times;
contact warden, tel. 01-650 6695
All year

An interpretation centre and nature trail are features of this woodland, scrub and grassland area, a reserve that has been created along a railway cutting.

Downe Bank

Permit only; 7ha; KTNC reserve
Chalk grassland, beech and oak woodland with hazel
coppice
All year

The reserve is predominantly hazel coppice and chalk grassland bank: the latter has a rich flora including several species of orchid chronicled by Charles Darwin who lived for 40 years in nearby Down House.

Duck Wood Community Nature Reserve

Sheffield Drive, Harold Hill, Romford; 9.5ha; LWT reserve
Woodland
Leaflet available from LWT
Spring, summer

Right on the edge of London's built up area, the wood is very popular with local people. An ancient coppiced hornbeam woodland, it includes a series of nine ponds which are being restored. The site is very good for overwintering birds and often boasts large flocks of finches, including the rare and impressive hawfinch.

Epping Forest

Chingford Plain, Rangers Road, Chingford, E4; 2430ha; Corpn of the City of London
Ancient wood pasture, grassland and wetland
Spring, early summer

Situated inside the Greater London boundary at the southern tip of the Forest, Pole Hill is one of the outstanding parts of the area, the rest of which is described in greater detail under Essex. The hill provides a vantage point offering extensive views over the Lea Valley and its rich grassland includes plants such as dyer's greenweed.

Fir and Pond Woods

Permit only; 27ha; HMWT reserve
Woodland and grassland
Spring, summer

Part of the ancient Enfield Chase Forest, the woodlands are predominantly oak and hornbeam, with birch and other occasional species. Pond

Wood contains a small lake surrounded by marsh and willow carr. The lichen is particularly interesting, and breeding birds include little grebe, all three British woodpeckers and tree pipit.

Fox Wood

Hillcrest Road, Ealing, W5; 2.7ha; LWT reserve
Leaflet from LWT
All year

Woodland has developed on the banks of the former Fox Reservoir, drained in 1943 and, rather sadly, infilled as Ealing council playing fields in the 1980s despite its wealth of wildlife. The remaining fringe has, however, been retained and is now traversed by a nature trail. The trees include wild cherry; rotting wood is used by many invertebrates and a wildflower meadow attracts butterflies. A lively birdlife includes visiting fieldfare and redwing, willow warbler, chiffchaff, blackcap, spotted flycatcher and breeding tawny owls. More than 40 fungi species have been recorded.

Fryent Country Park

Fryent Way, NW9; 20ha; LB Brent reserve
Woodland and farmland
Nature trail leaflet from council's leisure department, tel. 01-903 1400 ext. 529
All year

Not far from BRENT RESERVOIR is Fryent Park, an area bought by the local council in 1927 and managed for its wildlife interest. The nature trail that guides you round the woodland also covers the 82ha of hay meadows and hedgerows across Fryent Way.

Hornbeam, beech, oak and hazel form a canopy over Old Park Wood's fine bluebell display.

Gillespie Road

Highbury, N5; 1ha; LB Islington reserve
Grassland, scrub, whips and pond
May–July

A fine specimen of progressive landscape architecture, this nature park on old railway sidings abounds in naturalised lupins rooted in the clinker. Whitethroat find the planting of alder, birch and field maple attractive, and a new pond is lavishly planted with species such as waterplantain, water-soldier and yellow iris.

The Grove

Royal Lane, Hillingdon; 2ha; LWT reserve
Woodland, lake and grassland
Access for disabled. Leaflet from LWT
Spring, summer

Part of a former private house now mostly built on. Regenerating since the 1950s, the woodland includes exotics as well as a flora of foxgloves, bluebells, lords-and-ladies and such like. A brook runs through the reserve forming a lake and marshy areas. Bird life includes kestrel, tawny owl, all three woodpeckers and heron.

Gunnersbury Triangle

Bollo Lane, Chiswick, W3; 2.4ha; LWT reserve
Damp woodland, scrub and pond
Leaflets from interpretation centre, tel. 01–747 2881
All year

Bounded by railways, this triangle of wet birch and sallow woodland is to be served by a field studies centre. The damper zones give rise to lush vegetation, including ferns, horsetails and sedges as well as hemp-agrimony, celery-leaved buttercups and nettles. Thickets of bramble, elder and holly provide nesting places for blackcaps, chiffchaffs, willow warblers and sedge warblers, while the more open grassy areas attract butterflies such as orange-tip, small copper and holly blue.

Hainault Forest Country Park

Fox Burrows, Romford Road, Chigwell Row; 387ha; Essex CC–LB Redbridge
Ancient wood pasture, scrub and grassland
All year

While the area accommodates active recreational facilities such as golf, fishing and horse riding, the northern part retains characteristic features of its past as a royal hunting forest. Bought by the former London County Council in 1903, there is an extensive woodland of old hornbeam pollards bordered by younger secondary woodland with clearings of acid grassland. These habitats support a wide variety of breeding birds including nightingale, wood warbler and tree pipit.

Ham Lands

Riverside Drive, Ham, Richmond; 80ha;
LB Richmond–local management committee reserve
Grassland and scrub
All year

An extensive area of grassland with patches of scrub has colonised infilled diggings next to the Thames and supports a large population of bee orchids plus some pyramidal and common spotted-orchids. Other uncommon plants recorded here include moth mullien, bloody crane's-bill, hairy vetchling, dittander and salad burnet. Woodpeckers, spotted flycatcher and various warblers are among the 100 birds recorded here. A relict flood meadow survives near the Thames bank.

Hampstead Heath

NW1 and NW3; 324ha; Corpn of the City of London
Woodland, sandpit and meadow
All year

One of the earliest conservation battles saved the Heath from development, and areas of special interest include Ken Wood, with its massive old oaks and beeches; a valley bog and its *Sphagnum* mosses; and the South Meadow grassland and scrub which are visited in season by migrants such as yellowhammer.

Hanwell Springs

Church Road, Hanwell, W7; 1ha; LWT reserve
Lake and woodland
Access restricted, contact LWT
All year

A delightful area alongside the former course of the River Brent survives as part of the grounds of a house called The Hermitage. The two ponds, which include an oxbow on the old river course, are fed by a spring whose pool contains a rare moss among other ferns and mosses. The main area has been woodland of some sort for a long period as evidenced by its collection of primary woodland indicator plants, but is now predominantly sycamore. Lying on the boundary of the Brent River Park south of the Brent Valley golf course, it is a valuable refuge for birds.

Harefield Place

Uxbridge Golf Course; 6.4ha; Hillingdon Nat. Hist. Soc. reserve
Woodland, pond and wet meadow
May–July

Originally established as a bird sanctuary based on its woodland; a pond and marsh now increase its interest, and an additional area of woodland has been added. Animals include an unexpectedly wide range of small mammals and good insect fauna.

Hither Green

Green Chain Walk, Baring Road, Lewisham, SE12; 2.4ha;
LB Lewisham–local management committee reserve
Woodland, scrub, grassland and pond
Nature trail leaflet from warden, tel.01-650 6695
All year

The mixture of habitats on a former railway siding now form an educational reserve with a nature trail and an interpretation centre in prospect.

Hutchinson's Bank

Featherbed Lane, New Addington; 40ha; LWT reserve
Grassland, scrub and woodland
Leaflet from LWT
Spring, summer

The reserve is one of the best examples of chalk grassland within the London boundary. The good quality grassland supports orchids such as pyramidal, man and common spotted- and common twayblades.

The adjacent Chapel Bank contains ancient woodland (Bogram's Wood) plus a damp scrub-woodland mostly of hawthorn and dogwood with a rich herb layer including mosses, sanicle, primrose, violet and yellow archangel. The sites are particularly important for their butterfly populations which include brimstone, gatekeeper, ringlet, large, small and Essex skippers, speckled wood and common and small blue.

Isleworth Ait

Church Street, Isleworth; 3ha; LWT reserve
Wooded island
Can be viewed from London Apprentice Public House
All year

Largest of the islets, or eyots, in the Thames between Richmond and Kew Bridge, the area was acquired from the Duke of Northumberland's Syon House estate by the Thames Water Authority in the 1930s.

The island has retained a woodland cover dominated by sycamore with crack willow and elder on the wetter edges; herons, cormorants and kingfishers use the overhanging vegetation as perches and roosts, and the sand and mud banks are feeding grounds at low tide. The site has probably the country's largest population of two-lipped door snail, and a beetle species occuring in only two other British localities.

Lavender Pond

Rotherhithe Street, SE16; 1ha; Trust for Urban Ecology reserve
Pond and reedbed
July-September

Lavender Pond is a prime example of a wholly artificial nature reserve; its Thames-water pond supports shoals of fish, four species of dragonfly and various water birds. Other communities represented here are alder carr, together with plants typical of floor meadows and species commonly found on waste ground.

Litten

Oldfield Lane, Greenford; 1.6ha; LB Ealing reserve
Thicket, grassland and pond
May-July

This small educational reserve packs an interesting variety of habitats into a small space: two ponds, a grove of oak and elm, thickets and grassland are the basis for a range of plant and animal inhabitants.

Lonsdale Road Reservoir

Lonsdale Road, Barnes, SW13; 9ha; LB Richmond-local management association reserve
Shallow lake
Permit only from council
All year

The margins of the lake show the stages of plant succession. Pochard, tufted duck, goosander and goldeneye are among the diving ducks that feed on the reserve in winter, and raft-type islands have been provided for breeding purposes. A classroom is planned.

Middlesex Filter Beds

Lea Bridge Road, Clapton, E5; 4ha; Lea Valley Regional Park Authority reserve
Disused filter beds
Restricted access, contact LWT
All year

The filter beds have a range of wetland plant communities from open water through emergent marginal species to willow carr. The bird record of 62 species includes some rarely seen in inner London such as sparrowhawk, little owl, little grebe, little gull, jackdaw, rook and grasshopper warbler; little ringed plover is attempting to breed here. The site lies between the Lea and the Hackney Cut of the River Lea Navigation or canal, and the relatively undisturbed bank of the river supports a variety of riverside plants. On the other side of the river, the Essex Filter Beds, where plentiful birdlife can be observed, are to be managed by the LVRPA as an educational reserve.

North Cray Woods

Ladbrook Crescent, Sidcup; 8ha; LB Bexley-LWT reserve
Woodland
All year

Set within the larger grounds of Footscray Meadows, the predominantly oak and ask woods have a history stretching back to the Domesday Book and have been in fairly poor shape. They are now being restored by the coppicing of the ash and sweet chestnut, and the improving ground flora includes wood anemone, wood-sorrel, bluebell, pignut, dog's mercury and wood speedwell.

Nunhead Cemetery

Linden Grove, Peckham, SE15; 11ha; LB Southwark reserve
Wood and grassland
May-July

Though the nature reserve area is dominated by sycamore, 100-plus plants have already been recorded which include dog's mercury, meadow crane's-bill and meadow vetchling. Foxes and up to seven butterfly species, including speckled wood, red admiral and meadow brown, may be seen. Conservation work is being carried out by the Friends of Nunhead Cemetery.

Barking power station's disused chimneys stand over remnant saltmarsh at Thameside.

Oak Hill Woods

Church Hill Road, Barnet; 37ha; LB Barnet LWT reserve
Woodland and stream
All year

A north London equivalent of the NORTH CRAY WOODS, this reserve is now being managed to enhance its wildlife character. Though the woodland structure is poor it contains mainly oak and some wild service-tree, hazel and field maple, while on the ground wood anemone and yellow archangel flower. Two arms of a stream provide other interesting wildlife habitats.

Old Park Wood

TQ 049913; 7.7ha; H and MWT reserve
Woodland
April–June

Ancient oak woodland with hazel understorey: its rich ground flora includes coralroot as well as thin-spiked wood-sedge. This wood is one of the best places in London for spring flowers.

Parkland Walk

Alexandra Palace, N22, to Cranley Gardens, N10 (0.7km) and Holmesdale Road, N6, to Finsbury Park, N4 (2.8km); LB Haringey
Woodland, scrub, grassland and ecological corridor
All year

Disused as a railway line for more than 20 years, the site is now managed on an ecological basis, and is colonised by woodland, scrub and coarse grassland. One section runs from Alexandra Park to Highgate Woods, the second section from Highgate tube station to Finsbury Park, passing the information centre at Stapleton Road, N4.

Perivale Wood

Permit only; 11ha; Selborne Soc. reserve
Ancient woodland
April–October

One of the oldest nature reserves in Britain, for it has been owned and managed since 1904 by the Selborne Society; their name is a tribute to Gilbert White whose *Natural History of Selborne* still inspires new generations of naturalists. Sandwiched between the railway and the Paddington arm of the Grand Union Canal, the mainly oak woodland is interspersed with patches of hazel coppice, ash and wild service-tree.

A profusion of bluebells in spring is accompanied by large numbers of breeding blackcap and other birds. Other woodland flowers including red campion make a vivid display, while grasses such as wood millet are an indication of the wood's age. Coppicing of the hazel is being reinstated; the hazel wands are used for hedging around the fields next to the wood. The grassland on the south and east sides encompasses a marshy pond and associated plants such as cuckooflower.

To be visited as part of any trip to Perivale is nearby Horsenden Hill, whose unimproved hay meadow includes dyer's greenweed and ragged-Robin. Its hedgerows, survivors of ancient woodland, are fringed with herbs such as dog's mercury.

Queen Mary Reservoir

Permit only; 283ha; TWA
Open water
All year

Part of the reservoir is a protected area for birds, with black-necked grebe a regular, and shoveler and goosander among the range of waterfowl that winter in nationally important numbers.

Ruislip

Permit only; 4.5ha; Ruislip and District Nat. Hist. Soc. reserve
Open water and marsh
All year

This segment of former reservoir offers open water and surrounding marshland of unusual richness containing a range of plants, insects and molluscs. Drier parts consist of heathland vegetation and developing scrub. As added interest excavated chalk debris supports characteristic chalk grassland. Breeding willow tit and kingfisher are among the birds to be seen here.

The reserve, one of London's two oldest Local Nature Reserves, is surrounded by the complex of Ruislip Woods and by other ancient vestiges. A pre-Roman greenway runs through Mad Bess Woods and a medieval trackway crosses Poor's Fields between Ruislip and North Woods. One of the largest oak-and-coppiced-hornbeam areas left, it presents a contrast to the pollards of EPPING FOREST. Whereas Epping was open for grazing, Ruislip Woods were enclosed and pannage laws restricted the areas to pigs rooting for acorns.

In winter the woodland is a haven for woodcock, and water rail lurk in the densest part of the swamp. Summer sees breeding woodpeckers, hawfinch, wood warbler and tree pipit, and sometimes a nightingale in Poor's Fields.

Ruxley Gravel Pits

Permit only; 20ha; KTNC reserve
Open water and marsh
All year

The contrasting textures of these flooded gravel-pits, which act as flood storage lagoons for the River Cray, are an exciting spectacle for visitors looking from the Sidcup side towards the wooded banks on the Kent side of the valley. The ponds are frequented by migrant wildfowl such as gadwall and tufted duck, and by grey wagtail; they also support many freshwater invertebrates. Surviving marshland vegetation from before the days of water authority drainage schemes is of special interest. But above all it is the atmosphere of this oasis on the edge of the built-up area of south east London which makes Ruxley a source of such immense pleasure to the visitor.

St Philomena's Lake

Shorts Road, Carshalton; 1ha; LWT reserve
Open water
Permit only, except on open days
All year

This large spring-fed pond within the grounds of Carshalton House, now a convent school, has been desilted and its weir reconstructed. The original vegetation – mostly small reed-grass, water mint and watercress – is being replaced along with more plantings of water dock, water celery, large bittercress and the nationally rare water sedge. Newts, toads and frogs are also found, as well as a rare aquatic snail *Limnea palustris* and good numbers of dragonflies.

Scadbury Park

Perry Street, Sidcup; 60ha; LB Bromley reserve
Woodland, meadows, pools, streams and hedges
All year

Opened by the council in 1985, the park includes oaks from Elizabethan times when the estate was a hunting park, 58 acres of woodland managed by Bromley's forestry department, and farmland including old hedgerows. The wide range of habitats supports a diversity of plant and animal life and is particularly rich in bird species.

Selsdon Wood

Court Wood Lane, Selsdon, Croydon; 81ha; NT–LB Croydon reserve
Woodland and bird sanctuary
May–July

The woodland ranges from 200-year-old oaks to recent plantings of beech, larch and spruce, with rotational coppicing in parts, and ground flora including early-purple orchid. Breeding birds to be found in the wood include long-tailed tit, blackcap, treecreeper, whitethroat and spotted flycatcher. Grassland pasture occupies a quarter of the reserve.

The surroundings of Ten Acre Wood in London's Green Belt, an essential buffer between town and country.

Staines Reservoirs, North and South

Hanworth; 172ha; TWA
Open water
All year

A winter count here recorded 5000 pochard – one of the largest concentrations in the British Isles – and 4000 tufted duck – only 500 less than the highest national count at LOCH LEVEN (Tayside). Other regulars are teal, wigeon and common sandpiper.

Stanmore and Harrow Weald Commons and Bentley Priory

Common Road, Harrow Weald; 133ha; H and MWT (reserve only)
Heathland, scrub and woodland
Permit only to reserve
All year

This common land supports oak woodland on Harrow Weald, and a more varied association of birch scrub, developing oak and beech woodland and secluded grassland glades on Stanmore Common. Cattle still graze on the floristically rich grasslands at Bentley Priory next to the formal reserve, consisting of a lake fringed by bulrush.

Stave Hill Ecological Park

Salter Road, Rotherhithe, SE1; 3ha; Trust for Urban Ecology reserve
Recreated habitats
All year

A new reserve replacing the former William Curtis Ecological Park is being established next to the local council's ambitious new Russia Dock Wood. The part next to the wood has open access while the remainder will become an educational site with a planned interpretation centre.

Sydenham Hill Wood

Sydenham Hill, SE26; 11ha; LWT reserve
Woodland
All year

The wood includes areas once known by individual names such as Fernbank and Lapsewood. Originally oak forest, the wood is now a patchwork of oak, hazel and hornbeam coppice together with holly and impressively large beeches. Rhododendron and bamboo have invaded from the Victorian garden which protected it from development.

The rich bird life in the wood includes great spotted woodpecker, thought to breed here, together with marsh tit, long-tailed tit, treecreeper, nuthatch, chiffchaff, willow warbler, blackcap and spotted flycatcher, and with winter woodcock. Woodland flowers include wood anemone, Solomon's-seal, southern wood-rush and ramsons; wood melick is among the unusual grasses.

One of the reserve's curious features is the track of the railway built to take visitors to the Crystal Palace. A long tunnel, barred against intruders, may provide a good harbourage for bats. Alongside the railway embankment path an undrained

marsh where grey wagtail once bred has been excavated to form a pond.

Other parts of the wood are being restored to the working wood that existed before Victorian encroachments. The hazel is being coppiced once again, and the sycamore is also being controlled.

Tarleton's Lake

Permit only; 2.8ha; H and MWT reserve
Lake, marsh, sandpit and wood
June–July

Birds abound here, and while orchids are a special feature other rare species include flowering-rush and moschatel.

Ten Acre Wood

Charville Lane, Hayes; 7.6ha; LWT reserve
Oak woodland and meadow
All year

A fine stand of oak standard woodland with hazel coppice and Midland hawthorn on the edge of Yeading Brook includes herb-Robert in its ground flora. Higher up the stream, Gutteridge Wood (9ha) is ancient woodland managed by LWT, as are Hare's Hollows further downstream on the Yeading Meadows – wetlands with characteristic plants including the rare narrow-leaved water-dropwort.

Thameside Community Farm Park

River Road, Creekmouth, Barking; 13.2ha; Thameside Assn. reserve
Grassland, lagoon and dykes
All year

On the unpromising foundation of wasteland on the site of the old Barking power station, the reserve already has an unexpected variety of plants such as the hybrid between common spotted-orchid and southern marsh-orchid growing on a soil which is mostly pulverised fuel ash. The area is drained by dykes but marsh and pools remain. Skylark and meadow pipit feature among the grassland birds and in winter short-eared and barn owl quarter the flats, alert for unsuspecting mice and voles.

An active management scheme is developing a spectrum of habitats while at the same time making them accessible to visitors and students. In the often grim terrain left in the wake of obsolete industries in this part of eastern London, an urban farm is an added attraction.

Nearby, Barking Bay survives as a short but rewarding stretch of estuary mud and sand where diving duck congregate. Their refuge is, however, threatened by possible development.

Tower Hamlets Cemetery

Southern Grove, Bromley, E3; 11ha; LB Tower Hamlets
Disused cemetery
All year

Opened in 1841 and closed for burials in 1965, the cemetery was acquired in the following year for a public park. Over 100 plant species are found here, and its birdlife includes greenfinches, blackcaps and long-tailed tits. The profusion of ivy is an attraction to holly blue butterflies.

Tump 53

Carlyle Road, Thamesmead, SE28; 1.4ha; Thamesmead
Town Trust LWT
Small island
By arrangement with LWT
All year

The Tump, an island surrounded by a moat on the Woolwich marshes, was once used to store explosives. Retained amid the new housing development at the centre of Thamesmead for its amenity and nature conservation interest, it is being managed by an LWT warden with responsibility for promoting its educational use and keeping an eye on other sites of ecological value in the area.

Upper Wood

Farquhar Road, Crystal Palace, SE19; 3ha; Trust for
Urban Ecology reserve
Woodland
All year

Mature trees including oak, lime and horse-chestnut are among the 20-plus species forming a woodland which, after years of neglect, is being managed to increase plant and animal diversity and provide a range of wildlife interest for visitors.

Walthamstow Marsh

Spring Hill, Clapton, E5; 35.2ha; Lea Valley Regional
Park Authority reserve
Flood meadow
All year

The marsh has joined WALTHAMSTOW RESERVOIRS as a Site of Special Scientific Interest – it forms the last ancient grassland in the Lea Valley. The plant life includes fen-type communities of sedges, meadowsweet and reedbeds, and over 350 plant species have been recorded. Sedge warbler are present in summer, snipe and teal in winter.

Walthamstow Reservoirs

Permit only; 133ha; TWA
Open water and wooded islands
All year

In addition to its famous heronry this group of reservoirs is an important breeding site for mute swan, Canada goose, pochard, mallard and tufted duck. Other nesting birds include kestrel, yellow and grey wagtail and sand martin. Other major attractions at this site are the large numbers of tufted duck which gather to moult in late summer and the concentrations of migratory waterfowl present during the winter months.

Walton Reservoirs

Permit only; 90ha; TWA
Open water
All year

The nine reservoirs offer late summer and winter concentrations of diving duck and other wildfowl plus sightings of the rarer grebes and many rare ducks.

The Warren

Sheepcote Lane, St Mary Cray, Orpington; 35ha; LWT
reserve
Acid grassland, woodland and lake
Leaflet from LWT
All year

Part privately owned and part belonging to LB Bromley, the Warren is gradually being restored. The woodland is a haven for the three woodpecker species and the lake for amphibians, including the endangered great crested newt.

West Kent Golf Course

Luxted Road, Leaves Green, Bromley; 111ha; West Kent
Golf Club LWT
Woodland and downland
Access restricted to public footpaths
All year

While not a formal reserve, the golf course is an interesting example of a golf club encouraging appropriate managment of its wildlife areas. Set in the valleys of the northern slopes of the North Downs adjacent to Biggin Hill airfield, the area includes beech and oak woodland and rich ancient downland supporting man and bee orchids as well as common spotted-orchids.

Wilderness Island

River Gardens, Mill Lane, Carshalton; 2ha; LWT reserve
Wooded island
All year

The island lies between two branches of the Wandle and survives because of the railway line forming an eastern barrier. While it contains a patch of broadleaved woodland, its main interest is in its watery habitats. Willow carr gives way to a pond surrounded by beds of sedge and the river banks themselves. Abundant birdlife includes redpolls, goldfinches and linnets as well as bankside grey wagtails and kingfishers.

Wimbledon Common

Parkside, Wimbledon, SW19; 341ha; Wimbledon and
Putney Commons Conservators
Heath, woodland, scrub and bogs
All year

Higher, gravelly areas support an extensive mosaic of open wet heath and acid grassland with gorse and birch scrub in places, while the lower clay slopes feature oak woodland with hornbeam and birch – redstart are among the large breeding bird population. A couple of valley bogs harbour bogbean, water horsetail and bog mosses. Animals include badger, grass snake, common lizard, and a large insect population including many butterflies.

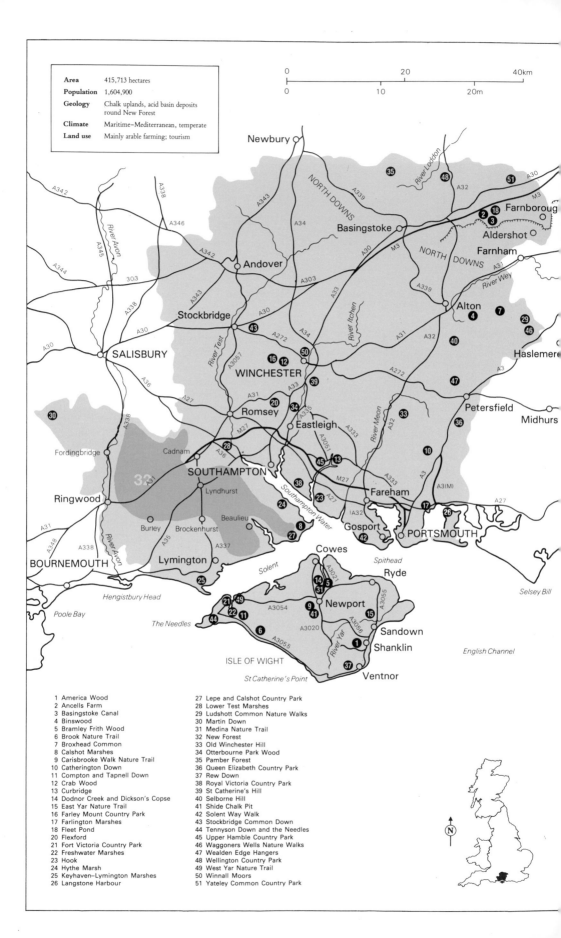

Area	415,713 hectares
Population	1,604,900
Geology	Chalk uplands, acid basin deposits round New Forest
Climate	Maritime–Mediterranean, temperate
Land use	Mainly arable farming; tourism

1 America Wood
2 Ancells Farm
3 Basingstoke Canal
4 Binswood
5 Bramley Frith Wood
6 Brook Nature Trail
7 Broxhead Common
8 Calshot Marshes
9 Carisbrooke Walk Nature Trail
10 Catherington Down
11 Compton and Tapnell Down
12 Crab Wood
13 Curbridge
14 Dodnor Creek and Dickson's Copse
15 East Yar Nature Trail
16 Farley Mount Country Park
17 Farlington Marshes
18 Fleet Pond
20 Flexford
21 Fort Victoria Country Park
22 Freshwater Marshes
23 Hook
24 Hythe Marsh
25 Keyhaven–Lymington Marshes
26 Langstone Harbour

27 Lepe and Calshot Country Park
28 Lower Test Marshes
29 Ludshott Common Nature Walks
30 Martin Down
31 Medina Nature Trail
32 New Forest
33 Old Winchester Hill
34 Otterbourne Park Wood
35 Pamber Forest
36 Queen Elizabeth Country Park
37 Rew Down
38 Royal Victoria Country Park
39 St Catherine's Hill
40 Selborne Hill
41 Shide Chalk Pit
42 Solent Way Walk
43 Stockbridge Common Down
44 Tennyson Down and the Needles
45 Upper Hamble Country Park
46 Waggoners Wells Nature Walks
47 Wealden Edge Hangers
48 Wellington Country Park
49 West Yar Nature Trail
50 Winnall Moors
51 Yateley Common Country Park

Hampshire and the Isle of Wight

The stark white pinnacles of the Needles present a marked contrast with the flat mudlands and marshes of the mainland coast, epitomising the dramatic variety of landscape and wildlife to be found in the two counties. Additionally the Isle of Wight contains eroding cliffs and the only piece of rocky shore in the area, as well as sandy beaches and estuaries.

Although the central chalk ridge dominates the Isle of Wight scenery, as do the South Downs in Hampshire, the presence of other geological formations gives rise to a range of soil types supporting varied plant and animal communities. The poorer soils in the west of Hampshire bear the unique NEW FOREST, a mosaic of ancient oak and beech woodland intermixed with lowland heath and valley bog, modified by human influence over many centuries and currently under considerable recreational pressure. In the other area of poor soil, in north east Hampshire, it is heathland species that predominate.

The richer soils derived from chalk strata support the WEALDEN EDGE hanging woodlands near Petersfield, with their abundant specialised flora and fauna. More woodland, less diverse but still interesting, grows on the Hampshire Basin tertiary strata. These woods are remnants of one of Hampshire's Royal Forests, the Forest of Bere, and indeed the county contains about 10 per cent of all the ancient woodlands of England and Wales. Viewed from the high points of Hampshire the well-wooded appearance of the landscape is remarkable, especially since large tracts of countryside, including some parts of the chalk downs, are farmed intensively. The shortage of plant and animal life on farmland makes another contrast with the exceptional richness of the remaining semi-natural chalk grassland. Some of this valuable habitat type is conserved in a number of reserves, large and small, in both Hampshire and the Isle of Wight. Orchids, butterflies and a

wide range of animals and plants, together with the yew and whitebeam woods on the slopes, provide a further aspect of wildlife diversity.

Rising in the chalk hills and flowing into the Solent are several large rivers and many smaller streams. Most are noted for their trout fisheries, implying a wealth of small aquatic animals, and the unpolluted state of most of Hampshire's rivers is a direct result of their importance to anglers. Otter still occur on some of Hampshire's rivers, and havens are being established.

The equable climate of central southern England enables a number of species to survive at the northern end of their range: four plants and two insects occur nowhere else in England. Similarly the position of Hampshire and the Isle of Wight places them where the eastern continental and western Oceanic–Lusitanian floras overlap. The North Sea and Atlantic waters mix in a zone surrounding the island and washing the shores of the mainland; the considerable variety of marine fauna and flora, which includes a number of introduced species, is probably connected with this.

The population increase in Hampshire, resulting from London overspill in the north and urban expansion in the south, forms yet another sharp distinction from the sparsely settled agricultural regions of the county. The Isle of Wight, on the other hand, experiences seasonal population differences, with a massive influx of holiday-makers in the summer and relative peace and quiet in the winter. Residents are not slow to appreciate the natural environment and its wild-life, carrying on the tradition of study started by Hampshire's two best-known naturalists, Gilbert White of Selborne fame and W.H. Hudson.

In addition to their local and national importance for wildlife conservation, several sites are of international significance. Notable among them are the New Forest and the three linked harbours of Portsmouth, LANGSTONE and Chichester – the last actually in West Sussex – where wintering wildfowl and waders occur in considerable numbers.

These rich and varied wildlife resources are safeguarded by reserves, owned and managed by a range of agencies: parts of the coastline are under the protection of the Nature Conservancy Council, Hampshire County Council, the Forestry Commission, the Royal Society for the Protection of Birds and the National Trust, as well as the Hampshire and Isle of Wight Naturalists' Trust. Similarly the woodlands and chalk grassland are protected by one or more of these organisations. But general public awareness of the value of wildlife is perhaps the best safeguard of all, ensuring the retention of these habitats.

FAY R. STRANACK

America Wood

SZ 568819; 11ha; WdT
Deciduous woodland
Spring, summer

The wood is a fine example of ancient pasture dominated by mature and pollarded oaks.

Ancells Farm

SU 824557; 2ha; H and IOWNT reserve
Wet heath
Summer

This small site is alive with wildlife. The ponds support many dragonfly species and aquatic plants, while on the heath early marsh-orchid and intermediate and round-leaved sundews flower. Snipe and marsh fritillary butterflies are present.

Ashford Chace

Part of the WEALDEN EDGE HANGERS

Basingstoke Canal

SU 719514–784513; 12km; HCC reserve
Reopened canal
Spring, summer

The canal and towpath pass through woodland and fields, adding their wildlife interest to the little grebe and moorhen, dragonflies and damselflies.

Basingstoke Canal Flashes

Permit only; 1.4ha; H and IOWNT reserve
Shallow pools adjoining the canal
Spring, summer

When the canal was dredged these wetlands were conserved as sanctuaries for such uncommon plants as frogbit, flowering-rush, narrow-leaved water-plantain, water-soldier and water-violet. The insects are particularly varied and interesting.

Binswood

SU 764370; 62ha; WdT
Pasture woodland
Spring, summer

The ancient wood pasture common is still managed in a traditional manner, with cattle grazing among the old pollarded trees. It offers visitors a rare glimpse into the medieval world, and is part of one of King John's deer parks in the old royal hunting forest of Woolmer.

Blackdam

SU 654516; 4ha; H and IOWNT reserve
Streamside, marshland and scrub
Spring, summer

All stages from open water through marsh to dry land are represented at Blackdam, which contains a fine range of plant and animal wildlife. Adder's-tongue, water avens, bluebell and cowslip are among the attractive plants while birds include corn bunting and water rail among 50 species recorded on the reserve.

Bramley Frith Wood

SU 513920; 27ha; CEGB reserve
Deciduous woodland
Educational or youth groups only
Nature-trail leaflet from nature centre
Spring, summer

An electricity substation has been sited in the centre of the wood. The wood is of ancient origin and consists mainly of coppice with oak and a few ash standards. In spring there are many bluebells, primroses, Solomon's-seal and common spotted-orchids. Speckled wood and white admiral butterflies may be seen along the sunny rides, and mammals include dormouse and roe and fallow deer.

Brook Nature Trail

SZ 391839; 3.2km; IOW Nat. Hist. and Arch. Soc.
Countryside trail
Leaflet from IOW Tourist Board
Spring, summer

The circular walk includes land on both lower greensand and chalk, showing the contrast of the brilliant small downland plants such as clustered bellflower, lady's bedstraw and common centaury with the more robust and common flowers of the farmland.

Broughton Down

Permit only; 14.4ha; H and IOWNT reserve
Chalk grassland, scrub and woodland
Spring, summer

A fine chalk grassland, which includes the unusual field fleawort, grades through scrub into beech woodland. Insects to be found here include chalkhill blue and dark green fritillary butterflies with moths such as ruby tiger and large yellow underwing.

Broxhead Common

SU 806374; 44ha; HCC reserve
Dry heathland
Spring, summer

Situated on rising ground, this small remnant of dry heathland enjoys fine views over the well-wooded landscape of east Hampshire. Mature and regenerating heather occupies the higher ground while common and dwarf gorse, birch and pine have colonised the lower slopes, providing nest sites for tree pipit, whitethroat and redpoll.

Calshot Marshes

SU 480010; 48ha; HCC reserve
Saltmarsh and mudflats
Spring, autumn, winter

A wide area of cord-grass saltmarsh and tidal mudflats which may be overlooked from the Calshot end of the LEPE AND CALSHOT COUNTRY PARK, it is good for migrants and winter birds.

Carisbrooke Walk Nature Trail

SZ 484876; 6.4 8km; IOW Nat. Hist. and Arch. Soc.
Countryside walk
Leaflet from IOW Tourist Board
Spring, early summer

A wood where badgers breed, a shady deep-sunk lane and a sunlit stream are characteristic island features of the circular walk, which in early summer is loud with songbirds.

Catherington Down

SU 689141; 12ha; HCC H and IOWNT
Chalk grassland
Spring, summer

The unploughed banks of the ancient field system bear chalkland flowers such as clustered bellflower, round-headed rampion and dropwort. Several orchid species include autumn lady's-tresses. A good range of butterflies may be present.

Chappetts Copse

Permit only; 13ha; H and IOWNT reserve
Woodland
Summer

The beech wood was planted only about 100 to 150 years ago but it now supports large populations of orchids including white and broad-leaved helleborine, and fly and bird's-nest orchids. Spurge laurel and sanicle are also found, and the latter is the food-plant of a rare moth.

The Chase

SU 444627; 47.6ha; H and IOWNT NT reserve
Conifer woodland and lake with alder wetland
All year

The reserve is most interesting for its bird life which includes all three native woodpeckers, a good range of warblers, kingfisher near the lake, and wintering siskin and redpoll in the alder carr.

Compton and Tapnell Down

SZ 368854; 54ha; NT
Chalk grassland
Spring, summer

Compton and Tapnell Down forms part of the most southerly flank of chalk in the country, crowned with a turf of herbs and grasses and looking out across the Channel. The soil is sometimes deep enough for gorse and coarse grasses to grow, sometimes a shallow broken cover over open, herb-rich rubbles.

The deeper soils are filled with plants such as cowslip, flowering before the grass grows tall, salad burnet, small scabious and pyramidal orchid, later plants which can lift above the shade, or common rock-rose, leaning on the stronger stems to raise its yellow flowers to the light. Ragwort and gorse grow with occasional hawthorn and taller lime-loving species such as wild parsnip.

The thinner soils are filled with small, more delicate bright flowers such as wild thyme, harebell, quaking-grass and yellow-wort. The soft pink of restharrow complements the blue selfheal, the tiny eyebright, clusters of horseshoe and kidney vetch, lady's bedstraw and squinancywort. Clustered bellflower and bee orchid contrast with the prickly carline and dwarf thistle. While the summer show of chalkland flowers is wonderful, in spring the down is decorated with a spread of early gentian and early-purple and green-winged orchid to add to the vivid colour provided by the cowslips.

The southerly position of the down makes it an ideal site for migrant butterflies. Clouded yellow and Berger's clouded yellow are both attracted by the wealth of vetches, while other butterflies include Adonis, chalkhill and little blue with dark green fritillary. The blue butterflies, too, are attracted to leguminous plants such as vetches and trefoils, both Adonis and chalkhill blue particularly associated with horseshoe vetch. The dark green fritillary feeds as a caterpillar on violets like most of the British fritillaries, but an exception to this rule, and one which in Britian is limited to the Isle of Wight, may stray on to the down: the Glanville fritillary generally feeds on plantains and breeds on the undercliff nearby. Marbled white may also occur on these southern slopes although the breeding colony prefers a more northerly aspect.

The juxtaposition of the down and the sea implies a maritime influence which adds to and varies the characteristics of the chalk, reflected in the variety of the insects which includes such uncommon species as the rare weevil *Apion millum*.

Coulters Dean

Permit only; 5.2ha; H and IOWNT reserve
Chalk grassland and scrub
Spring, summer

A rich variety of chalkland plants includes clustered bellflower and round-headed rampion with orchids such as bee and fragrant. The butterflies include Duke of Burgundy and dingy skipper.

Glanville fritillary occurs only on the Isle of Wight.

Crab Wood

SU 436298; 36ha; HCC–H and IOWNT reserve
Old oak woodland
Spring, early summer

Many of the higher chalk areas are covered by clay with flints, where deeper soils have developed than on the bare chalk. These soils once carried dense oak forest, of which Crab Wood is a remnant. Most of the larger oaks have been felled but some remain, together with a number of fine old beech trees, overtopping the hazel understorey. The diversity of plants reflects the varying depth of soil, the nutrient status and water-holding capacity. Ash, field maple, spindle, wayfaring-tree, yew and privet interlaced with traveller's joy grow where the soil is rich. Holly, hawthorn and willows with aspen, birch and honeysuckle reflect the damper state of the soils with lower nutrient content.

Where glades have been opened up in the course of management, primrose, violets and the local specialities Solomon's-seal and lily-of-the-valley flower in spring. Where the light is less dog's mercury and enchanter's-nightshade grow, while under the dense shade of the beeches bluebell flourishes with scattered bird's-nest orchid and early-purple orchid. On richer soils woodruff, sanicle, pignut and wood spurge appear, and in damper hollows pendulous sedge, perforate St John's-wort and common spotted-orchid are found. Wood melick and nettle-leaved bellflower border the paths.

The wide range of birds also reflects the differing habitats. Open areas suit nightjar, scrub attracts nightingale, and all three woodpecker species are found as well as the more common woodland birds. Roe and fallow deer have been seen; dormouse, hedgehog and the usual woodland small mammals are also present.

Moths include some rarities; among the butterflies are white admiral, a melanistic form of silver-washed fritillary and Duke of Burgundy.

Curbridge

SU 528118; 5.6ha; H and IOWNT–NT reserve
Mixed woodland and wetland
Spring, early summer

A good variety of spring flowers is matched by the riverbank plants, with freshwater species grading into saltmarsh where the unusual marsh-mallow may be found. There is a wide range of bird and insect species.

Dodnor Creek and Dickson's Copse

SZ 505915; 8.8ha; IWCC reserve
Freshwater ponds and woodland
Permit from Planning Unit IWCC
Leaflets from Planning Unit IWCC
Spring, summer

A former mill pond associated with cement mills on the bank of the Medina River has reverted to freshwater marshes and now provides a habitat for breeding wetland birds, including mute swan and reed and sedge warbler. Dickson's Copse provides a wooded fringe of pedunculate oak noted for mosses, liverworts and ferns.

Eagleshead and Bloodstone Copses

Permit only; 6.9ha; H and IOWNT reserve
Woodland
Spring

This superb ash and hazel coppice contains over 30 ancient woodland indicator plants including a very large population of toothwort. Both badgers and dormice are present.

East Yar Nature Trail

SZ 576857; 4.8km; IOW Nat. Hist. and Arch. Soc.
Riverside walk
Leaflet from IOW Tourist Board
Spring, summer

A delightful walk along the eastern River Yar is bright with the flowers of comfrey, water forget-me-not and yellow iris. Damp meadows may show the flower spikes of common spotted-orchid while reedbeds give cover to reed and sedge warbler, little grebe and moorhen.

Emer Bog

Permit only; 25ha; H and IOWNT reserve
Bog and heathland
Summer

Duke of Burgundy, a mainly southern butterfly, lays its eggs on cowslip and primrose.

The reserve is nationally important for its extremely varied moth populations, while silver-studded blue butterflies are found on the wet heath. The bog itself holds interesting plants such as marsh cinquefoil and bottle sedge, and water rails breed in the marginal reedbeds.

Farley Mount Country Park

SU 409293 433293; 106.5ha; HCC
Chalk downland and woods
Spring, summer

The chalk downland is spangled with characteristic plants, including the uncommon bastard-toadflax and beautiful pyramidal orchid, while the woods include CRAB WOOD.

Farlington Marshes

SU 679045; 120ha; H and IOWNT reserve
Damp grassland and scrub, freshwater marsh, and pools
Spring, autumn, winter

An integral part of LANGSTONE HARBOUR.

Fleet Pond

SU 816553; 56ha; Hart DC reserve
Open water, heath and woodland
Spring, early summer

Heathland, with mixed broad-leaved and coniferous woodland, covers roughly half of the reserve while the pond itself forms a fairly large body of water. Great crested grebe and Canada goose are among the breeding species and the reserve has been visited by such rarities as great reed warbler from Europe and transatlantic blue-winged teal.

Fletchwood Meadows

Permit only; 4ha; H and IOWNT reserve
Grassland
Summer

In these peaceful meadows beside the Bartley Water are to be found flowering many green-winged and lesser butterfly orchids, as well as corky-fruited water-dropwort.

Flexford

SU 424220; 9.3ha; H and IOWNT reserve
Alder carr woodland and grassland
Spring, summer

Carpets of ramsons, opposite-leaved golden saxifrage and wood anemones cover the woodland floor in summer, with scarce wood club-rush and Solomon's-seal also present. The peaty grassland is equally rich in wood horsetail, water avens and marsh-orchids. Butterflies such as the ringlet and white admiral have all been recorded.

Fort Victoria Country Park

SZ 339898; 20ha; IWCC
Wooded coastal landslips
Nature trail leaflet from information centre
Spring, early summer

Below the limestone of the clifftops are beds of sands and clays which periodically collapse when water drains down from above. This has led to a tumbled overgrown wilderness, full of wildlife, which is explored by the nature trail laid out within the woods. The area is rich in tangles of lime-loving traveller's-joy.

Bramshaw Wood in the New Forest: high-forest woodland where fallow, roe and red deer may be seen.

Freshwater Marsh

SZ 347862; 16ha; South Wight BC reserve
Rich marsh and river course
Nature trail leaflet from SWBC
Spring, summer

A nature trail overlooks the main body of the marsh, an attractive spread of common reed and marsh plants such as bulrush, flowering-rush, yellow iris and yellow loosestrife, purple-loosestrife, meadowsweet and water-plantain. Alder and birch woodland fringes the western River Yar, which rises in the marsh, and, with the reedbeds, encourages a variety of birds including reed, sedge and willow warbler, reed bunting and nightingale. Butterflies are well represented, with a chance of migrants such as clouded yellow and Berger's clouded yellow, and several characteristic wainscot moths breed in the marshy reedbeds.

Holmesley Gravel Pits

Permit only; 3.2ha; H and IOWNT reserve
Scrub and flooded diggings
Spring, summer

Common duck such as mallard overwinter here but the muddy foreshore is attractive to waders and has drawn breeding redshank while the shingle banked islands are a suitable site for nesting little ringed plover. Willow scrub around the pits provides sites for many songbirds and encourages a good range of insects on which they feed.

Hook

SU 490060; 200ha; HCC reserve
Estuary shore
Winter

The reserve includes a wide range of habitat from the mudflats and saltmarsh of the tidal shore, through brackish meadows and freshwater marsh, to woodland. A great variety of birds may be seen throughout the year, from winter wildfowl and waders such as curlew and dunlin, to summer sedge warbler, stonechat and yellowhammer.

Hythe Marsh

SU 433073; 8.8ha; H and IOWNT reserve
Cord-grass saltmarsh
Summer

This area of specialist interest supports a wide range of genetically varied populations of cord-grass.

Keyhaven–Lymington Marshes

SZ 300908-333945; 277.6ha; HCC-H and IOWNT
Estuary coastal strip
No access off rights of way
All year

Hurst Spit is a long shingle ridge which forms the western limit of the area and shelters a wide spread of mudflats. The mudflats stretch on, outside the sea wall, to the Lymington River some 5km north eastwards and are backed by grazing marshes and coastal scrub.

From Hurst Castle, the mudflats stretch in a gullied, puddled, inhospitable-looking spread. The channels turn and twist, cutting deep into the muds.

A narrow saltmarsh has developed along the edge of the shingle where glasswort, sea aster, sea plantain and annual sea-blite begin to stabilise the muds and grade into the typical plants of the pebble spit. Here and in the grass of the castle area is a wealth of fascinating plants including sea campion, sea-kale, sea-lavender, sea-purslane and sea wormwood, with yellow horned-poppy, golden samphire, thrift, hare's-foot clover, kidney vetch and wild thyme. The sea wall, too, is faced with many of these species and is backed by grazed grasslands and marshy, heathlike scrubs of gorse and birch. Pools behind the sea wall provide an extra habitat and some have developed stands of common reed. A number of unusual plant species occur, including a subspecies of little-Robert, *Geranium purpureum forsteri*, which has a very limited distribution on stabilised shingle.

Spring passage may bring red-throated diver, common scoter, arctic and great skua, little gull and black tern, while autumn brings numbers of waders such as black- and bar-tailed godwit, greenshank and grey plover, spotted redshank, ruff, common and curlew sandpiper, little stint and whimbrel.

In winter up to 500 Brent geese may be present with similar numbers of shelduck and teal and smaller flocks of duck such as goldeneye, long-tailed duck, mallard, pochard and wigeon. Huge flocks of dunlin may be here and large numbers of lapwing. A few Slavonian grebe and goosander are recorded and there is a November gathering of red-breasted merganser. There have been sightings of surf scoter and whiskered tern.

Langstone Harbour

SU 697058; 554ha; RSPB reserve
Inter-tidal marshes and mudflats
Spring, autumn, winter

No access is possible to the reserve itself but the area is easily overlooked from the coast footpath along the north shore. In winter over 6000 dark-bellied Brent geese may be present, with spring and autumn passages of waders such as black-tailed godwit and grey plover. The reserve also supports Britain's second largest colony of little terns which numbered over 100 pairs in 1986.

Lepe and Calshot Country Park

SZ 456986 and SU 480012; 49.5ha; HCC
Cliff top and foreshore
Winter

The park itself, in two separate sections, is mainly used as a picnic spot from which to view the Isle of Wight and the Solent. In winter, however, low tide may provide good feeding grounds for waders such as turnstone and oystercatcher.

Long Aldermoor

Permit only; 2.4ha; H and IOWNT reserve
Wet woodland and grassland
Spring, early summer

The small but interesting reserve, with a range from heathland to marsh, contains species such as bog asphodel and heath spotted-orchid.

Lower Test Marshes

SU 364150; 110ha; H and IOWNT reserve
Reedbeds, water meadows, grassland and saltmarsh
Permit only beyond footpaths
All year

Over 450 plant and 170 bird species have been recorded on this very varied reserve. The water meadows include marsh-marigold, water avens and green winged orchid while the birds range from wintering wildfowl and waders to breeding reed warbler and snipe.

Ludshott Common Nature Walks

SU 850360; various lengths; Ludshott Common Committee NT
Heathland walks
Leaflet from Grayshott post office and newsagents
Spring, summer

An interesting range of heathland plants and bird life may be seen on the common, which adjoins the woodland surrounding WAGGONERS WELLS.

Mapledurwell Fen

Permit only; 0.25ha; H and IOWNT reserve
Fen
Summer

Despite its size, this reserve holds a spectacular list of rare plants. It is one of the only two sites in Hampshire for the common butterwort, while marsh helleborines occur in dense clumps. Other rarities include dioecious sedge, flat-sedge and various marsh-orchid hybrids.

Martin Down

SU 058192; 249ha; NCC reserve
Chalk downland, chalk heath and scrub
Leaflet from NCC
Spring, summer

A very wide range of habitat, from a superb mix of chalkland scrub, with ash, buckthorn, dogwood, hawthorn, privet, spindle and wayfaring-tree, through spreads of dense gorse, of chalk heath with heather, and gorse, to tall or short-grazed grassland, the reserve is rich in plant life and animal species. Among the downland plants are local species including chalk milkwort, early gentian, field fleawort and dwarf sedge, with a variety of orchids; among the insects is an outstanding range of butterflies, with Adonis, chalkhill and small blue, silver-spotted skipper and Duke of Burgundy. The bird life varies from songbirds such as nightingale in summer to winter predators such as short-eared owl and hen harrier.

Medina Nature Trail

SZ 501895; 3.2-4.8km; IOW Nat. Hist. and Arch. Soc.
Riverside trail
Leaflet from IOW Tourist Board
Spring, summer

The trail runs from Newport Quay beside the tidal waters of the River Medina which show good examples of saltmarsh, with typical plants such as Townsend's cord-grass, sea-purslane and sea beet, and in late summer may be visited by cormorant, dunlin, bar-tailed godwit and ringed plover.

Micheldever Spoil Heaps

Permit only; 7.6ha; H and IOWNT reserve
Old chalk rubble, scrub and woodland
Spring, summer

The beech woodland contains such characteristic species as bird's-nest orchid, while the spoil heaps contain a good range of chalkland plants and include less usual species, for instance cut-leaved germander.

New Forest

See map; 37,560ha; FC and others
Woodland, heath and wetland
Leaflets from FC
All year

To walk in the New Forest is to walk in the largest spread of old lowland woodland in north west Europe, in one of the richest reservoirs of wildlife in Britain today.

Just under half of the forest is covered by varied woodland which forms a mosaic among and around wide spreads of grass and heather heathland or bowls of marsh and bog. The main woodland trees are beech and oak, trees around 200 to 300 years old which stand as high-forest woodland fringed with a younger mix of oak with beech, birch and other species such as ash, sweet chestnut, sycamore, hawthorn and Scots pine. The understorey is mainly holly, which stands above a very thin ground cover often limited by grazing pressure to nothing but grey-green cushions of the moss *Leucobryum glaucum.* On deeper soils there may be thick tangles of bramble and bracken or, where the woods are growing on richer clays, a more general spread of common woodland plants.

Although uncommon plants occur, such as narrow-leaved lungwort, coral-necklace and beech fern, together with a superb range of western species of lichens at their eastern limit, the woods are perhaps most outstanding for their richness of animal life. A small number of red, a few hundred roe and perhaps around 600 fallow deer remain as a memorial to the original purpose of the forest. The fallow has always been the chief member of these, at least partly because it tends to wander less. Sika deer, having spread from Beaulieu, now add to the numbers of forest deer, but modern grazing will not sustain the herds that lived here in the seventeenth century.

The deer are seldom seen or heard but in early summer the birds will be hard to miss. The forest woodlands contain both large and small timber, riven and rotting pollards, young trees and shrubs in a pattern of copses and clearings; suitable habitat is therefore available for outstanding numbers of woodland birds. Hawfinch, redstart, wood warbler and lesser spotted woodpecker are all rather locally spread in southern England – all may be present here, together with green and great spotted woodpecker, treecreeper and nuthatch. There are good numbers of predators and the forest has for a long time been a breeding site for buzzard and honey buzzard, hobby, kestrel, sparrowhawk and tawny owl.

The woods are also outstanding for their insects – for the presence of Britain's only cicada, the New Forest cicada, for a wide variety of moths and butterflies, and for a range of beetles probably unique in the British Isles; more species of beetle have been identified here than in any similar area in Britain.

The heathlands vary between wide acid grasslands filled with bristle bent, a characteristically south western fine-leaved grass, and spreads of heather with dwarf gorse or with cross-leaved heath in damper sites. A contrast with the summer cool of the woodlands, they are warm wide levels or shallow slopes, sheltered by occasional breaks of gorse and scattered with Scots pine, oak or hawthorn scrub. Purple moor-grass is spread throughout the heathlands, replacing bristle bent where the land is wettest, while deeper soils are marked by stands of bracken. Although the sandy heathlands support uncommon plants such as wild gladiolus and yellow centaury, the greatest variation appears in wet heathland, or where the heathlands grade into bog and marsh.

These valley mires are as richly varied as the other main habitats with lawns of *Sphagnum* mosses below the wet heath and with richer areas of fenlike marsh. These richer areas usually lie where slow streams run through the centre of a bog, where alder and willow grow above clumps of greater tussock sedge, a linear wet woodland fringed with common reed, or where black bog-rush, marsh St John's-wort and uncommon species such as broad-leaved and slender cottongrass show the course of the water. Touch-me-not balsam, our only native balsam, occurs in these alder carrs, together with a local speciality, Hampshire-purslane, a small creeping shallow-water plant, which grows only here and on Jersey. These stream-fed or spring-fed central areas vary according to the richness of the water supply and may show as a stand of common reed, tall above *Sphagnum* and sharp-flowered rush, or as a swamp of bog myrtle and purple moor-grass.

All three British sundews occur while, scattered among heather and cross-leaved heath, scented bog myrtle, tussocks of purple moor-grass and slender white beak-sedge and deergrass, are plants such as lesser skullcap, bog asphodel and meadow thistle, with more uncommon species including bog-sedge and slender sedge, brown beak-sedge and bog orchid, rare in the south of England.

The animal life of the open plains and the wetlands of the forest is no less varied and is equally specialised. The valley bogs and pools are rich in insects, from the biting midges and mosquitoes of late summer, to the dragonflies and damselflies, which include two species better known in Mediterranean areas, *Ceriagrion tenellum* and *Ischnura pumilio*. The relatively undisturbed deeper parts of the forest hold several species which survive at the northern limits of their range. The Dartford warbler is an example, a non-migratory warbler which lives and breeds on heathlands; in good years the population builds, but one bad winter can almost wipe it out.

Redshank, curlew and snipe are better adapted birds which breed in these open parts of the forest, together with heathland species such as stonechat, linnet and yellowhammer and less common birds such as nightjar. In winter the berry-bearing shrubs may be feeding posts for fieldfare and redwing, while the heathlands may be hunted by predators – hen harrier, merlin, peregrine and occasional red-footed falcon.

Newtown

Permit only, 338ha; IWCC NT reserve
Mudflats and saltmarsh
Permit from site or IWCC; reserve can be overlooked from public right of way
Leaflets from reception centre
Winter

The old harbour contains an interesting range of plants, including Townsend's cord-grass, sea-heath and golden samphire, and provides a nest site for black-headed gull and a wintering area for wildfowl such as Brent goose, teal and wigeon, and for waders such as curlew, redshank and black-tailed godwit.

Old Winchester Hill: a superb example of chalk downland varied with scrub and woods.

Gilbert White once walked on Selborne Hill, a varied Hampshire woodland.

Newtown Ranges

SZ 429915; 64ha; MOD
Grassland, marsh and woodland
All year

The Clannerkin, a tidal stream, is a haven for wader and wildlife. Green-winged orchid and adder's-tongue are abundant in the nearby meadows. In Locks Copse 5ha are coppiced for the spring display of wild daffodils. Red squirrel and dormouse are present and 34 species of butterfly including Glanville fritillary occur.

Noar Hill

Permit only; 12ha; H and IOWNT reserve
Old chalkpits and scrub
Spring, summer

Yellow-wort, autumn gentian and kidney vetch are typical of the chalkland flowers which grow here and attract a good variety of insects. The butterflies include both marbled white and Duke of Burgundy.

Normandy Farm

SZ 330940; 36ha; HCC reserve
Coastal grazing marshes
All year

Part of KEYHAVEN–LYMINGTON MARSHES.

North Solent

Permit only; 640ha; NCC reserve
Saltmarsh and grazing marsh
All year

Breeding colonies of terns, together with the largest colony of black-headed gulls in Britain, provide summer interest in an estuary reserve which contains an exceptional variety of fresh-water and saltmarsh plants while supporting large numbers of passage and wintering waders and wildfowl. Part of the reserve may be overlooked from the public footpath from Beaulieu to Bucklers Hard.

Old Burghclere Lime Quarry

Permit only; 6ha; H and IOWNT reserve
Disused chalk quarry
Spring, summer

Colonising chalkland plants include kidney vetch and fly orchid and attract such butterflies as little blue. Slow-worm is usually present.

Old Winchester Hill

SU 647210; 60ha; NCC reserve
Chalk downland, scrub and woodland
Visitors must keep to marked pathways: danger from unexploded missiles
Leaflets from car park or information centre
Spring, summer

The highest point of the reserve, within the ramparts of the Iron Age hill fort, overlooks the valley of the Meon with views across to the NEW FOREST and to the Isle of Wight. Below this point the downland falls in slopes and folds of scrub and woodland, a rich mosaic of chalkland habitat.

The woodland is in blocks separated by grass-land and generally fringed by hawthorn scrub.

Yew is the classic Hampshire downland tree and, left to itself, the whole reserve might develop into yew forest. This is prevented by careful management which also sustains some areas of broad-leaved woods, beech and ash over coppiced hazel, to give the greatest degree of variation. The hawthorn scrub is rich in other shrubby species, filled with buckthorn, dogwood, privet, spindle, wayfaring-tree, whitebeam and tangling traveller's-joy. A large area of juniper scrub is important for insects. The range of grassland, scrub and woodland here is a classic demonstration of the transition from one stage to the next.

Near the car park a layer of clay above the chalk is deep enough for tormentil and gorse but, lower down and on the ramparts of the fort, the soils are thin and highly alkaline and superbly dressed with lime-loving species. Here are yellow-wort and clustered bellflower, fine spreads of horseshoe and kidney vetch, late-summer-flowering autumn gentian and, on the ramparts, a speciality of the reserve, one of the largest populations in the country of round-headed rampion. In the sheltered slopes between the woods are dark mullein and musk mallow while the reserve boasts some 14 orchid species. There are unusually large colonies of fragrant and frog orchid and greater butterfly-orchid.

Woodland birds include all three native wood-peckers while the wood edge and scrub attract a good range of warblers and other small birds. Kestrel and sparrowhawk are frequently seen. Harvest and yellow-necked mouse have been recorded and larger mammals include roe deer and badger. Butterfly species include chalkhill blue, dark green fritillary and Duke of Burgundy.

Otterbourne Park Wood

SU 458223; 24ha; WdT
Deciduous woodland
Spring, summer

Some very old oak coppice is found in this ancient wood. There are also areas of oak, ash and silver birch with an understorey of hazel, and in wetter areas aspen, alder and willow grow. A Roman road runs through the reserve.

Oxenbourne Down

Permit only; 83.6ha; HCC–H and IOWNT reserve
Chalk grassland, scrub and yew woodland
Spring, summer

The main woods contain mixed-age yew trees, with other lime-loving species such as whitebeam and juniper, allied with areas of chalk grassland and contrasting with oak woodland and small areas of chalk heath. Breeding birds include blackcap, lesser whitethroat and nightingale.

Oxey and Pennington Marshes

SZ 330940; 71.6ha; HCC reserve
Coastal grazing marshes
All year

Part of KEYHAVEN–LYMINGTON MARSHES.

Pamber Forest

SU 616605; 115ha; Englefield Estate–Pamber Forest Management Committee
Mixed woodland
Spring, summer

The reserve is an extensive acid oakwood with a few plantations of Douglas fir, larch and sweet chestnut. It is probably primary woodland as it was recorded in Roman times and is a remnant of the much larger thirteenth-century royal hunting forest of Pamber. More recently it has been managed as hazel coppice with oak standards, some of which are very large. There is a great variety of trees and shrubs, including aspen, wild service, whitebeam, butcher's-broom and alder buckthorn. In addition to the usual flowers of ancient woodland there are lily-of-the-valley, early-purple orchid, nettle-leaved bellflower and orpine. Wide rides and glades are ideal areas for butterflies, and white admiral and silver-washed fritillary can be plentiful; purple emperor and purple hairstreak also occur.

Queen Elizabeth Country Park

SU 717186; 560ha; HCC–FC
Mixed woodland, downland and scrub
Leaflets from HCC or park centre
Spring, summer

A good variety of habitat may be observed from the trails within the park which interpret the nature of the woods and downland.

Reston Roundhill and Happersnapper Hangers

SU 749271; 17.6ha; HCC reserve
Beech–ash hanging woodland
Spring, early summer

Part of WEALDEN EDGE HANGERS.

Rew Down

SZ 552775; 4.6ha; IWCC reserve
Chalk grassland
Spring, summer

The nature reserve is situated on the steep south-facing chalk slope above Ventnor and gives commanding views over the English Channel. A wide range of basic alkaline and acid soils supports a rich variety of chalk grassland flora and fauna. Large populations of early gentian and horseshoe vetch provide seasonal colour, the latter supporting a colony of Adonis blue butterflies.

Royal Victoria Country Park

SU 457080; 58ha; HCC
Woodland, parkland and coastal shores, nature trail
All year

Inland, there is a contrast between open beech woodland and marshy areas where common reed and wet alder and willow scrub give shelter to birds such as reed bunting, blackcap, willow warbler and nightingale. A further range of habitat is added by parkland trees and by the saltmarsh, shingle, muds and gravels of the shoreline, where birds such as curlew, oystercatcher and redshank may be seen.

Roydon Woods

Permit only; 340ha; H and IOWNT reserve
Mixed deciduous woodland, heathland, grassland and river banks
Spring, early summer

This large and very varied reserve has a magnificent mix of tree and shrub species with a great variety of smaller plants. Specialities include royal fern and narrow-leaved lungwort, with buzzard and sparrowhawk among the birds.

St Catherine's Hill

SU 841275; 30ha; H and IOWNT reserve
Chalk grassland and scrub
Spring, summer

A steep grassy knoll just outside Winchester, the reserve contains a wide variety of chalkland flowers and shrubs, including privet, dogwood, kidney vetch and common rock-rose. Beautiful downland butterflies may be seen, including a small colony of the rarer little blue.

The Salterns

SZ 330940; 14ha; HCC reserve
Coastal grassland and marsh
All year

Part of KEYHAVEN–LYMINGTON MARSHES.

Selborne Hill

SU 735337; 97.4ha; NT
Mixed woodland and beech hanger
Spring, early summer

No natural history of Hampshire could leave out the territory of Gilbert White. Selborne Hill, composed of Selborne Common and Selborne Hanger, is a fine example of woodland on the clay-capped Hampshire chalk. The common occupies the more level land, a plateau which falls abruptly to the village where beechwoods hang upon the slope.

The plateau varies from open scrubland around wide grassy clearings to high-forest woodland and areas of coppice. Old pollard beech trees argue the common status, when pigs and cattle roamed and the stems were cut above their browsing height to provide both poles for firewood and fencing and herbage for winter stock feed. Coppicing must have started later, when animals no longer grazed, and new young shoots could grow uneaten from the lower hazel stools. The clay supports such acid-loving species as tormentil, gorse and birch with sweeps of bracken around the grassy clearings, grading into elder, hawthorn and hazel scrub.

The woods themselves, chiefly beech or oak standards over a rich variety of species including ash and blackthorn, holly, buckthorn, dogwood and spindle, stand above a ground cover which varies both with the density of the shade and with the depth of the clay over chalk. Under pure beech cover there is very little that can survive, but ride edges and clearings show white drifts of greater stitchwort, bright red campion, woodsorrel, dog's mercury and enchanter's-nightshade, yellow archangel, ferns and foxglove, wild rose and honeysuckle. The clay thins higher up and traveller's-joy replaces honeysuckle, with wood spurge, sanicle and woodruff beneath the trees.

The hanger is a steep one, of tall straight beech trees with an understorey of ash, young beech, yew, holly, hazel, hawthorn, dogwood, wayfaring-tree and spindle. The ground cover is mainly woodruff and ivy, dog's mercury and sanicle but, where the light strikes through, wood melick lines the pathways while wood spurge, spurge-laurel, violets and nettle-leaved bellflower, with Solomon's-seal, wall lettuce and ferns such as hart's-tongue, hard shield-fern and male-fern, occur.

Shide Chalk Pit

SZ 506882; 5ha; IWCC reserve
Abandoned chalk quarry
Spring, summer

The deep man-made pit sunk into an escarpment of the Upper Chalk exhibits all stages of succession from bare chalk, important for geological research, through a chalk grassland plant community to tall scrub. Over 160 flowering plant species have been recorded, including, at the pit floor, some unusual flora associated with spring.

Shutts Copse

Permit only; 4.4ha; H and IOWNT reserve
Old hazel coppice
Spring, early summer

A rich woodland plant life, including such species as Solomon's-seal and greater butterfly-orchid, is encouraged by continued coppicing.

Solent Way Walk

SZ 569994; MOD
Coastal walk which passes through Browndown
Ranges at high-water mark
All year

No live firing, but when training is taking place and flags are flying follow public highway (Browndown Road and Privett Road) between Stokes Bay and Lee-on-Solent. The coastal walk is not dedicated as a public highway.

Stag Copse

Permit only; 2.4ha; H and IOWNT reserve
Mixed woodland
Spring, early summer

Woodland is not now widespread on the Isle of Wight. The reserve, home to a variety of common mammal and bird species, has a good range of trees over hazel and holly with a ground cover which includes bluebell and butcher's-broom.

Stockbridge Common Down

SU 377347; 89ha; NT
Ungrazed downland and scrub
Spring, summer

A long sweep of ungrazed grassland with tilted mixed rich scrub and a thick shrub cover on the highest land, the down gives a picture of the ancient Salisbury Plain edge before ploughing turned the turf to endless cereals.

The upper scrub on the clay cap of the chalk contains hawthorn, gorse and blackthorn, an excellent shelter for birds, while the scrub on the sloping chalk is a mix of species such as dogwood, privet, spindle and juniper, wild rose and hawthorn, with an occasional young oak. Giant hogweed and wild parsnip stand above the grasses here, together with other plants sufficiently robust to reach for light. Agrimony, ragwort and common toadflax show varied shades of yellow to contrast with the blue small scabious. Dark purple heads of greater knapweed stand beside tall spikes of knapweed broomrape, a curious parasite which lives upon their roots and lifts its flower spikes perhaps some 60cm high. Lady's bedstraw puts up a vivid fizz of yellow flowers but cannot compare in delicacy with the exquisite pale dropwort, which grows on the downland in great profusion.

The spread of grassland, although so much of it is deep and coarse, is filled with these elegant flowers, with the tall columns of wild mignonette, with yellow rattle and occasional dark mullein. Marjoram and betony may be found with the beautiful nodding musk thistle while path edges and shallow turfs have squinancywort and wild thyme, common rock-rose, kidney vetch and common bird's-foot-trefoil.

The varied slopes and scrubland areas prove attractive for butterflies, including marbled white and species of blue, for mammals such as short-tailed vole, for hunting kestrel and owl species and for a vareity of other birds such as skylark and meadow pipit in the grassland or linnet and yellowhammer in the scrub.

Swanpond Copse

Permit only; 4.4ha; H and IOWNT reserve
Small coppice-with-standards woodland
Spring, early summer

Goldilocks buttercup and narrow-leaved lungwort are among the interesting plants in this mainly damp woodland. There is a good range of tree and shrub species with an attractive variety of woodland birds.

Tennyson Down and the Needles

SU 324855; 77.6ha; NT reserve
Coastal chalk downland and scrub
Spring, summer

Tennyson Down differs from COMPTON DOWN to the east in not curving steeply towards the sea but rather dropping sheer into it. On the northern side the land falls steeply to Alum Bay but the sea has carved the south side into shining cliffs of chalk. At the western end the cliffs are weathered into the stacks of the Needles.

The sheltered northern side of the down has a fine development of mixed scrub species which suddenly stops when it reaches the height of the grassland plateau above. The chalkland plants on top are stunted by the sea winds – pigmy clustered bellflowers which open in the very short turf, short-stemmed harebells and the well-adapted dwarf thistle.

Lower, and less exposed, is a fine mixture of species, carline and musk thistle, lady's bedstraw and salad burnet, milkwort, eyebright, wild thyme and squinancywort, yellow-wort, quaking-grass and hoary plantain. In the Needles reserve, overlooking the stacks themselves, masses of kidney vetch, thrift, wild mignonette and pyramidal orchid sway in the breezes together with an unexpected plant for a chalk sea headland, yellow horned-poppy.

Areas of chalk heath, with heather, bell heather and tormentil or wind-pruned blocks of gorse, occur on the down and gorse again may be found in the dense mixed scrub. This scrub is a steep

A tree-lined hammer pond at Waggoners Wells.

rich mixture of privet, hawthorn, ash, spindle and small-leaved cotoneaster, tied and tangled with traveller's-joy and honeysuckle. Path edges are thick with wild madder and fringed with stinking iris and ivy.

The scrub is of great interest as one of the very few areas where gorse and blackthorn grow together with privet, a highly lime-loving species. The site is also notable for large colonies of early-purple orchid and for bastard-toadflax and heath-grass in the maritime chalk grassland.

The downland is some 147m above sea level and rather exposed for much bird life, but skylarks may still be seen, together with a variety of gulls, and cormorant and shag. The guillemot, razorbill and puffin colonies are now depleted but there is scope for seawatching at passage times.

Titchfield Haven

Permit only; 86.26ha; HCC reserve
Lagoons, marshes and grazing meadows by River Meon
The lower part of the reserve may be overlooked from SU 533024
Permit and leaflets by prior arrangement from the Naturalist Ranger, Haven Cottage, Cliff Road, Hill Head, Fareham (tel. Stubbington 2145)
Chiefly winter but interesting all year

The reedbeds and marshes, grazing meadows and lagoons of Titchfield Haven form an oasis of quiet between the urban spread of Southampton and the Gosport–Portsmouth complex to the east. The major part of the reserve remains a sanctuary area, grazing marsh and reedbeds along the winding River Meon. These marshes, where winter wigeon feed, are overlooked from the Meadow hide, are often hunted by kestrel or barn owl and are the most northerly stretch of the reserve to which the public has access.

The Suffern hide overlooks the Meon, with sweet-grass marshes on the nearer side and common reed filling the further bank. Here are duck and gulls, heron, coot and moorhen, with an occasional wader on the muddy, tidal shores. The Meon shore and Pumfrett hides overlook lagoons, islanded scrapes with flats and shallows for the dabblers and waders, with deeper waters for the diving ducks.

Over the last few years the reserve has become an important wintering site for curlew, godwit, bittern, shoveler, mallard, teal and wigeon. Breeding birds include reed and sedge warbler, little grebe and water rail, together with an increasing colony of bearded tit, while spring migrants include a great variety of small birds, for instance warblers, together with such waders as curlew and greenshank, and seabirds such as black, common and little tern. Autumn brings the return of several of these species with others including spotted redshank, common and green sandpiper, hobby and short-eared owl. The closeness of the Solent affords the chance to see great crested and Slavonian grebe, divers, and Brent geese in winter.

Insects include holly blue butterfly, the unusual wainscot moths, *Nonagria algae* and *Leucania obsoleta*, and dragonflies and damselflies.

Deadly nightshade's sombre flowers give way to highly poisonous black berries.

Upper Hamble Country Park

SU 490114; 163ha; HCC
Riverside woodland
Spring, early summer

An area of mature oak stands above the River Hamble, with small-leaved lime and wild service-tree, uncommon in the county. The rich ground cover includes good spreads of bluebell and primrose in spring, with more unusual plants such as butcher's-broom and hard shield-fern. The insects to be found in the Park include white admiral while a typical range of woodland birds is present.

Upper Titchfield Haven

Permit only; 16.8ha; H and IOWNT reserve
Freshwater marsh, meadow and scrub
Spring, autumn, winter

Contrasting with the LOWER TEST MARSHES, Upper Titchfield is not tidal but still contains an interesting range of plants and attracts a good variety of bird life.

Waggoners Wells Nature Walks

SU 863354; 2km; Ludshott Common Committee–NT
Lakeside, woodland and heath walks
Leaflet from Grayshott post office and newsagents
Spring, summer

Two trails show the natural history interest of a chain of small lakes, originally hammer ponds, set among woodland on the edge of LUDSHOTT COMMON.

The Warren

SU 728288; 24.8ha; HCC–H and IOWNT reserve
Beech–yew–ash hanging woodland
Spring, early summer

Part of WEALDEN EDGE HANGERS.

Warren Bottom Copse

Permit only; 4ha; Mereacre Ltd–H and IOWNT reserve
Coppice woodland
Permit holders must contact the estate before visiting
site
Spring

A classic ancient oak–hazel coppice carpeted in spring with bluebells, primroses and Solomon's-seal.

Wealden Edge Hangers

SU 729266, 749271 and 728288; 129.2ha; HCC reserves
Steep woodlands on chalk slopes
No access off rights of way
Spring, early summer

These are spectacular steep woodlands, chiefly of beech, ash and yew, which cling to the sides of the weathered mass of chalk that overlooks the farmland of the Weald. The chalk which covered the dome of the Weald has been worn away to leave a fluted, steep escarpment. Woodland once covered the plateau above and spread across the plain beneath, but only the slopes were steep enough to avoid the plough and now the scarp stands, dark with trees, between the open fields and spreading villages, a haven for chalkland wildlife.

Yew, if left alone, would probably replace all other trees and clothe the slopes in dark forest. Groves of yew spread down the scarps, showing as a deep green mass among the paler deciduous trees.

Beech also forms a dense canopy and only early spring bluebell or adapted plants such as bird's-nest orchid or white helleborine survive beneath its shadow. Ash is far more open and lets in light for privet and field maple, dogwood and whitebeam, spindle, hawthorn and blocks of coppiced hazel.

Mixed woodland thus gives the widest range of species. The slopes of the hangers lean at all angles, steep, sunny, shaded, shallow, and so afford a great deal of variety. Sunny open banks are thick with hart's-tongue or show chalk-loving species such as tutsan, deadly nightshade and nettle-leaved bellflower, while in the shaded areas the ground cover is full of plants such as wood spurge and ramsons, dog's mercury and enchanter's-nightshade, climbing traveller's-joy and carpets of ivy.

Bracken, above, marks the clay cap of the plateau, while birds sing in the treetops or in the deep clear air, but the slopes of chalk have a special thrill of their own.

A tall woodland of beech may open on to a clear-felled hillside aflame with yellow mullein and rosebay willowherb. The heat of the clearing is suddenly lost in the green gloom of a yew copse or found again on a flowery bank where yellow-wort and common rock-rose, common bird's-foot-trefoil and wild thyme defy the dark of the woods and where musk mallow stands among tangles of wild rose.

Wellington Country Park

SU 724626; 244ha; Wellington Enterprises
Lake, woodland and meadowland
Leaflets from Wellington Office, Stratfield Saye, Reading, RG7 2BT
Spring, early summer

Five nature trails show the variation of beech, oak and coniferous plantations, open parkland and the lake. Roe and fallow deer occur in the woodlands, where open rides provide sites for such butterflies as comma, white admiral, purple emperor and speckled wood, and the lake attracts great crested grebe, feral Canada goose and goosander. There are also many species of fungi.

West Yar Nature Trail

SZ 354897; 8km; IOW Nat. Hist. and Arch. Soc.
Riverside trail
Leaflet from IOW Tourist Board
Spring, summer

The trail follows the West Yar River to FRESHWATER MARSH, passing from the tidal area to fresh water above the sluice valve, and includes much of interest. Among the plants are the rather uncommon marsh-mallow, and the saltmarsh species sea arrow-grass and sea-purslane. A fine range of birds includes curlew, dunlin, redshank and ringed plover.

The Wildgrounds

Permit only; 30.4ha; Gosport BC reserve
Woodland and pond
Spring, early summer

Birch and pollarded oak form a bird-rich woodland above a rather acid ground cover of bracken and bramble, while hazel and sweet chestnut are grown for coppicing and young oak saplings have also been planted to revitalise the woods. All three native woodpeckers, bullfinch, linnet and goldfinch occur. The pond encourages nesting mallard and adds to the insect life of the reserve.

Winnall Moors

Permit only; 43ha; H and IOWNT reserve
Freshwater marsh and water meadows
Spring, early summer

The moors represent the remnants of now redundant water meadows, lying between the city of Winchester and the River Itchen. The site is dissected by many drains and dykes with raised drier strips between. Plants of freshwater marsh are abundant both in species and numbers: marsh-marigold, southern marsh-orchid, meadowsweet, yellow loosestrife, purple-loosestrife, water avens and yellow iris occur together with common reed, rush and sedge species. The alien monkey flower also grows here, mixed with great willowherb. The damp grassland carries a wide range of grass species accompanied by angelica, ragged-Robin, hemp-agrimony, comfrey, gipsywort, valerian, greater bird's-foot-trefoil and common spotted-orchid. Some tree species have been planted in the past, including the hybrid black Italian poplar, in addition to the existing native willows, alder, ash, hawthorn and guelder-rose.

The reserve supports a wide range of birds at all seasons: winter visitors include wildfowl and waders, migrants pass through in spring and autumn, while many species stay to breed in spring and summer. Little grebe, moorhen, duck and mute swan nest beside the river; on the open grassland some waders breed and, in the reedbeds, sedge warbler and reed bunting rear their young.

Winnall Moors (southern area)

SU 486300; 16.2ha; H and IOWNT reserve
River and water meadows
Summer

The land here differs from that in WINNAL MOORS (the northern area) in that it is not grazed and supports a rich, tall fen vegetation. Reeds and sedges are plentiful and provide a rich bird and insect habitat with many of the taller-growing marsh plants adding their burst of colour. The River Itchen flows beside this section and the birds noted in WINNAL MOORS occur here as well. However, great densities of reed, sedge and grasshopper warblers are to be seen and heard in the taller vegetation.

Woolmer Pond

SU 788320; 26ha; MOD
Lake and woodland
All year

The fishpond recently restored by the Army attracts curlew and redshank. The surrounding forest contains the only site in the British Isles where all 12 reptiles and amphibians can be found.

Yateley Common Country Park

SU 822597, 838594; 197ha; HCC
Heathland and pools
Nature trail leaflet from site or HCC
Spring, early summer, autumn

The heathland of south Hampshire is echoed north of the great chalk mass by the part of the county which lies within the heathy London Basin. A fine show of acid heather land may be found at Yateley Common where a nature trail demonstrates the interest of the site.

The 2km trail begins at Wyndham's Pool, an artificial lake popular for fishing and picnics. Away from the valley the scrub opens out as heathland; the gravelled sandy ground is thick with heather and bell heather by thickets and belts of birch and Scots pine. Gorse and broom form a colourful lower scrub and provide a sheltered area for many small heathland birds. Both downy and silver birch are found together with gorse and dwarf gorse–plants with narrow leaves evolved to withstand the water shortages on such quick-draining sands and gravels.

Where the ground becomes damper cross-leaved heath replaces bell heather, although in some parts all three species may be found. Tussocks of purple moor-grass mark the damper ground while a small area near the pool edge is acid enough for *Sphagnum* mosses to grow, together with typical bog plants such as common cottongrass and round-leaved sundew. The pools in general, though, are richer than the heath above and support a marshy vegetation rather than that of a bog. Horsetail species and bulrush grow around the margins with marsh St John's-wort and marsh pennywort, water-plantain, yellow iris and floating white and yellow water-lily. A willow swamp stands at the head of the pool, varied with alder buckthorn, but once away from the wetland area the common returns again to open heathland or to a woodland of birch and grey willow with occasional rowan.

Low regrowing heather, the patches of acid grassland, the open rides between woodlands and the scrubland belts make fine hunting grounds for predators – kestrels may often be seen hovering over the clearings. Jay and magpie scavenge the common and typical heathland birds such as linnet and stonechat with goldfinch, dunnock and many small woodland and garden birds may be found. Butterflies include peacock, red admiral and painted lady with common and silver-studded blue, small heath, brimstone and comma. The pool encourages a good variety of dragonflies and damselflies.

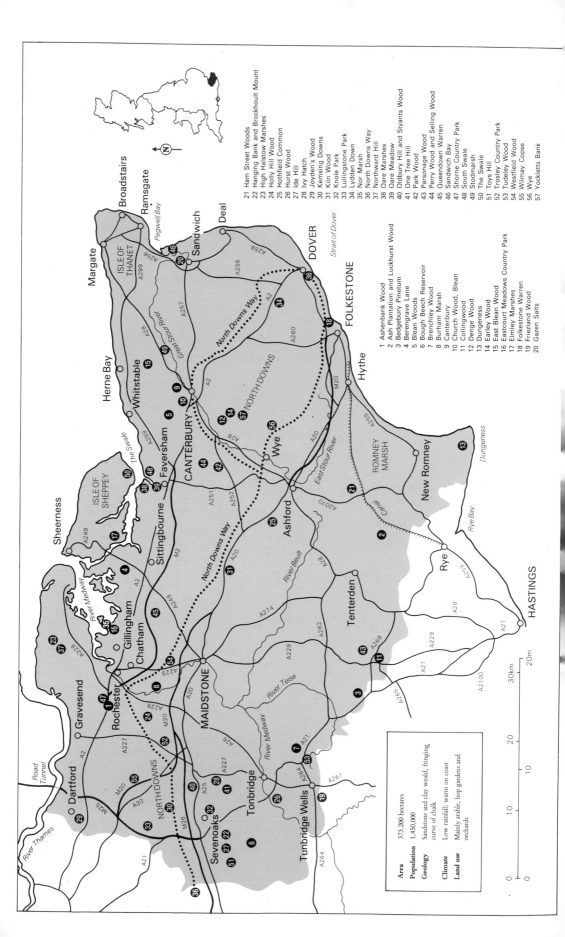

Kent

Known as the Garden of England because of the extensive orchards which thrive on the favourable southerly climate and rich soils, the county is famous for beautiful countryside, from the rolling hills of the North Downs and the white cliffs of Dover to the broad, flat, reed-fringed pasture of north Kent. The characteristic wildlife habitats of Kent, notably the old deciduous woodland of the Weald, the chalk grasslands of the North Downs, and the marshlands of north Kent and Romney Marsh, relate to the geology of the county, which changes to the north east following the contours of the High Weald sands, the Low Weald clays, the greensands, the chalk and finally, on the eastern edge of the county, the tertiary beds of gravel and sands, laid down over the soft white upper chalk. It is this change of bedrock that accounts for much of the diversity of land use, habitat and wildlife found in Kent.

The county is still extensively wooded. Stands of the ancient oakwood remain, but commercial chestnut coppice and plantation forest account for most of Kent's woodlands. Many areas of semi-natural woodland are still found, from the steep-sided, spring-fed valleys or ghylls of the High Weald, clothed with oak and ash, crab apple and wild cherry, bluebell and bracken, to the beech hangers on the summits and slopes of the Downs.

The main agricultural activities are fruit growing, arable farming, dairy cattle and sheep. Hedgerows still fragment the agricultural landscape. On the flat clay vale of the Low Weald sheep and cattle feed in the wet meadows edged by broad and blooming hedges of blackthorn and hawthorn, wild service-tree, elm, ash and hazel, while in the fruit-growing belts along the Medway Estuary and in central Kent tall shelter hedges of alder and poplar stand upright between orchards of bowed apple and cherry. Where the pasture has escaped the ravages of herbicides and chemical fertilisers traces of the agricultural past can be found. Remnants of downland rich in yellow vetches, sweet-scented herbs and orchids are reminders of intensive sheep farming, and the network of narrow roads linking the small Kentish towns and villages reflects former agricultural wealth. Old hay meadows, not used for silage or turned over to barley but still cut annually and fertilised lightly with manure, support many plants. Grass species such as barley and oat-grass, oxeye daisy, buttercup, ragged-Robin and cowslip, and more often than not the heady-scented pepper-saxifrage and the curious adder's-tongue, are all vulnerable to drainage and the plough and remain only in these meadows.

The coastline is as varied as the rest of Kent. The sharp chalk cliffs of Dover and Deal are constantly eroding but suppport a diversity of plants, some, such as the early spider-orchid, seeking lime-rich pastures, others, for instance rock samphire, the constantly changing cliff faces, and still others, such as sea-kale, the shingle beaches. The Stour Estuary around SANDWICH is a mosaic of pasture, saltmarsh and sand dunes, but the adjacent cliffs of Thanet indicate the presence of chalk, reflected in the flora. The coast at Romney Marsh in the south is remarkable for its history of reclamation as well as its special flora and fauna. Both marsh-mallow and marsh frog are common, and the Marsh's ornithological importance relies on the intricate field and dyke system which still remains in some areas. The marshes and estuaries provide wintering grounds for birds such as bar-tailed godwit, hen harrier and Brent goose, and breeding sites for shelduck, redshank and garganey; few other areas are so rich in both numbers and species.

Kent's natural history relates closely to its proximity to continental Europe. The southerly winds carry over unusual insects: painted lady and red admiral butterflies often arrive in this way, and many of the recordings of unusual moths made in central Kent can be attributed to this migration. Bird migrants travelling across continental Europe seek the nearest land mass and so direct themselves towards Sandwich and DUNGE-NESS. Bird observatories have been established at both places to monitor their movements, and both areas are now protected by official status and the establishment of nature reserves.

Plants, though less mobile, still reflect the continental influence. The abundant roadside weed hoary cress is sometimes known as Thanet weed because it first became established there after being brought over in straw from Europe. Other species are on the most northerly limit of their range, and subject to the wild fluctuations in population size caused by small climatic changes which are characteristic of species at the edge of their distribution. Orchids are the most striking example. At least five species are more abundant in Kent than anywhere else in Britain. At least twice as many more are commonly found here. Orchids of woodland pasture occur, but the best representatives are those of the chalk downland. Common spotted-orchid, man, pyramidal, fragrant, bee and fly orchid are all frequently found on the Downs.

Kent also provides the only remnants of habitat suitable for many other plant and animal species. FOLKESTONE WARREN and ORLESTONE FOREST support unique assemblages of plants and insects; BLEAN WOODS contain one of the last British breeding colonies of heath fritillary, and subangled wave and lesser bell moths are restricted to Orlestone Forest. Other species in decline in Britain still remain common here; wild servicetree is found frequently in hedgerow, woodland and coppice; dormouse and harvest mouse are still often recorded in Kent; and nightingale, although found throughout southern Britain, is most abundant in east Kent.

Kent is under severe pressure from urban development and population expansion, from intensification of agriculture, and from the expansion of communications with Europe, especially the development of motorways. All these influences threaten wildlife, but conservation bodies throughout the county continue to protect its variety and uniqueness.

P. EVANS

Ashenbank Wood

TQ 677694; 32ha; WdT
Deciduous woodland
Spring, summer

An unusual feature of the reserve is the extremely large hornbeam and sweet chestnut pollards; there are also some good specimens of cherry and oak. Birch, ash and other species have regenerated on the formerly grazed areas.

Ash Plantation and Luckhurst Wood

TQ 934282 and TQ 933277; 2ha; WdT
Deciduous woodland
Spring, summer

These two woods are very close to each other but quite different in character. Luckhurst contains hornbeam, hazel and sweet chestnut coppice, while Ash Plantation, true to its name, still contains many coppiced ash trees.

Bedgebury Pinetum

TQ 715338; 40ha; FC
National pinetum established by FC and Royal Botanic Gardens, Kew
Booklet at site or from FC
All year

This reserve contains over 200 tree species with a further 200 varieties of conifers all of which are ranged within an area that includes two streams and a lake.

Berengrave Lane

TQ 820670; 10ha; Gillingham BC reserve
Former chalkpit with small pond and trees
All year

In the 30 years since the quarry closed a great variety of habitats has developed. The ponds contain breeding populations of frogs, toads and newts, and a number of species of dragonflies. A reedbed has grown up around where reed warblers and reed buntings nest. Much of the rest of the area has reverted to woodland of birch, ash and sycamore with shrubs such as dog rose, clematis and dogwood.

Blean Woods

TR 118611; 66.5ha; NCC reserve
Coppiced woodland
Permit only off paths and rights of way
Leaflet from NCC
Spring, early summer

This woodland consists of oak standards over coppiced ash, beech, sweet chestnut and hornbeam which is spread across the London clay with small areas of acid heath where gravels overlie it. A good range of woodland wildlife is present and the area is important as a beach-head from which continental species may spread into Britain. The reserve of CHURCH WOOD, BLEAN is part of the same woodland complex.

Bough Beech Reservoir

TQ 495494; 18ha; KTNC reserve
North lake and part of reservoir
Booklet from information centre (open April–October)
All year

The information centre illustrates the importance of the reserve both as a breeding and wintering site for birds and as a staging post for migrants. Garganey, common scoter and osprey are occasionally recorded on passage, together with a good range of waders.

Brenchley Wood

TQ 648418; 2.8ha; KTNC reserve
High Weald woodland
Spring, early summer

In contrast to the clay and chalk of much of Kent, the High Weald is acid sandstone, reflected here by the intrusion of birch into the oak–beech woodland and by boggy areas with *Sphagnum*.

Burham Down

TQ 735624 82.5ha; KTNC reserve
Woodland, scrub and chalk grassland
Permit only off paths and rights of way
Leaflet from KTNC
Spring, summer

The reserve contains the characteristic plants, wild thyme, trefoils and vetches, which attract a good range of butterflies. The scrub and woodland provide nest sites for small birds while the cliffs of disused chalkpits are breeding sites for kestrel.

Burham Marsh

TQ 714614; 40ha; KTNC reserve
River bank, marsh and reedbeds
No access off public footpath
All year

The vegetation is interesting, particularly for the rare marsh sow-thistle, but the reedbeds and river probably provide the greatest interest, for wetland birds and resting migrants.

Burnt Oak Wood

Permit only; 28ha KTNC reserve
Damp oak woodland
Mid, late summer

The wood is chiefly oak standards over hazel and hornbeam coppice on heavy clay. There is little ground cover, due to the dense canopy, but pathway edges and open glades are attractive to woodland butterflies such as white admiral.

Canterbury

TR 159596; 12ha; CEGB reserve
Freshwater lakes, grassland, recent woodland and river
Restricted site for use by Kent Education Authority and KTNC
Nature-trail guide from CEGB and study centre
All year

The site is noteworthy for freshwater life, resulting from recolonised abandoned gravel workings, but the recent woodland and open grassland add diversity. Over 200 plants have been recorded and 90 species of birds, including kingfisher, water rail and Cetti's warbler.

Chiddingstone

Permit only; 6.8ha; KTNC reserve
Woodland, marsh and pools
Spring, early summer

A series of old brickpits provides a range from open water through bulrush reedswamp to dry ground and woodland, containing wild service-tree and oak with an area of conifers. Wood sandpiper has been recorded on passage while breeding species include kestrel and tawny owl.

Church Wood, Blean

TR 123593; 142ha; RSPB reserve
Deciduous woodland
Spring, summer

The reserve is part of one of the most extensive ancient oakwoods in southern England; BLEAN WOODS is also a piece of this complex. The structure of the wood is mixed, including areas of oak high forest, with scattered wild service-trees, oak standards over coppice of hazel, chestnut and hornbeam; there are also blocks of pure chestnut coppice, and scrub spindle and dogwood have developed in areas of recent felling. Small stands of beech occur on gravelly soils, while alder and sallow grow along the streams. There is a good breeding population of nightingales and a variety of warblers, including wood warbler, which, like the redstart, is scarce in this area. Hawfinches and crossbills are seen occasionally and long-eared owls have nested in a small conifer plantation. Among the woodland flowers there are large colonies of lily-of-the-valley and lesser periwinkle. Cow-wheat is common and supports the threatened heath fritillary butterfly.

Collingwood

TQ 760292; 2.4ha; KTNC reserve
Woodland and lake
Spring, early summer

The wood contains a variety of planted exotics, together with native trees, and the lake is bright with water-lilies, fringed by bulrush. Spotted flycatcher and several tit species breed and the lake may be visited by kingfisher.

Denge Wood

TR 108525; 25.6ha; WdT
Coppiced woodland, scrub and grassland
Spring, early summer

The woodland, composed of hornbeam and sweet chestnut coppice, includes an area of chalk scrub and grassland together with old earth banks topped with hornbeam pollards. Active coppicing encourages a rich variety of wildlife.

Denton Bank

Permit only; 3.6ha; KTNC reserve
Steep chalk grassland
Spring, early summer

A show of cowslip and early-purple orchid in the spring is followed by characteristic chalkland species.

Dungeness

TR 063196; 821ha; RSPB reserve
Extraordinary shingle expanse with scrub and lagoons
Leaflet from information centre or RSPB
All year

Dungeness, often described as the largest shingle ridge in Britain, perhaps in Europe, is a desert plain of shingle, a great expanse of rounded stones combed into lines and curves by a giant hand. It looks inhospitable and yet it is a special, magical place, the best in Britain for sea-kale, fine-leaved sheep's-fescue and dwarf broom, a site for the uncommon Nottingham catchfly and stinking hawksbeard. It is a place for scrub and stony grassland, for sweeps of open shingle, for natural and man-made pools, for huge skies and sea-breezes, above all for migrant insects and for birds. .

Spring and autumn bring the passage migrants: black tern, wryneck, bluethroat and hosts of other birds. In autumn the numbers are higher, and the reserve is noted for whitethroat, lesser whitethroat and firecrest.

Some 40 to 45 species usually breed on the reserve, although some 60 in all have been recorded, with the shingle and shingle islands in the lagoons providing sites for black-headed, common and Mediterranean gull, and common tern. Hides have been built overlooking some of the lakes and a trail laid out from which the range of habitat can be observed. Gorse, blackthorn, elder and bramble scrub provides nest sites for many birds, including magpie and carrion crow in the absence of taller trees, while the wetland areas contain breeding shelduck and little grebe, occasionally shoveler and water rail. Throughout the summer the croaking of marsh frogs can be heard. Eight of these European animals were brought to Romney Marsh in 1935; since then they have spread up waterways to colonise Dungeness. Newts also live in the pools and grass snake and common lizard may often be seen.

In winter the lagoons hold sheltering flocks of wildfowl including mallard, pintail, pochard, teal, tufted duck and wigeon with occasional gadwall, goosander and smew. Hen harrier, merlin and short-eared owl may hunt the area for smaller birds such as shore lark and snow bunting.

Migrant butterflies such as painted lady, clouded yellow and the rarer pale clouded yellow add seasonal interest to the resident species, which

Dungeness: an oasis of shingle wilderness visited by many spring and autumn migrants.

Rare wart-biter cricket occurs on Lydden Down.

include Essex skipper, while moths include brown-tail. Among rarer moths are toadflax brocade, pigmy footman and Sussex emerald.

Earley Wood

TR 120505; 15.2ha; WdT
Coppiced woodland
Spring, early summer

Coppiced hazel, hornbeam and sweet chestnut encourage a wide range of plants to follow the carpets of spring bluebell. An avenue of fine old beech runs through the wood which harbours a large badger sett.

East Blean Wood

TR 188643; 112ha; KTNC reserve
Old coppiced woodland
No access off rights of way and marked woodland walk
Spring, summer

Oak and ash standards, over a variety of coppice species including hornbeam and field maple, stand above a ground cover rich in spring with wood anemone, bluebell, lesser celandine and lesser periwinkle. Typical woodland birds are present. Sweet chestnut is still actively coppiced in the wood and provides valuable habitat for the heath fritillary.

Eastcourt Meadows Country Park

TQ 805684; 24ha; Gillingham BC
Estuary-side grassland, scrub and trees
All year

The country park lies on the southern edge of the Medway Estuary and overlooks the various marshes, islands and creeks.

Elmley Marshes

TQ 926704; 1360ha; RSPB reserve
Grazing marsh, lagoons, saltmarsh and mudflats
All year

Gadwall, mallard, pochard, shelduck, shoveler and tufted duck are among the breeding species of

Elmley, together with lapwing, ringed plover, oystercatcher and redshank. All are present in some numbers throughout the year but another important nesting species, yellow wagtail, flies south to winter in West Africa. In summer the breeding birds provide the greatest interest here, with perhaps an occasional marauding marsh harrier, and it is then that the plant life of the reserve is at its best.

The wide grasslands, generally dry now, are scattered with daisies, buttercups, clovers and thistles, whose autumn heads will provide food for later small migrant birds. The shallow margins of the ditches and lagoons are fringed with sea club-rush while deeper areas have stands of common reed and lesser bulrush, waving above water-crowfoot species. The saltmarsh areas are filled with sea aster, sea lavender and thrift contrasting with the grey-green sea-purslane, with the fleshy spikes of glasswort and, in one site, the yellow heads of golden samphire.

As the colours fade in autumn the migrant birds begin to arrive, moving away to warmer places or driven down from the colder north. Curlew, redshank and greenshank, golden plover and lapwing, black-tailed godwit, spotted redshank, ruff and snipe, common, green and wood sand-piper – there is a continual movement into and out of the reserve. Smaller birds such as linnet, greenfinch and reed bunting move in flocks across the area, at peril from hunting short-eared owl, hen and marsh harrier or other predators.

By midwinter the resident species have been increased in numbers and others flock in to rest and feed, either on the flooded marshes or the mudflats of the Swale. White-fronted and Brent geese winter with red-breasted merganser and pintail, with dunlin, knot, turnstone and grey plover; bitter weather may bring in a host of other birds to add to the variety. In spring the flow of migrants reverses direction, the wintering birds disperse and the annual round of breeding and rearing young begins again.

Folkestone Warren

TR 242373; 140ha; Shepway DC reserve
Chalk cliffs, chalk grassland and scrub
Spring, summer

One of the best southern sites for migrant butterflies and moths, the Warren also contains areas of chalk grassland, landslips and open cliffs, with plants including sea-heath, rock sea-lavender and privet.

Friezland Wood

TQ 565383; 7.9ha; WdT
Mixed woodland
Spring, summer

A rich mixture of oak, ash, holly, yew, alder, hazel and willow offers a good varied habitat for other forms of wildlife.

Gazen Salts

TR 327587; 4.8ha; Dover DC
Wet meadow with ponds and ditches
Spring, summer

The reserve is noted for its birdlife, and over 150 species have been seen, including such rarities as osprey, spoonbill, bittern and great grey shrike. In summer reed and sedge warbler, whitethroat, willow warbler, yellow wagtail and swallow fre-quent the area, and redwings and fieldfare, water rail, short-eared owl and snipe are winter visitors.

The old Pilgrims' Way followed the curve of the North Downs above the Weald.

Wildfowl on the lake include pochard, shoveler, shelduck and barnacle and greylag geese. There is a good selection of butterflies, including Essex skipper, holly blue and wall.

Ham Fen

Permit only; 3.6ha; KTNC reserve
Relict fenland
Spring, summer

A fine show of marsh fern, with areas of sedge, distinguishes the marsh while birch and alder, ash and grey willow woodland attracts many species of birds. Little grebe, mallard, teal and occasional kingfisher may be seen at the central stream.

Ham Street Woods

TR 004337; 97ha; NCC reserve
Coppice-with-standards woodland
No access off paths and rights of way
Leaflet from NCC Regional Office, Church Street, Wye
Spring, early summer

The woods are chiefly oak over hornbeam, hazel and sweet chestnut, though many other species may be found, over a fine spring display of woodland plants. Birds include hawfinch, nightingale and nuthatch while the varied nature of the woods makes the reserve a site for many moths and butterflies.

Hanging Bank and Brockhoult Mount

TQ 497518; 38.8ha; NT
Mixed woodland
Spring, early summer

The mixed woodland, clothing the crest of a hill, is attractive both for its wildlife interest and for its splendid views across BOUGH BEECH RESERVOIR and the Weald.

High Halstow Marshes

TQ 799763; 52ha; NCC reserve
Saltings and mudflats
No access off right of way
Winter

The spread of reclaimed saltings and saltmarsh is a breeding site for birds. Those known to breed here are gadwall, garganey, mallard, pochard, pintail, shelduck, shoveler and teal; winter wildfowl may include white-fronted geese with waders including curlew, grey and golden plover, dunlin, knot and redshank. Heron from adjoining NORTHWARD HILL may frequently be seen feeding or flying across the marshes.

Holly Hill Wood

TQ 667627; 12.8ha; Tonbridge and Malling BC reserve
Mixed woodland
Spring, summer

The woodland, at one of the highest points in Kent, has extensive views across the Downs to the Medway Valley.

Hothfield Common

TQ 969459; 56ha; KTNC-Ashford BC reserve
Heathland and bog system
Nature trail leaflet from KTNC
Spring, early summer

Heathland and bog are uncommon in Kent but the reserve is an excellent example of these habitats, safeguarded by careful management.

Acid sands are spread across a layer of impermeable rock to give a pattern of raised ground separated by narrow bogs. The higher ground is wooded, with ancient beech, oak, planted Scots pine and sweet chestnut, while much of the drier lower areas are covered with bracken and birch. Areas of the original cover, heather grading into purple moor-grass, can still be seen but, without control, the birch and bracken will spread.

The drier areas slope down into the bogs where cross-leaved heath joins the heather and purple moor-grass fringes the wetter parts. Here is the typical bog development, a spread of *Sphagnum* mosses decorated with tiny plants such as heath milkwort, yellow tormentil and bog asphodel. Common cottongrass in the wettest places shows white-plumed heads while all around are heath spotted-orchid and bog pimpernel. Here also is round-leaved sundew, quite rare in Kent.

Below the mires is a more marshy area with clumps of tussock-sedge, spreads of marsh pennywort, stands of rushes, marsh bedstraw and greater bird's-foot-trefoil, water mint, yellow iris, ragged-Robin and devil's-bit scabious. The marsh grades into an area of willow and alder swamp.

The range of habitat encourages a variety of birds, with 35 species recorded as breeding. The high-forest woodland of the ridge tops is suitable for nuthatch, treecreeper and green woodpecker while the open scrub and wetland areas attract reed bunting, tree pipit, yellowhammer and a variety of warblers. Common lizard and grass-snake occur and the insects include dragonflies and damselflies, together with several sand wasps and the day-flying orange underwing moth.

Hunstead Wood

Permit only; 9.3ha; KTNC reserve
Dry and wet woodland
Spring, early summer

Steep sloping beech woodland falls to a stream and pond, thick with alder and birch, sharp-flowered rush and *Sphagnum* mosses. Solomon's-seal is one of the attractive plants of the dry woodland while birds include breeding nightingale and occasional woodcock.

Hurst Wood

TQ 568405; 17ha; WdT
Mixed woodland
Spring, summer

The woodland lies in a small valley with a stream running through it. Over the last 40 years most of the mature trees have been felled, but the Trust has replanted with oak, sweet chestnut and hazel.

A small area of land was planted in 1963. There are some open glades in the woodland which are covered by a sea of bluebells in spring.

Ide Hill

TQ 487517; 12.8ha; NT
Mixed woodland
Spring, early summer

A stand of mature trees, a mix of oak, sweet chestnut and conifers, the woodland lies on a ridge of greensand overlooking the Weald.

Ivy Hatch

TQ 588548; 0.8ha; KTNC reserve
Wet woodland
Spring, early summer

Grey willow and alder grow in the main wet part of the wood while drier areas have hazel, ash and oak. American skunk-cabbage has spread within the reserve, most of which was formerly a nut orchard.

Joyden's Wood

TQ 500715; 130ha; WdT
Mixed woodland
Spring, summer

This large area of woodland lies only 21km from the centre of London, and the Forestry Commission, its previous owners, developed the area for all types of recreation. Although largely replanted, this ancient site still retains much of its interesting wildlife.

Kemsing Downs

TQ 550594; 14.4ha; KTNC reserve
Woodland and chalk grassland
Spring, summer

Chalkland scrub and a disused chalkpit add to the variety of the reserve which includes lime-loving oak, birch, ash and yew woodland, containing characteristic species such as spurge-laurel, and a fine area of chalk downland. Butterflies include brown Argus, chalkhill blue, Essex, dingy and grizzled skipper.

Kiln Wood

TQ 888515; 6ha; KTNC reserve
Coppiced and old-coppice woodland
Spring, early summer

Kiln Wood lies on gault clay, a rather level very wet wood, actively coppiced to encourage a fine array of woodland plants. Among the new growth are spreads of damp-loving and woodland plants: bugle, rushes and sedges, including pendulous sedge, stands of rosebay and great willowherb and clusters of square-stalked St John's-wort. Willow, ash and hazel are the main coppice species here and the presence of antiquated farm machinery, together with meadow plants such as cuckooflower, suggest a secondary wood grown up on once-cleared farmland.

The older part of the wood, less recently coppiced, is mainly oak, ash and hornbeam with occasional field maple and birch over an understorey of hawthorn, hazel and elder. The drier parts have a splendid show of springtime bluebell with wood anemone and primrose. A characteristic plant of the damper clays is yellow archangel. Wild rose tangles and climbs around clearings and path edges, where openings in the canopy let in the light and guelder-rose adds its colour to the woods. Early-purple orchid, common twayblade and common spotted-orchid are present, with herb-Paris.

Buckler-fern species grow thick in the valley where a small steam runs, together with the delicate lady-fern, while further wetland interest is added by a small pond which lies across the boundary of the reserve. The pond is fringed with marshlike vegetation such as gipsy-wort but its chief interest is a fine colony of water-violet.

Birds include species of woodland and scrub: nuthatch and treecreeper, warblers and nightingale. Kingfisher may visit the sheltered pool.

Knole Park

TQ 532543; 400ha; NI
Extensive deer park
Access on foot only
Spring, summer

The old parkland still holds deer, and the park trees and woodland attract a range of birds and insects.

Lullingstone Park

TQ 515636; 120ha; Sevenoaks DC
Parkland and woodland
Spring, early summer

Areas of woodland and stretches of parkland afford a good range of wildlife habitat.

Lydd Ranges

Permit only; c. 450ha; MOD
Holly wood on shingle
All year

The area includes a unique group of holly trees growing on the shingle beach which is carefully protected by the Army.

Lydden Down

TR 278453; 21.2ha; KTNC reserve
Superb chalk grassland
Spring, summer

Too steep for ploughing, the long slopes of downland have probably stood unchanged since man first cleared them to graze his flocks of sheep. This is fine chalk grassland, the pride of Kent, where typical lime-loving plants such as yellow-wort and salad burnet grow with the less common chalk milkwort and dropwort. Common rock-rose grows here with wild thyme, cowslip, dyer's greenweed, common bird's-foot-trefoil and horse-shoe vetch. Wild mignonette is found in the deeper grassland while the shorter swards are flecked with tiny eyebrights, common centaury and small violets.

One of the specialities of Kentish downland is its magnificence of orchids. Fragrant orchid and autumn lady's-tresses both occur, standing among the commoner plants with the strange elegance of their kind.

Gorse scrub with occasional hawthorn and dogwood tops the downland and, with a narrow belt of hawthorn on the deeper soils below, provides shelter and nest sites for birds. The grassland flowers are attractive to butterflies including marbled white and common and chalk-hill blue. Among the other insects are two of particular note: the reserve contains populations not only of great green bush cricket but also of wart-biter cricket.

Marden Meadow

Permit only; 1.5ha; KTNC reserve
Unimproved meadow with hedgerows and ponds
Spring, early summer

Green-winged orchids, dyer's greenweed and adder's-tongue are all found on this rich meadow.

Nor Marsh

TQ 812688; 102ha; Gillingham BC–RSPB reserve
Estuarine island
No access–may be viewed from B2004
Autumn, winter, spring

The Medway estuary is made up of a vast complex of bays, peninsulas and islands of which the reserve is one of the largest. Despite being very close to the Medway towns, it provides an important refuge for wildfowl and waders.

North Downs Way

TQ 428557–TR 319412; 123km or 139km; CC
Long-distance way
Leaflet from CC or booklet from HMSO bookshops
Spring, summer

Based on the old Pilgrims' Way from Winchester to Canterbury, the way follows the line of the Kentish Downs and winds through Rochester and Canterbury to Dover. An alternative route from Boughton Lees takes the walker south to Folkestone and along the sea coast of the white cliffs to Dover.

Northward Hill

TQ 784761; 54ha; RSPB reserve
Oak woodland and scrub
Spring, early summer

The reserve is chiefly important for its heronry, the largest in Britain and possibly western Europe, but also contains breeding nightingale, hawfinch and long-eared owl.   A nature trail affords views of the estuary, and there are guided walks to see the heronry.

Oare Marshes

TR 011645; 68ha; KTNC reserve
Grazing marsh
Access along Saxon Shoreway public footpath
Leaflet from Trust office
All year

An interesting area of grazing marsh, reedbeds and dykes with small areas of saltmarsh which is being developed to encourage wildfowl and waders. Already it is used by good populations of wintering birds including short-eared owls.

The Devil's Kneading Trough is a fine example of a dry valley at Wye and Crundale Downs.

Oare Meadow

TR 007627; 2.8ha; KTNC reserve
Small grazing meadow
Spring, early summer

A small tidal stream adds to the interest of the rather acid grassland while wet flushes, fed by springs, provide a habitat for freshwater plants such as brooklime. Trees and scrub attract a variety of birds.

Oldbury Hill and Styants Wood

TQ 578559; 60.7ha; NT
Mixed woodland
Spring, early summer

An Iron Age hill fort adds archaeological interest to this large area of varied woodland.

One Tree Hill

TQ 560532; 13.6ha; NT
Mixed woodland
Spring, early summer

Broad-leaved woodland crowns the spine of a hill with wide views across the farmland, hedges and woods of the Kentish Weald.

Orlestone Forest

Permit only; 11.2ha; KTNC reserve
Oak–hornbeam woodland
Summer

An area of old coppiced woodland now being allowed to grow on to high forest, the reserve is a notable site for butterflies including the white admiral.

Park Gate Down

TR 168459; 6.9ha; KTNC reserve
Woodland, scrub and unimproved chalk grassland
Spring, summer

The scrub and woodland areas shelter songbirds such as nightingale while the grassland is rich in typical chalkland species, for instance cowslip and early-purple orchid, together with bee and pyramidal orchid.

Park Wood

TR 045525; 22ha; WdT
Coppiced woodland
Spring, early summer

A fine remnant of the old Challock Forest, the wood is chiefly hazel, hornbeam and chestnut coppice with a rich variety of other shrubs and plants. Active coppicing increases the interest.

Parsonage Wood

TQ 797329; 9.2ha; KTNC reserve
High Weald woodland
Spring, early summer

Clay overlies the High Weald sands, supporting an oak–beech woodland with rich-wood species

Stodmarsh: mining subsidence has brought back rich wetlands to the Stour Valley.

such as ash and field maple. Small pools add a wetland interest and a stream-cut ghyll, rich in liverworts, mosses and ferns, cuts down to the sandstone beneath. The oak and beech is being managed as high forest while hornbeam is being coppiced elsewhere in the wood.

Perry Wood and Selling Wood

TR 045556; 60ha; Swale BC reserve
Mixed woodland
Spring, summer

In this attractive area of woodland, with a good range of rich wood plants, active sweet chestnut coppicing is practised.

Queendown Warren

TQ 827629; 7.2ha; KTNC reserve
Chalk, grassland, scrub and woodland
Leaflet from site or KTNC
Spring, summer

The records of Queendown Warren stretch back to the time of Henry III when it was, in fact, a commercially managed rabbit warren – a source of meat and fur.

Around the grasslands dense spreads of hawthorn, beech and elder are laced together with traveller's-joy; tall beech trees stand in a mixed scrub of broom, birch and hawthorn, hornbeam, oak and sweet chestnut; ash, dogwood, hawthorn and hazel, hornbeam, oak and wayfaring-tree are clustered in the deeper soils at the foot of the slopes. The grassland slopes themselves are banked and terraced with impressive beeches standing like parkland trees among the rich array of smaller plants. Cowslip and violet are followed by the typical range of downland plants, common rock-rose and wild thyme, marjoram and common milkwort, common bird's-foot-trefoil, horseshoe vetch and a splendid range of orchids. Bee and fly orchid and early spider-orchid are all well represented together with burnt, green-winged and man orchid. Scrub and woodland add extra habitats and both white and broad-leaved helleborine occur.

The woodland is very varied with blocks of high-forest beech and oak contrasting with areas where oak, ash, birch and wild cherry have been left as standards above an understorey of coppiced sweet chestnut. Bluebell, honeysuckle and yellow archangel are encouraged by active coppicing.

This wide range of habitat provides suitable food and shelter for a great variety of animals. Grasshopper populations are good and there are breeding colonies of both common and chalkhill blue butterfly. Despite myxomatosis, there are large numbers of rabbits, hunted by fox, stoat and weasel. Adders enjoy the warmth and shelter of the slopes and there is a good range of typical scrub and woodland birds such as breeding warblers, tit species and woodpeckers.

Sandwich Bay

TR 351620; 413ha; KTNC–RSPB–NT reserve
Grassland, beach and foreshore, dunes and saltmarsh
Toll levied on access road
All year

Shingle and dunes contain plants such as sea bindweed, sea-holly and sea sandwort, old slacks may have a show of southern marsh-orchid and pyramidal orchid. A spectacular plant is the giant sharp rush while among the most fascinating are the parasitic bedstraw and carrot broomrape. The reserve lies on a bird migration route and has long been famous among ornithologists.

Sevenoaks Wildfowl Reserve

Permit only; 54ha; Jeffery Harrison Memorial Trust
Flooded gravelpits
Permit and leaflet from warden
All year

Flooded gravel workings have been developed as a wetland reserve, where floating rafts provide nest sites for waterbirds and the shores have been designed to give the best conditions for breeding species.

Shorne Country Park

TQ 684698; 70ha; Kent CC
Woodland, ponds and grassland
Leaflet available on site
Summer

The rich woodland consists of oak, ash, sweet chestnut, field maple and hazel, with a characteristic old woodland flora. An area of clay pits, long since abandoned, now form an interesting area of scrub and ponds which is especially good for insects including twelve species of dragonflies.

Smallman's Wood

Permit only; 12ha; KTNC reserve
Old coppiced woodland
Spring, summer

A remnant of the old ORLESTONE FOREST, the reserve is now actively coppiced again, and contains some fine oak standards over a spring show of bluebell. Woodpeckers and treecreeper are plentiful.

South Swale

TR 035647; 413.1ha; KTNC reserve
Beach and foreshore
Permit only off rights of way particularly during breeding season
Winter

An attractive range of plants such as yellow horned-poppy and sea-lavender adds interest in summer, but the reserve is chiefly notable for its winter wildfowl and waders, for perhaps 500 Brent geese, and for migrants such as shore lark and snow bunting.

Stockbury Hill Wood

Permit only; 2.8ha; KTNC reserve
Rich chalk woodland
Spring, early summer

Bird's-nest, fly, butterfly and lady orchid add their special beauty to this small area of yew, hornbeam, oak and beech woodland.

Stodmarsh

TR 222607; 160ha; NCC
Open water and dykes, reedbeds and grazing meadows
No access off Lampen Wall and riverbank footpaths
Leaflet from NCC
All year

The Stodmarsh is a superb wetland area through which a flood protection bank, the Lampen Wall, winds to join the riverbank flood wall and from which the whole wide marsh is overlooked. The wetlands of the Stour Valley were all but eradicated by drainage but subsidence due to underground coal workings has lowered much of this area and recreated the marshes which are so attractive to many birds.

The edges of the lagoons and the wide reedbeds are filled with common reed and bulrush. The open dykes contain bogbean, greater bladderwort and greater spearwort, water forget-me-not, flowering-rush, marsh cinquefoil and frogbit. Marsh stitchwort and common meadow-rue grow on the banks, with hawthorn, willow and alder scrub along the waterways.

The list of birds breeding on the reserve is long and varied, with lapwing, redshank and snipe on the meadows, reed bunting, reed and sedge warbler in the reedbeds, coot, moorhen and great crested grebe by the lagoons. Cetti's warbler has colonised the scrub, with grasshopper warbler in the drier marshland, while the reedswamp proper gives cover for rare breeding species – bittern, bearded tit and Savi's warbler. Nesting duck include gadwall and garganey, mallard, pochard, teal, shelduck and shoveler.

In winter dabbling duck frequent the flooded meadows while the lagoons are dotted with diving birds such as tufted duck and pochard. Occasionally winter will bring flights of wild swans or geese from the north and birds may be driven in from the sea by storms. Passage birds such as arctic, black and common tern pass through in spring and autumn together with ruff and black-tailed godwit; migrant swallow, swift or martin may be pursued by hobby; seasonal visitors such as hen and marsh harrier or osprey may hunt the marshes.

The Swale

TR 032662; 220ha; NCC reserve
Grazing marshes, saltmarshes, lagoons and mudflats
Permit only off right of way
Leaflet from NCC
Winter

Like SOUTH SWALE the reserve has impressive winter numbers of waders, wildfowl and smaller migrant birds. The grazing marshes provide breeding sites for many species while the shell beach holds birds such as ringed plover. The large lagoon contains one of Britain's largest populations of sea club-rush.

Toys Hill

TQ 469517; 152ha; NT
Mixed woodland
Spring, summer

Beech, oak, sweet chestnut and coniferous woodland stand on the brow of a greensand ridge; the wood is attractive both for its wildlife and for its splendid views across the Weald.

Trosley Country Park

TQ 634613; 64ha; Kent CC
Chalk woodland, scrub and grassland
Nature trail leaflet from information centre
Spring, summer

High-forest beech, hornbeam, oak and ash woodland, with whitebeam, wild cherry and coppiced hazel, caps the steep escarpment which shows good examples of chalkland scrub and grassland.

Tudeley Wood

TQ 6244; 121ha; RSPB reserve
Woodland and heathland
Access to be arranged
Spring, summer

An old coppice wood of oak, ash and hazel which in spring is a mass of bluebells and primroses – more unusual plants include bird's-nest orchid. Great and lesser-spotted woodpeckers, nuthatches and marsh tits nest in the rotting branches, while nightingales sing from the shrubs on the woodland edge. On fine summer evenings roding woodcock can be seen and nightjars and tawny owls call.

Westerham Mines

Permit only; 2000m; KTNC reserve
Old mine tunnels
Winter

These old tunnels are an important site for hibernating bats. Five species are known to occur: Natterers, Daubentons, whiskered, brown long-eared and Brandt's.

Westfield Wood

TQ 754607; 5ha; KTNC reserve
Steep yew woodland with areas of mixed wood
Spring, early summer

Westfield Wood, on the flanks of the Medway Gap, is a good example of Kent's steep chalk woodlands. Yew has colonised the main part of the slopes.   Nothing grows beneath them, for too little light can penetrate, but there is a special quality of ancient, almost sepulchral, peace within the wood. Where the canopy opens the woodland floor is filled with plants: carpets of dog's mercury are patterned with sanicle and common twayblade, ivy or stinking iris. The fringes of the yew-wood get most light and here young saplings and shrubs of ash, privet, sycamore and wayfaring-tree are tangled with traveller's-joy above yellow archangel and stinking hellebore. Burnet rose, guelder-rose, spindle, whitebeam and beech also occur here.

Above the yew-wood the soils deepen to allow a spread of ash and beech, oak, wild cherry and field maple with an area of coppiced hazel. The ground cover is varied with tangles of bracken, bramble and rosebay willowherb, with the woodland plants wood anemone and bluebell, wood-sorrel, yellow pimpernel and with the less common species butcher's-broom and green hellebore.

This variety of woodland is typical on chalk where a cap of clay with flints encourages more acid plants such as bracken and bluebell with, lower down, a spread of lime-loving ash and beech, grading into dense yew woodland. Yew is probably the climax here and, left to itself, would eventually spread and shade out everything else. The structure is rich and varied and provides a range of habitat for many woodland animals.

Most of the old badger setts have been taken over by rabbits but a small population of badger still uses the wood. The yew woodland is not attractive to many birds, although goldcrest may be present and the red fruits may draw thrushes in the autumn. The mixed woodland above is rich in typical birds, as are the fields and hedgerows around.

Wilmay Copse

TQ 582655; 3.9ha; WdT
Woodland and grassland
Spring, summer

Lying within the Green Belt area of London, this rough pasture and rather neglected coppice of hazel, ash, hornbeam and field maple is an important local amenity.

Wye

TR 077455; 100ha; NCC reserve
Chalk downland scrub and woodland
No access off rights of way
Leaflets and nature trail guide from information centre or
NCC
Spring, summer

The general effects of millennia of weathering would probably have produced a fairly regular slope to these chalk downs but one of the features of the scarp today, well shown at Wye, is the series of spectacular coombs and deep gullies which run towards the plain. These were almost certainly caused by the ice ages which did so much to form our modern landscape. Although the ice cap never reached this far south, the Downs were still subjected to arctic conditions. When snow and ice on the tops of the Downs began to thaw, the water would have run off on the surface, cutting the coombs in the chalk. At the same time, frozen moisture held in the surface would cause frost shattering and flake away the rock. Magnificent fluted slopes were carved on the edge of the Downs in this way and the Devil's Kneading Trough at Wye is a fine example.

The chalk poses problems for plant life, particularly in coping with its dryness, and the first plants to grow here, before a soil develops, must be highly adapted for these conditions. Sheep's fescue, one of the typical grasses of the short turf of chalk grassland, keeps its stomata hidden from the drying effect of the wind by rolling the edges of its leaves. Other plants, such as hoary plantain and dwarf thistle, grow low rosettes of leaves, keeping their stomata safe from the wind close against the ground, lying low to avoid grazing, and preventing other plants from growing too close to them; around one-third of all chalk-sward plants conform to this low rosette pattern. Some plants form mats, which carry the same advantages – wild thyme and common bird's-foot-trefoil, for example – while others have fleshy water-storing leaves, like biting stonecrop, or slow down the drying airstream by being hairy, like lesser hawkbit.

Unless it is continually grazed, this short chalk sward will be colonised by taller plants, such as torgrass, which shade the small herbs out. Much of the colour is lost, although some special plants prefer this habitat, but the coarser grasses are less liable to grazing and in their shade and cover shrubs can begin to find a foothold. Eventually an open scrub of elder, blackthorn, hawthorn, dogwood, spindle, wild privet and wayfaring-tree will spread, an area where many attractive plants can survive in the glades and a splendid site for blackcap, willow warbler and whitethroat, as well as nightingale.

In the shelter of the scrub, forest trees begin to seed and the down grows on towards woodland. Beech or yew will eventually form a densely shaded wood where only specially adapted plants can survive but ash, until taken over by one of these two, lets in more light and may form an airy woodland rich in plants.

For its orchids alone the reserve is a site of exceptional interest and beauty. In the short dry turf of the Kentish Downs, and generally only in the Wye and Folkestone districts, late spider-orchid is a very special plant: on the reserve it is possibly at its most north westerly site. Early spider-orchid also grows here but flowers before its cousin and is rather more widespread: it prefers to grow fairly near to the sea and is found as far west as Dorset. Bee and burnt orchid, musk and man orchid are also short-turf plants, although man orchid may sometimes be found growing in open scrub on steep slopes.

The deeper grasses, scrub and woodland are sites for shade-tolerant plants, for commoner species such as fragrant and pyramidal orchid, although these are often found in the shorter swards, and a habitat for the more uncommon fly orchid. In the scrub and woodland clearings lady orchid grows: almost wholly restricted to Kent, it is among our most beautiful plants.

Yockletts Bank

TR 125477; 25.1ha; KTNC reserve
Particularly fine chalk woodland
Spring, summer

This is a classic Kentish site, one of the best chalk woodlands in the county. It is comprised of slopes of chalk capped with deposits of clay and, although yew is present, it has never achieved the density of WESTFIELD and active coppicing of the other species has increased the range of habitat.

The clay grows springtime drifts of bluebell, ramsons, wood anemone, common figwort and lords-and-ladies. Oak trees stand over coppiced sweet chestnut with thickets of blackthorn.

The lower woodland, on the chalk, is chiefly of ash, beech and hornbeam above an understorey of coppiced hazel. Dogwood, field maple, yew and wild rose, with hawthorn, elder and wayfaring-tree, contribute to the variety of shrubs and spread above a typical range of varied rich-wood plants. Primrose and wood spurge, violets and woodruff make an attractive show in spring, together with ramsons, sanicle, dog's mercury, enchanter's-nightshade and yellow archangel.

The open banks and pathway edges retain their grassland species: cowslip and common milkwort, common rock-rose, wild thyme and salad burnet. Chalkland grasses and sedges grow, surrounded by sapling spindle, wayfaring-tree and dogwood. Yockletts Bank has splendid colonies of common twayblade and common spotted-orchid, of early-purple, fly and pyramidal orchid. Greater butterfly-orchid may also be found but the chief excitement is the population of lady orchid, probably one of the finest in the county. Lady orchid is one of our most beautiful orchids and is virtually limited to Kent, where it is found mainly in woods and shady places growing on the chalk.

Green and great spotted woodpecker nest in the larger trees while the areas of scrub and coppice provide sites for nightingale and warblers. There is a flourishing badger population.

Fly-orchids: these delicate flowers are found in the woods and on the chalk downlands of Kent.

Oxfordshire

One of Britain's most inland counties, Oxfordshire comprises a large slice of the scarplands that lie between the Cotswolds in the west and the London clay of the lower Thames basin in the east. To travel to London from Banbury, in the extreme north of the county, involves a journey across rocks that represent millions of years of geological history, and explain the basis of Oxfordshire's present-day wildlife.

First come the lower Jurassic or lias rocks, then the middle lias that yields iron ore, still mined in parts of north Oxfordshire. These are succeeded by oolitic rocks which produce the lovely honey-coloured stone that has made Cotswold villages and Oxford colleges world-famous. A sandwich of upper Jurassic rocks follows, consisting of corallian limestone set between the Kimmeridge and the Oxford clay – the latter is quarried for a brickworks at Calvert, just across the Buckinghamshire border. The layered effect of the scarplands continues with the next sandwich, the gault clay enclosed between the lower and upper greensands. The upper greensand makes a distinct small escarpment between Postcombe and Watlington, rising to 144m at Adwell Cop.

Next come the great cretaceous system of rocks and the steep Chiltern escarpment, whose summits lie on average 100m above the Icknield Way at its foot. The beech-clad chalk hills of the Chilterns are quite distinct from those of the Berkshire Downs, now administratively in Oxfordshire. Whereas the Berkshire Downs recall the 'blunt, bow-headed, whale-backed' South Downs, the Chilterns, whose summits are covered with a thick deposit of clay with flints, are almost all wooded, except where farmland has replaced the trees. From the crest of the Chilterns the landscape slopes downhill all the way, and the chalk is progressively deeper down and covered with thicker layers of clays, sands and gravels.

The point of this geological odyssey across Oxfordshire is to show that most of the county consists of calcareous rocks. The first acid soils are not encountered until the clay with flints and scattered tertiary deposits on the top of the Chilterns. The plant and animal life of the county is almost entirely lime-loving, which makes common heather, for instance, one of the rarest plants in Oxfordshire, found only in a few spots – such as a small area of ASTON ROWANT – where rain has leached all the lime out of the topsoil. The naturalist will find bee, pyramidal and fragrant orchid, typical species of chalkland, and butterflies such as chalkhill blue and marbled white, whose larvae feed on chalk-loving plants, but not such plants as sundews and *Sphagnum* mosses or such butterflies as grayling or silver studded blue.

While Oxfordshire is still rich in wildlife, as in most counties this richness is entirely the result of the ability of plants and animals to adapt to conditions created by man through the centuries. Excluding the large towns such as Oxford and Banbury and their associated industry, the county consists either of completely artificial habitats, for instance arable fields or grass leys (though traditional grassland management, still carried on at Coleshill Meadow and FOXHOLES, preserves old-meadow plant and butterfly species), or at best of semi-natural habitats. Among the latter are chalk grassland – a fine example of which can be found at Aston Rowant; beech and oak woodland; scattered fens – for instance the famous one at COTHILL, west of Abingdon; and the River Thames and its tributaries. Old sand- and claypits, such as those at DRY SANDFORD PIT and HENRY STEPHEN, and former railway lines such as HOOK NORTON RAILWAY CUTTING, become useful wildlife refuges when no longer needed for their original purpose.

Modern Oxfordshire is now more than ever the county of the Isis or Upper Thames. To the lower reaches of the Windrush, Evenlode, Cherwell, Ray and Thame on the north bank have been added the Ock on the south bank, together with its whole drainage basin, the Vale of the White Horse.

No part of the county can by any stretch of the imagination be called wilderness, but there are still places, such as the Isis Valley around Chimney and parts of the RIDGEWAY PATH on the Berkshire Downs, where, despite the intensive agriculture all around, with stuttering tractors and barbed wire fences, it is possible to feel remote from the everyday world. Naturalists in Oxfordshire can still find plenty to occupy them in its range of landscape and wildlife habitats, including a number of reserves owned or managed by BBONT,

the Trust responsible for the three adjacent counties of Berkshire, Buckinghamshire and Oxfordshire; however naturalists are more and more likely to find themselves sharing the countryside with other users. The Ridgeway Path, for instance, has brought many newcomers to the county to enjoy the traffic-free walk along England's oldest road, that starts on the north coast of Norfolk and finishes far away on the Channel coast of Devon, and the County Council has pioneered the way-marking of circular walks from Banbury, Wantage and Witney.

RICHARD FITTER

Aston Rowant

SP 741967; 124ha; NCC reserve
Chalk grassland, scrub and woodland
No access off nature trail or rights of way
Leaflets from site or NCC
Spring, summer

While PEWSEY DOWN (Wiltshire) is a celebration of short-grazed open downland, Aston Rowant is a fine example of more varied Chiltern scarpland.

A small area of chalk heath occurs where heather and other acid plants such as heath bedstraw are mixed with more lime-loving species, but most of the grassland and scrub lies on the long slopes where chalk is too close to the surface for acid plants to survive. The grassland is tightly grazed, containing typical downland plants or a slightly deeper, dense, colourful turf with common bird's-foot-trefoil, clovers and vetches, lady's bedstraw, common centaury, oxeye daisy and marjoram, wild mignonette, common spotted-orchid, squinancywort, yellow-wort and kidney vetch.

Tiny close-pruned sprays of dogwood, privet and hawthorn point to the efforts of scrub to invade the grassland, and a block of less closely grazed downland does indeed show more vigorous invasion. Where the nature trail climbs towards the woodland on Beacon Hill, a further step in the change from grassland may be seen. Rabbit-grazed clearings still show the typical small herbs but most of the slope is filled with a mix of scrub ash, beech, elder, hawthorn, wild privet, wild rose, wayfaring-tree, common whitebeam and yew. Approaching the woodland proper, woodland plants begin to appear and under the scrub, to which hazel, oak, rowan and willow are added, spreads of dog's mercury begin to show, together with deadly nightshade.

An even more important area of scrub contains a fine population of juniper which, with a mixed scrub of ash, beech, blackthorn, bramble and buckthorn, dogwood, hawthorn, wild privet and spindle, wayfaring-tree, common whitebeam and yew, forms the most northerly representative of such a community in Britain.

The woodland proper has developed on the cap of clay with flints. Beech, typical of the Chiltern chalk, dominates the woodland and, casting a heavy shade, tends to deny a varied ground cover.

Where light can penetrate, plants such as yellow archangel, bluebell, enchanter's-nightshade, wood melick, sanicle and woodruff may be seen or tangles of bramble grow under the trees and spread across the clearings. In clearings, too, guelder-rose may occur and, although the under-storey tends to be thin, young beech, hawthorn, holly, rowan and sycamore may survive the shade.

Two plants of the deep beech woodland seem to delight in the lack of sun – both white and violet helleborine often occur on the bare forest floor. Two unusual grasses also grow at Aston Rowant, wood barley in the woodland and the rare mat-grass fescue in the pastureland, while downy oat-grass, generally a plant of damp lime-rich sites, may be found unexpectedly on a north-facing slope. Other uncommon plants include Chiltern gentian and candytuft, together with the better known but rather local pale toadflax. Chiltern gentian is limited to this area and to a part of the North Downs.

The outstanding butterfly is probably silver-spotted skipper, a species which occurs only locally on southern chalk, but there are also good populations of dingy and grizzled skipper. Numbers of chalkhill blue are not as great as at Pewsey Down, which has larger colonies of horseshoe vetch, but the abundance of common rock-rose here encourages good numbers of brown argus while the chalk heath attracts green hair-streak which does not occur at Pewsey. Two other notable species are dark green fritillary, a large and beautiful insect, and Duke of Burgundy, like silver-spotted skipper mainly restricted to the south of England.

The scrub is the richest area for bird life, where the low shelter and abundance of insects provide nesting sites and plentiful food for many song-birds, but the woods also have their complement of birds and provide a habitat for great spotted woodpecker and nuthatch, for kestrel and spar-rowhawk which hunt across the reserve, and for the rather uncommon hawfinch.

Fox and badger are fairly common, fallow and muntjac deer may be present and the small mammals include harvest mouse. The main impression on the visitor, however, will probably be of the chalkland flowers and scrub, the butter-flies and birds, and the cool shade of the woodland.

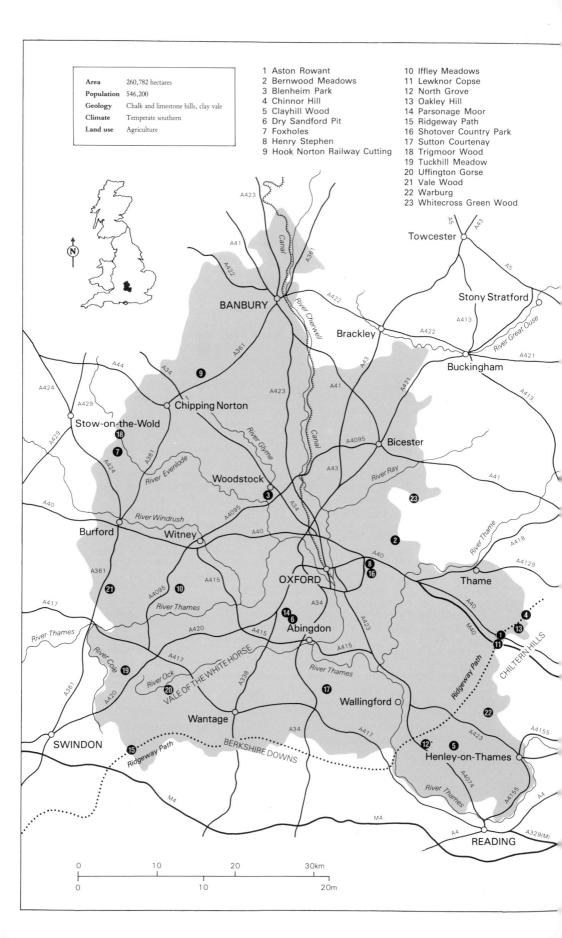

Area	260,782 hectares
Population	546,200
Geology	Chalk and limestone hills, clay vale
Climate	Temperate southern
Land use	Agriculture

1 Aston Rowant
2 Bernwood Meadows
3 Blenheim Park
4 Chinnor Hill
5 Clayhill Wood
6 Dry Sandford Pit
7 Foxholes
8 Henry Stephen
9 Hook Norton Railway Cutting
10 Iffley Meadows
11 Lewknor Copse
12 North Grove
13 Oakley Hill
14 Parsonage Moor
15 Ridgeway Path
16 Shotover Country Park
17 Sutton Courtenay
18 Trigmoor Wood
19 Tuckhill Meadow
20 Uffington Gorse
21 Vale Wood
22 Warburg
23 Whitecross Green Wood

Bernwood Meadows

SP 606110; 7.3ha; BBONT reserve
Neutral grassland
Keep to footpaths from mid-May until hay is cut; dogs
not allowed when stock grazing
Spring, early summer

Over 100 species of plants have been recorded, including 23 grasses and there is a good display of green-winged orchids and adder's-tongue. Both fallow and muntjac deer frequent the reserve and rutting stands are clearly visible in the autumn.

Blenheim Park

SP 442168; 897ha; Duke of Marlborough
Parkland, woodland and lake
Self-guided nature trail
Spring, early summer

A good variety of birds may be seen around the park or on the lake but the special interest of the site lies in its parkland oak trees, centuries old.

Chinnor Hill

SP 766002; 26ha; BBONT reserve
Chiefly chalk scrub and woodland with some grassland
Spring, summer

There is a fine range of lime loving trees such as whitebeam, wayfaring-tree and yew with a scrub that includes juniper and grassland species such as autumn gentian. The varied cover provides nest sites and territories for breeding songbirds while the berry-bearing species attract winter migrants.

Clayhill Wood

SU 687835; 4.3ha; WdT
Deciduous woodland
Spring, summer

The reserve is only part of this typical Chiltern beech wood. Some of the area has been felled but a replanting programme is in progress.

Cothill

Permit only; 2ha; NT–NCC reserve
Pond, fen and woodland
Leaflet from NCC
Spring, summer

Once known as the Ruskin reserve, the fragile rich wetland contains several uncommon species such as fen pondweed. Together with adjacent PARSONAGE MOOR it forms an outstanding area for the richness and variety of its plants and animals.

Dry Sandford Pit

SU 467995; 8ha; BBONT reserve
Old sand digging
Spring, early summer

A lime-rich wetland, rich in plants such as fen pondweed, marsh helleborine and several orchid species, has developed in the old working. The range of flora provides a habitat which is enjoyed by numerous insect species.

Foxholes

SP 254206; 72ha; BBONT reserve
Woodland and riverside meadow
Spring, early summer

Protected from disturbance by its position at the heart of a private estate, Foxholes contains a very wide variety of habitats. The reserve slopes gradually from a fairly level plateau down to the wet meadowland beside the Evenlode, showing a range from rather acid woodland above to limestone-influenced woodland and grassland below.

The woodland rides of Bernwood Forest, on the borders of Buckinghamshire and Oxfordshire, are famous for their butterflies.

The meadow has been neither ploughed nor dressed with chemical fertiliser for over a century, and species such as great burnet, marsh valerian and marsh speedwell may still be found here.

The lower wood lies immediately above the meadow, initially a narrow hedgelike strip, then widening, slopes up away from the river. The narrow belt contains mainly oak and ash over hawthorn, blackthorn and hazel with a variable ground cover according to the shade: dense bramble grows where the light is good but many woodland flowers survive among the bramble and along the pathway. Where the wood deepens more varied conditions occur; the good shrub layer is ideal for warbler species. The path is damp enough for meadowsweet to show in clearings, accompanied by a good display of common spotted-orchid. Above, the wood becomes more open, with oak and birch over dense bramble or bracken between coppiced hazel draped with honeysuckle, an ideal site for badger.

The rough grassland above the wood is thick with ragged-Robin and meadow crane's-bill while higher again the upper woodland climbs to the plateau. The wealth of woodland types provides suitable sites for small mammals. These are hunting grounds for fox, stoat, weasel, tawny owl and sparrowhawk as well as safe retreats for fallow deer. The plateau woodland, like the slope, has much birch and oak and contains areas of planted conifers, damper areas of oak and ash, scrub grassland, rich in vetches and meadow flowers such as cowslip and common spotted-orchid, and open park-like glades deep in bracken.

Henry Stephen

SP 560065; 2.8ha; BBONT reserve
Pond and woodland
Spring, early summer

An educational reserve formed by flooding old claypits, the pond and giant horsetail marsh is rich in wetland life while the woodland attracts many songbirds.

Hook Norton Railway Cutting

SP 360320; 7.6ha; BBONT reserve
Disused railway line
Spring, summer

Developing woodland, grassland and artificial rock faces, the old retaining walls afford a wide range of habitat utilised by lime-loving plants, insects and a good range of birds.

Iffley Meadows

SP 324037; 33ha; BBONT reserve
Ancient wet meadow
Early spring

Fritillaries are concentrated around the centre of the northern section, their numbers having been decimated mainly by picking but also by lack of appropriate management. Marsh thistle, marsh-marigold, great burnet, ragged-Robin and adder's-tongue flower here.

Lewknor Copse

SU 724976; 1ha; BBONT reserve
Small beech woodland
Spring, summer

The reserve protects a population of spurge-laurel and of white and narrow-lipped helleborine, uncommon and beautiful plants characteristic of undisturbed lime-rich woodland.

North Grove

SU 647832; 21ha; WdT
Deciduous woodland
Spring, summer

This attractive Chiltern beech wood has been well managed along traditional lines. Selective felling has encouraged natural regeneration of beech and allowed the remaining trees to grow into fine specimens. There are also areas of ash and hazel coppice, which add variety to the reserve.

Oakley Hill

SU 755995; 4.5ha; BBONT reserve
Chalk downland
Spring, summer

The downland has been mainly colonised by scrub but there are still open areas with plants, including rock-rose, thyme, Chiltern gentian, clustered bell-flower, spotted-orchid, yellow-wort, salad burnet and cowslips. There is a fringe of beechwood along the top of the slope.

Parsonage Moor

SU 461998; 5.2ha; BBONT reserve
Lime-rich fen
Spring, summer

The largest and most important section of an area which includes COTHILL Fen, Parsonage Moor is outstanding for the richness and variety it contains. Areas of tussocked purple moor-grass give way to small mires or to tall beds of common reed or seas of meadowsweet while reed-filled sedge-beds, wet underfoot, lift up to shoulders of drier ground thick with scrub. The whole is sheltered, full of aromatic wetland plants and filled with insects and the sound of songbirds.

The tussocks of purple moor-grass are spangled with yellow tormentil and patterned with the rounded heads of devil's-bit scabious, the food plant of the marsh fritillary caterpillar. In the mires the purple moor-grass gives way to *Sphagnum* mosses, sedges and rushes. Both common butter-wort and round-leaved sundew grow on the *Sphagnum*, representatives of two of our three families of insect-catching plants; common cotton-grass and meadow thistle nod above lousewort or spikes of early and southern marsh-orchid and the beautiful marsh helleborine.

The taller herb communities, dominated by common reed, include common comfrey, food plant of scarlet tiger moth, hemp-agrimony, marsh valerian, meadowsweet and a great variety of sedges, including brown and tawny sedge, glaucous sedge and long-stalked yellow-sedge, together with black bog-rush, a distinctive plant of rich calcareous fens. Invading scrub is species-rich, with lime-loving shrubs such as privet and spindle growing among hawthorn, hazel and willow, with ash and guelder-rose, birch, oak and alder. Drier scrub-covered banks have a typical woodland ground cover and include cowslip and quaking-grass. One of the particular interests of the reserve is the population of scarlet tiger moth which, with its variety *bimacula* has been studied here for many years.

Ridgeway Path

SU 259833–SP 770013; 58km (in two sections); CC
Long-distance way
Leaflet from CC or booklet from HMSO bookshops
Spring, summer

Generally following the line of chalk hills, past the White Horse of Uffington and the colourful slopes of ASTON ROWANT, the long distance foot-path gives a good idea of the richness of the wildlife to be seen in Oxfordshire.

Shotover Country Park

SP 561063; 1.2–4km (trails); Oxford City Council
Woodland, scrub, heath and grassland
Leaflet from site or from OCC
Spring, early summer

Five trails have been laid out to show the interest of the area, once part of a royal hunting forest, which contains a good range of habitat including ancient woodland still managed as coppice with standards, bird-rich scrub, heath containing heather, a species uncommon in Oxfordshire, and grassland where plants such as star-of-Bethlehem and musk mallow may be found. Mammals include both fallow and muntjac deer, while purple emperor and white admiral are among the butter-flies that occur, together with a good variety of other insects.

Sutton Courtenay

SU 643600; 14ha; CEGB reserve
Meadows, ponds and scrub
Educational or organised groups only; book with the Head Teacher, Sutton Courtenay Primary School, tel. (0235) 848333
Booklets from school and the PR Department, CEGB, SW Region Headquarters, Bridgewater Road, Bedminster Down, Bristol BS13 8AN
Spring, summer

Lying at the edge of Didcot Power Station, two ponds on the site provide feeding areas for mallard, teal, coot and little grebe, and both frogs and common newts breed. The stream, Moor Ditch, is known to be at least 900 years old and is a good place to see water voles and dragonflies. Cowslips, heath spotted orchids and meadow crane's-bill flower in the herb-rich grassland, while in the scrub willow warblers and chiffchaffs nest and thrushes feast on the hawthorn berries in winter.

Trigmoor Wood

SP 256229; 3.6ha; WdT
Mixed woodland
Spring, summer

A former area of railway sidings and track where planting of conifers and broadleaved trees has complemented natural regeneration.

Tuckhill Meadow

SU 240900; 5.3ha; BBONT reserve
Grassland, stream and spinney
Summer

The higher ground supports typical limestone grassland plants, while in the wetter areas there is southern marsh-orchid and marsh valerian; this section is excellent for dragonflies and damselflies. Kingfishers may breed on the reserve.

Uffington Gorse

SU 314900; 4ha; WdT
Mixed woodland
Spring, summer

This reserve lies in the Vale of the White Horse, an area lacking much woodland cover. The wood at present consists of a ring of Scots pine and oaks, the central section having been felled. Plans to replant this area with a mixture of native trees and shrubs will enhance the wood for wildlife and ensure its survival as a landscape feature.

Vale Wood

SP 237040; 0.2ha; WdT
Small plantation
Spring, early summer

In an area devastated by Dutch elm disease, a small plantation has been established to produce a future woodland.

Vicarage Pit

Permit only; 8.8ha; BBONT reserve
Flooded gravelpit
Can be overlooked from SP 400056
Winter

The reserve, easily overlooked from the road, is a favourite resting place for winter wildfowl such as mallard, tufted duck and pochard.

Warburg

SU 720880; 102ha; BBONT reserve
Chalk woodland, scrub and grassland
Visitors must keep to marked pathways
Information centre open periodically
Spring, early summer

The largest and one of the most varied of the BBONT reserves, Warburg lies in the chalk valley of Bix Bottom, sheltered, sunny and particularly rich in plant and animal life. Most of the reserve is wooded, much of it with beech, but there are wide grassy rides, old meadows, open banks and woodland clearings providing a varied habitat.

The open areas show the typical chalk grassland range of plants such as salad burnet, wild mignonette and cowslip, with more unusual plants including meadow clary, a tall spikelet of deep blue-violet flowers, and orchids such as bee and fly orchid.

The beech woodlands standing over shaded deep leaf-litter contrasts with areas of coppiced hazel or mixed varieties such as dogwood, privet, spindle, field maple, wayfaring-tree, ash, birch, hawthorn, sweet chestnut and sycamore or the dense shade of yew. Conifer plantations are being replaced with species more natural to the chalk.

Commoner rich-wood plants are plentiful throughout the reserve – plants such as dog's mercury, varieties of violet, wood spurge, looping ropes of traveller's-joy, path-edge plants such as bugle and delicate wood melick, deep green splays of ferns or tangles of bramble – but more unusual plants abound and include such species as yellow archangel, columbine, green hellebore, herb-Paris and Solomon's-seal.

Breeding birds here include kestrel and sparrowhawk, woodcock, willow tit and wood warbler; the larger mammals include fallow and muntjac deer, with fox, badger, stoat and weasel; adder, grass snake, slow-worm and common lizard may be found. The insects are equally varied and a good range of butterflies is complemented by a variety of moths which include maple prominent, scarce footman, clay triple-lines, large twin-spot carpet and map-winged swift.

Whitecross Green Wood

SP 603145; 62ha; BBONT reserve
Mixed woodland and pond
Spring, summer

Straddling the county boundary between Oxfordshire and Buckinghamshire, a small portion of this reserve once formed part of the ancient Royal forest of Bernwood. Unfortunately some 60 per cent of the wood at the north-west end was planted with conifers between 1963 and 1965 by the Forestry Commission, but the reserve still boasts over 200 species of flowering plants. Wood white, purple emperor and black hairstreak

Scarlet tiger moth, a subject of special study at Parsonage Moor.

butterflies have all been recorded. Birds are well represented, with most woodland warblers, nightingale and, in very recent years, the nightjar. Mammals include fallow and muntjac deer and a large population of foxes.

Wychwood Forest

Permit only; 647ha; NCC reserve
Mixed woodland
Spring, early summer

Formerly a Royal Forest and at one time managed by coppicing, the wood is very varied, containing oak and ash together with large areas of hawthorn and Midland hawthorn, of blackthorn, elder, field maple and willow. Four small lime-rich ponds add a wetland interest and the site is important for a number of old-woodland lichens.

Juniper scrub and woodland vary the chalk grassland of Aston Rowant.

Somerset

To the naturalist and country-lover, Somerset is a region of contrasts. The landscapes range from the Mendip hills in the north which are carboniferous limestone deposits rising in places to 300m, to the Somerset Levels – once an extensive marsh. There is Taunton Deane, a vale of rich agricultural land and the three gentle ridges of the Quantocks, the Brendon Hills, and Blackdown; wild windswept Exmoor reaches to 516m on Dunkery Beacon and the coastline is still remarkably unspoilt.

A rough quadrilateral drawn between Weston-super-Mare, Glastonbury, Taunton and Bridgwater contains the unique Somerset Levels, much of which is below high-tide level. The Rivers Axe and Brue and Parrett with its many smaller tributaries flow from the hills down to Bridgwater Bay and frequently flood this vast area. At one time the Levels were sea, then marshland, but now much of the area is drained and the rivers contained. Those pastures which have not been ploughed and reseeded are rich with many flowers in the summer. Numerous plants and insects, many of them very rare, flourish in some 8000km of ditch or 'rhynes' as they are called on the Levels. The cries of nesting curlew, lapwing, snipe and redshank are still heard here; and in winter, wildfowl which have bred in the far north may assemble in their thousands, including the Bewick's swans from Siberia to feed on the flooded fields. Agricultural improvements have had their effects on the wildlife, especially modern drainage techniques and lowered water-tables, but perhaps the designation of the Levels as an Environmentally Sensitive Area (ESA) may restore this rich wealth.

Much of the peat moors in this low lying area of central Somerset have been removed to provide us with 'Grobags' and other horticultural products. The peat industry has destroyed one wildlife habitat but there is a chance that the holes which are left can be developed into a different but almost as valuable wildlife area. The last decade of the century could, with careful planning which has already started, see the Somerset peat moors emerge as one of Europe's prime wetland sites for wildlife.

BRIDGWATER BAY, with its wide expanses of mudflats at low tide, is part of a major migration route and vast numbers of waders can be seen. The most remarkable sight in July is the hundreds of shelduck which assemble here to moult. The hides erected by the Nature Conservancy Council provide ideal viewing places for this wealth of wildlife. A Severn Barrage could change all this but one can only hope that the essential research on the impact will be completed and considered before any decision is taken.

At the north end of Bridgwater Bay is BREAN DOWN, a western outlier of the Mendip Hills. Several rare flowers grow here, the most spectacular being the white rock-rose which flowers profusely from April until July. Tens of thousands of migrating birds use Brean Down as a stopping-off and re-fuelling place, best seen early in the morning to appreciate the numbers involved.

Also bordering Bridgwater Bay is BERROW DUNES, Somerset's only dune system. People flock there in their thousands and lack of proper management by the local authority is causing damage to the very wildlife and beauty which they come to enjoy. In winter, when the human visitors have gone, the sea buckthorn, which provides food for large numbers of thrushes are well worth a visit.

The beautiful natural wealth of the Mendip Hills can be viewed from public trails on nature reserves at EBBOR GORGE, Black Rock and Long Wood (MENDIP CONSERVATION AREA). The rich limestone woodlands here contain a wide range of spring flowers, including herb-Paris, and butterflies such as brimstone, orange tip, fritillaries and speckled wood. Breeding birds include blackcap, willow warbler and chiffchaff, and there is a good chance of seeing roe deer. Woodland management at Long Wood has set out to encourage wildlife and in May and early June there are few woods with which to compare it for beauty and tranquillity. In nearby Velvet Bottom special plants such as alpine penny-cress and spring sandwort grow on the lead spoil heaps produced from pre-Roman times until the 19th century.

The Blackdown Hills of the southern fringe of Somerset is a relatively unknown area with numerous oases of wildlife habitat. Some of the ancient woodland remnants of Neroche Forest such as the Somerset Trust for Nature Conservation's reserves at BOON'S COPSE and at THURLBEAR WOOD to the east of Taunton are magnificent in the early summer. Perhaps the gems of the Blackdowns are its bogs with *Sphagnum*, bog asphodel, lousewort and sundew. These occur along a spring-line where water seeping through the greensand meets the clay in the keuper marl. Hopefully several will become Somerset Trust reserves and be opened for public viewing.

An idea of the Brendon Hills in west Somerset can be obtained at HURSCOMBE reserve at the northern end of the new Wimbleball Lake. With wildfowl on the lake, buzzard and raven above, and whinchat in the gorse, it is a birdwatcher's paradise, while the frogs and butterflies, and marsh plants of the rich, wet grassland ensure that there is something for every nature-lover.

FYNE COURT, in the Quantock Hills, is the headquarters of the Somerset Trust. Much modified by man, the estate nevertheless contains much of interest – from stately old beech trees to three artificial ponds and lakes. The snowdrop and foxglove seasons are two favourite visiting periods, and the interpretative centre helps visitors gain an understanding of the animal and plant life of the area.

Apart from its magnificent display of wildlife, Somerset is a region of great scenic beauty offering dramatic views. From Wills Neck, the highest point of the Quantocks, it is possible to see no fewer than three National Parks – EXMOOR to the west, DARTMOOR (Devon) to the south west, and the BRECON BEACONS (Powys) in Wales to the north.

C.E.D. SMITH

Aisholt Ring Walk

ST 182338; c.9km; STNC
Circular trail in the Quantocks
Booklet from STNC
All year

The walk includes Wills Neck, which is the highest point in the Quantocks and affords spectacular views over Somerset, Devon and Wales.

Aller Wood

Permit only; 23.5ha; STNC reserve
Mixed woodland
Spring, summer

The small reserve, set within a much larger area of ancient woodland, includes an attractive range of ground plants below a canopy of oak, ash and small-leaved lime.

Asham Wood

Permit only; 33.4ha; STNC reserve
Rich woodland
No access off public right of way
Spring, early summer

The wood contains a very good range of tree species with a particularly rich ground flora, including meadow saffron, which is encouraged by active coppicing.

Axbridge Hill

Permit only; 11.5ha; STNC reserve
Limestone grassland and scrub
Spring, summer

The south-facing steep grassland slopes above Axbridge support the rare Somerset hair-grass. The scrub area is important for breeding birds, and there is a cave (which is not open to the public) containing greater horseshoe bats.

Beer Wood

ST 413316; 13ha; STNC reserve
Ancient woodland
Spring

The reserve of oak, ash, small-leaved lime and maple has a rich understorey and ground flora. There are superb views over the Somerset Levels.

Berrow Dunes

ST 293540; 135.6ha; Sedgemoor DC reserve
Dunes and foreshore
Late spring, early summer

The dunes, slacks and pools support a good insect and plant life, including lesser bulrush, marsh helleborine and heath spotted-orchid; the foreshore and mudflats are best for winter bird life.

Bickenhall Old Churchyard

ST 286197; 0.2ha; WdT reserve
Trees, grassland
Spring, summer

Old churchyards can be important for wildlife and this one, now deconsecrated, is no exception. It contains areas of unimproved grassland with many meadow flowers. There is a massive ancient yew tree, in the tradition of churchyards.

Biddle Combe Nature Trail

ST 569488; 4km; Wells Nat. Hist. and Arch. Soc
Valley trail through grass and woodland
Leaflet from Wells Museum
Spring, summer

The often damp trail passes through a good range of habitats with opportunities to see grassland, woodland and streamside plants and animals, with the accent on lime-loving species.

Blackmoor

Permit only, 10ha; Bristol University reserve
Educational reserve
Spring, summer

A typical range of lime-loving plants grows around the pools and slopes of the old lead workings.

Boon's Copse

Permit only; 3.6ha; STNC reserve
Ancient woodland
Spring

The copse, a remnant of the medieval Neroche Royal Forest, is mainly ash and oak, with an abundance of wild service-tree and aspen. Careful management of the scrub of blackthorn, hawthorn, sallow and hazel, as well as the young aspen has

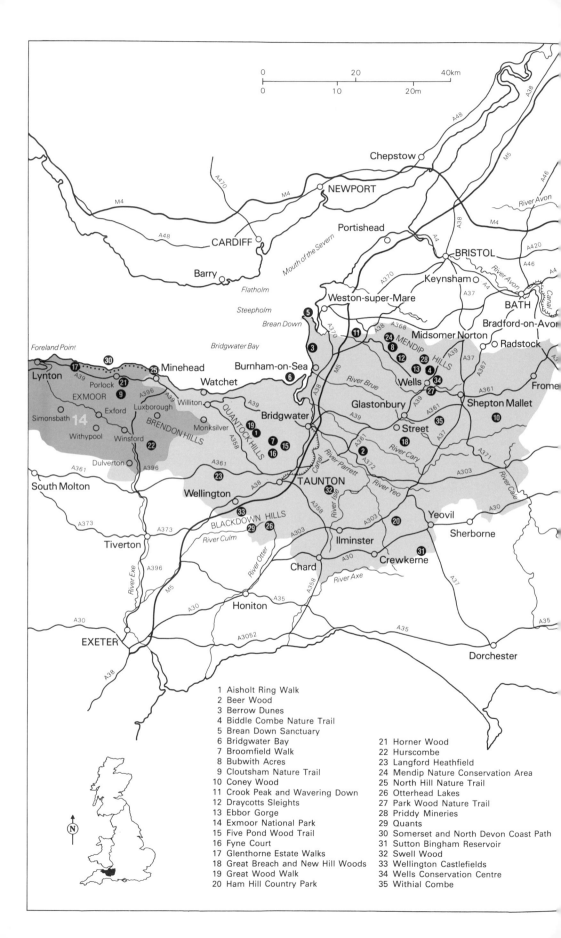

1 Aisholt Ring Walk
2 Beer Wood
3 Berrow Dunes
4 Biddle Combe Nature Trail
5 Brean Down Sanctuary
6 Bridgwater Bay
7 Broomfield Walk
8 Bubwith Acres
9 Cloutsham Nature Trail
10 Coney Wood
11 Crook Peak and Wavering Down
12 Draycotts Sleights
13 Ebbor Gorge
14 Exmoor National Park
15 Five Pond Wood Trail
16 Fyne Court
17 Glenthorne Estate Walks
18 Great Breach and New Hill Woods
19 Great Wood Walk
20 Ham Hill Country Park

21 Horner Wood
22 Hurscombe
23 Langford Heathfield
24 Mendip Nature Conservation Area
25 North Hill Nature Trail
26 Otterhead Lakes
27 Park Wood Nature Trail
28 Priddy Mineries
29 Quants
30 Somerset and North Devon Coast Path
31 Sutton Bingham Reservoir
32 Swell Wood
33 Wellington Castlefields
34 Wells Conservation Centre
35 Withial Combe

provided an ideal habitat for the increasingly rare nightingale. In 1987 two pairs of this celebrated songster established territories on the reserve. A wide ride through the wood provides a most interesting walk for the visitor and plenty of opportunities to see a good selection of woodland butterflies including the attractive white admiral.

Brean Down Sanctuary

ST 296586; 64ha; NT reserve
Limestone headland
Booklet from NT
All year

A great whale-backed ridge of limestone jutting out into the mudflats of the Severn Estuary, Brean Down forms an important landmark for migrating birds and insects. It is an outlier of the Mendip Hills with views of the island of STEEPHOLM and the Somerset Levels.

The plants vary according to the depth of soil and the exposure, which is so wild at times that only a few elder and hawthorn shrubs can survive. Privet and bramble form a low scrub which, together with bracken on the deeper soils and occasional heather, provides shelter for the smaller migrants. Rock samphire may be found on the seaward edges of the down, while grassy areas contain not only coastal plants such as thrift and buck's-horn plantain but also typical lime-loving herbs. The undoubted treasures of the area, though, grow in the shallowest, most rocky turf: dwarf sedge, Somerset hair-grass and white rock-rose all have very restricted distributions and are therefore of great interest to plant geographers.

The cliffs and rocky jumbles provide nest sites for birds such as jackdaw, kestrel and rock pipit while the scrubland and grassland are used by stonechat, meadow pipit and skylark. Mallard and shelduck breed in the area and are joined in spring and autumn by many migrant species.

Then the mudflats below the down and the saltmarsh behind it teem with birds. Redshank and oystercatcher, snipe and curlew, godwit, knot, lapwing and golden plover gather here for food or shelter. Geese may fly in from the Arctic to feed or a visiting peregrine may maraud the tired migrants.

Bridgwater Bay

ST 278464; 2400ha; NCC reserve
Estuary, saltflats and lagoons
Access limited to rights of way and public hides
Leaflet from NCC, Taunton
Winter and migration times

A rising tide, flooding the huge shallow bay, pushes vast numbers of wildfowl and waders into the shelter of the Parrett Estuary, where they may be watched from hides, or on to the scrapes by the hides. A feature of the reserve is that it is a moulting ground for shelduck, and at any time of year these strikingly beautiful birds may be seen feeding on the mudflats or flighting strongly across the estuary. Another important gathering is that of whimbrel in spring; up to 1000 pause here before moving northwards to breed; with perhaps around 200 curlew also present this provides an ideal opportunity to study the differences between the two birds.

Many thousand duck congregate in winter, with up to 2500 each of shelduck, mallard and wigeon together with smaller numbers of pintail, shoveler and teal. At migration times large flocks of dunlin, black-tailed godwit, lapwing, oystercatcher and redshank spread out across the mudflats or stand roosting in packed ranks when the tide drives them off their feeding grounds. Small numbers of bar-tailed godwit, knot, grey plover and turnstone are also usually present. Peregrines may be seen hunting over the reserve in winter.

The area is also one of note for the botanist

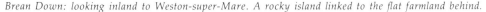

Brean Down: looking inland to Weston-super-Mare. A rocky island linked to the flat farmland behind.

with a variation of habitat from grassland to open mud and sand, including a spread of marsh and a shingle bank. Yellow horned-poppy occurs beside the path to the hides while other shingle species include henbane and knotted clover. Sea clover grows on the sea wall of the Parrett.

Broomfield Walk

ST 222322; c.8km; STNC
Country walk
Booklet from STNC
Spring, early summer, autumn

The walk passes through a range of agricultural land, woodland and coniferous forest with some spectacular viewpoints overlooking Somerset or over the River Severn into Wales.

Bubwith Acres

ST 470537; 5.2ha; STNC reserve
Limestone heath, downland and scrub
Permit only off right of way
Spring, summer

Outcrops of rock carry sprays of maidenhair spleenwort, wall-rue and the rather uncommon rustyback, while the limestone heath is character-ised by a mixture of acid and lime-loving plants such as salad burnet, heather and dwarf thistle. The scrub encourages a variety of birds including linnet, stonechat and whitethroat. The reserve is part of the MENDIP NATURE CONSERVATION AREA.

Burtle Moor

Permit only; 14.8ha; STNC reserve
Grazing marsh
Spring, early summer

Characteristic birds of the Somerset Levels, curlew, redshank and snipe, breed among a mix of marsh plants such as marsh-marigold, marsh pennywort, ragged-Robin and meadow thistle.

Catcott

Permit only; 14ha; STNC reserve
Fen meadow and heathy wetland
Spring, summer

The track which divides the reserve is a narrow straight drove, defined by low alders, bulrush, yellow iris and reed sweet-grass, sometimes almost a tunnel beneath the trees, sometimes an open peaty lane where the air is filled with the continual whizz of dragonflies.

After the last ice age, an acid raised bog developed in this area, overlying the rich fen peat beneath, but very little of the bog survived the drainage and peat digging which have turned the Somerset Levels to farmland. South of the drove, however, surrounded by a belt of wet woodland, a number of acid species still survive.

Broad stands of bog myrtle surround a mix of bog and fen plants, a luxuriant aromatic jungle sheltered by trees and shrubs. The acid-loving plants include cross-leaved heath and purple moor-grass, together with common cottongrass,

tormentil and creeping willow, with marsh penny-wort and devil's-bit scabious grading into a fenlike mix of bittersweet and meadowsweet, of hemp-agrimony, yellow loosestrife and yellow iris, purple-loosestrife, ragged-Robin, skullcap and milk parsley. The wet woodland, or carr, is mainly of birch, alder and grey willow but is varied with alder buckthorn and guelder-rose or, where drier, ash and hawthorn. The ground cover contains a variety of species including two uncommon ferns, the tall royal fern and the attractive small marsh fern.

One of the very few areas unspoiled by peat extraction or modern farming, the meadows at Catcott contain a wonderful mixture of plants associated with traditional management. The grazed meadows contain marsh bedstraw, marsh-marigold, jointed rush, common spike-rush and creeping-Jenny while the hay meadows have deep spreads of taller plants, wild angelica, common meadow-rue, meadowsweet and meadow thistle, with yellow loosestrife, water dock, marsh cinque-foil and southern marsh-orchid.

The rich dampness of the reserve encourages a great range of insects, together with a range of woodland birds with particularly good numbers of willow tit. The meadowlands offer breeding sites for curlew, redshank and snipe.

Cheddar Cliffs

Permit only; 80ha; NT reserve
Limestone cliffs
Spring, summer

The cliffs carry a variety of plants according to soil depth, light and dampness. Several unusual species occur including lesser meadow-rue, green-winged orchid and Cheddar pink.

Cheddar Wood

Permit only; 39.2ha; STNC reserve
Small-leaved lime woodland
Spring, early summer

Purple gromwell is a speciality among a fine range of lime-loving plants in an ancient coppice woodland which contains ash, hazel, small-leaved lime, field maple, oak and wild service-tree.

Cheddar Wood Fields

Permit only; 2.5ha; STNC reserve
Limestone grassland and scrub
Summer

The south-facing grasslands adjoin CHEDDAR WOODS and are important for blue gromwell, a British *Red Data Book* plant. Invertebrates are also of interest.

Chilton Moor

Permit only; 2.8ha; STNC reserve
Grazing marsh
Summer

A key area of the Somerset Levels, snipe and redshank regularly breed here, and the reserve is important for passage migrants. The damp Levels grassland is botanically very rich and plant species include tubular water-dropwort, meadow thistle, meadowsweet, cowslip and pepper-saxifrage.

Cloutsham Nature Trail

SS 903438; 5km; ENPC–NT
Moorland and woodland trail
Booklet from ENP Information Centre, Minehead
Summer, spring

Covering a small part of the Holnicote Estate on the edge of HORNER WOOD, the trail winds through moor and valley land, crossing the attractive East Water stream. It provides a range from damp oak woodland to open gorse moor with a rich animal life, which includes red deer and raven, brown trout and buzzard, not far from the bracken and heather top of Dunkery Beacon.

Coney Wood

ST 692389; 1.2ha; WdT reserve
Mixed woodland
Spring, early summer

This small attractive woodland stands beside a tributary of the River Alham and holds a resident population of badger.

Crook Peak and Wavering Down

ST 398558; 288ha; NT
Grassland, woodland and heath
Spring, summer

Along the steep, south-facing slopes of the Mendips deep valleys offer a wide range of habitats including chalk downland, chalk heathland, woodland and scrub. The grassland supports fairy flax, salad burnet and the rare Somerset grass; on more acid soils heather, bell heather and western gorse grow close to wild thyme, dropwort and common rock-rose. Kings Wood is ancient, with small-leaved lime, field maple, whitebeam and wild service-tree, and associated flowers include columbine and meadow saffron. There are interesting cave deposits at the southern end of the Peak where the remains of spotted hyaena, lion, mammoth, suslik and reindeer have been found.

Dommett Wood

Permit only; 13.8ha; STNC reserve
Beech woodland
Spring, early summer

The woodland, standing on a steep scarp slope, is varied with heathland clearings and is noted for bluebells. Badger and roe deer are present.

Draycott Sleights

ST 483513; 40ha; STNC reserve
Limestone grassland
Spring, summer

Sleights is a local word for sheep pasture and the reserve, lying on the south-facing slope of the Mendip Hills, is mainly limestone grassland. Some, on the deeper soils, was ploughed during

World War II, but much has been unaltered for probably hundreds of years. Over 200 species of flowering plants have been recorded.

Typical on the thinner soils are rock-rose, marjoram, bird's-foot-trefoil, horseshoe and kidney vetch, dwarf thistle and autumn lady's-tresses, while on the deeper soils oxeye daisy, knapweed, salad burnet and small scabious are found. Due to lack of grazing, a scrub of hawthorn, gorse and blackthorn has developed in the south-west corner and ash trees are also regenerating here. Ultimately, unless managed, this would form secondary woodland and destroy the grassland habitat.

The reserve is particularly important for butterflies and 34 species have been recorded including marbled whites, chalkhill blues and the occasional spectacular Adonis blue.

There is an active badger sett and a short cave (access strictly forbidden) is home to a colony of lesser horseshoe bats.

Birds are not particularly plentiful on the grassland but there are skylarks and meadow pipits. Flocks of linnets and goldfinches feed in the scrub and even the occasional cirl bunting. Buzzard and hobby can sometimes be seen.

Dundon Beacon

Permit only; 28ha; STNC reserve
Limestone downland, scrub and woodland
Leaflet from STNC
Spring, early summer

The ancient oak–ash woodland contains some splendid field maple, a tall contrast with the spread of scrub where nightingales may be heard, while the butterfly-rich grassland has lime-loving plants such as autumn lady's-tresses, bee orchid and musk mallow.

Durleigh Reservoir Sanctuary

Permit only; 31ha; WWA reserve
Birdwatchers' reservoir
Key available from reservoir ranger on request
All year

A hide overlooks the reservoir so that watchers may observe the extensive reedbeds and willow swamp where migrant warblers breed. Many species of duck together with Bewick's swan may visit the sanctuary in winter.

Ebbor Gorge

See map; 46ha; NT–NCC reserve
Wooded limestone gorge
Permit only off pathways
Leaflets from site or NCC
Spring, early summer

To see the gorge at Ebbor you must park, walk down through the green woodland and follow the climbing path through the rocks which form the walls of the chasm.

Despite the fact that the gorge has long been dry, it was cut by the action of water, and at one time the headwaters of the River Axe flowed through here. Now the Axe emerges at Wookey

Hole, having cut itself a new channel underground through the porous limestone.

The gorge is cut back into the Mendip plateau, and although much of this higher land is invaded by ash woods, near the edge of the scarp thinner soils show a remnant of limestone grassland. Gorse, heather and foxglove, heath bedstraw and common bent are found where rain has washed the lime out of the deeper soils, but where the soils are shallow and exposure has inhibited scrub a splendid variety of lime-loving plants may occur.

Below, in the damp shade of the gorge, are gardens of ferns, brittle bladder-fern, uncommon in the south, the rare Tunbridge filmy-fern, hart's-tongue, maidenhair fern, maidenhair spleenwort, polypody, rustyback and wall-rue. Other plants enjoy the shelter: wood melick, shining crane's-bill and wall lettuce grow here, together with hairy rock-cress and herb-Robert which also grow well on the screes. Although no river runs through the gorge, a stream will be seen in the Primrose Valley below the ravine, and this occurs because coal measures form the bedrock. Although lime-loving plants such as hart's-tongue and hard shield-fern occur on the coal measures' soils, so too do more general species such as male-fern, lady-fern and broad buckler-fern, while even the acid-loving hard fern can find a suitable habitat and marsh or moorland plants – small and plicate sweet-grass for instance – may be found near the source of the stream.

Small damp meadows provide a site for ragged-Robin, marsh-marigold, meadowsweet, greater bird's-foot-trefoil and lesser spearwort, together with fine stands of common twayblade in patches of scrub and an autumn display of meadow saffron. Other areas of the valley floor and the lower woodland slopes carry scattered oak and ash standards over a shrub layer of coppiced hazel.

The age pattern of the Ebbor woodlands seems to indicate a widespread planting, or a general regrowth, around the mid-nineteenth century, followed by a heavy thinning around the time of World War I. This has led to a high-forest woodland where large standards are scattered among a younger generation of trees to give a mix of ash and oak with smaller ash, wych elm, field maple and common whitebeam. Hornbeam occurs occasionally, thought to be native here at its western limit, and beech has long been established, shown by the use of beech stakes in the Bronze Age hazel-pole roadways. Small-leaved lime may be locally common in some places while the varying understorey includes a scatter of hazel and hawthorn but also the characteristic limestone species dogwood, privet, spindle and wayfaring-tree with guelder-rose and holly, tangles of honey-suckle and spreads of traveller's-joy.

Spring brings a carpet of bluebells to floor the woodland, varied with wood anemone, lesser celandine and primrose, and later drifts of dog's mercury, enchanter's-nightshade and bramble, woodland grasses, ferns and clumps of great wood-rush. Splashes of colour are added by yellow archangel, bugle, goldilocks buttercup, early dog-violet and wood-sorrel with less common plants

such as broad-leaved helleborine, greater butter-fly-orchid, nettle-leaved bellflower and purple gromwell. With its wide range of habitat, the reserve is obviously attractive to animals. The mammals include resident fox and badger, together with a typical range of small mammals such as wood mouse, voles and shrews. Among the birds are the characteristic western species such as grey wagtail and buzzard, together with woodcock which is uncommon in western England. Typical woodland birds include green and great spotted woodpecker, treecreeper and nuthatch, with tawny owl, kestrel and sparrowhawk; among the birds of scrubland and clearings are grasshopper warbler, whitethroat and goldfinch, cuckoo and meadow pipit.

Butterflies enjoy the range of woodland, scrub and grassland and over 30 species have been recorded. Woodland species include purple hairstreak, white-letter hairstreak, white admiral and the two fritillaries, silver-washed and high brown. The dark green fritillary is a fast-flying species which might be seen with marbled white, brown argus, common, chalkhill or silver studded blue around the plateau edge above the gorge.

Edford Wood

Permit only; 15.6ha; STNC reserve
Mixed woodland
Spring, early summer

The reserve protects a block of ancient woodland straddling a river, where ash and alder, birch and oak stand above a typical rich ground cover while the river adds its own wildlife interest.

Exmoor National Park

See map; 68,635ha; ENPC
Uplands, valleys, woods and coast
Booklets and leaflets from ENPC
Spring, summer

High on the north coast of Devon and Somerset, Exmoor stands as a land of heather and bracken, of peat bogs, mires and steep valleys draining south to the lowlands or, fast and sudden, cutting the hog-backed coastal hills to the sea. The valleys are dressed with splendid woods, rich in wildlife, while the uplands are the domain of the Exmoor pony and the woods and valleys home to red deer.

Ebbor Gorge: white rock contrasts with green shade.

The Exmoor, alone of British ponies, seems to have missed the improvements of modern breeding techniques and to represent a type of British hill pony which in many ways parallels the primitive Przewalski's horse. The red deer winter in the valley woodlands and roar at the autumn rut. Apart from the breeding season, hinds and stags remain separate, and at any time of year these beautiful animals are a magnificent sight on the hills.

The heathland is usually dominated by heather in association with plants such as bilberry, bracken, bristle bent and gorse. Near the coast bell heather and western gorse may be dominant. The wetter and more peaty moorland carries abundant purple moorgrass in association with deergrass, common and hare's-tail cottongrass and heath spotted-orchid. *Sphagnum* mosses are common in the patches of bog, where cross-leaved heath, round-leaved sundew, bog asphodel and large-flowered butterwort may also be found.

Raven, buzzard, merlin perhaps, curlew and ring ouzel, wheatear, whinchat and stonechat are among the birds of the moorland, while dipper and grey wagtail may be seen on the streams.

Where the streams cut down into the steep winding valleys, woodlands such as HORNER WOOD add a wide range of typical bird life and the coastal sites hold guillemot and razorbill, with ringed plover and dunlin where beaches or saltmarshes break the line of the cliffs.

Some of the fascination of the natural history of Exmoor may be seen in the presence of both northern and oak-eggar moths. The northern eggar is a heather-feeding upland race which here may be a glacial relict species while the oak eggar is a lowland race feeding on plants such as bramble and hawthorn. Both races remain as separate populations by having evolved different lifestyles.

The National Park Committee publishes several guides, such as that for the CLOUTSHAM NATURE TRAIL to explain the interest of the park.

Five Pond Wood Trail

ST 224275; 1.5km; NT–STNC
Woodland nature trail
Leaflet from STNC
Spring, early summer

The trail runs through a streamside woodland rich in bluebell, marsh-marigold and other spring flowers.

Fyne Court

ST 223321; c.9ha; NT–STNC reserve
Old estate woodlands and ponds
Leaflets from information centre
Spring, early summer

An arboretum, lake, ponds, beech woodland and old quarry area provide a wide range of habitat with a good variety of plants and animals. The buildings house the offices of STNC, a shop, lecture hall and an interpretative centre for the Quantocks.

Glenthorne Estate Walks

SS 794486; 1.6–3.2km; ENPC
Wooded coastline trails
Leaflet from ENPC
Spring, early summer

A nature trail, including the pinetum and the beach, together with two shorter walks, demonstrate some of the wildlife interest of this nineteenth-century estate with its views across the River Severn to South Wales.

Great Breach and New Hill Woods

ST 505325; 79.4ha; STNC reserve
Mixed woodland, and limestone grassland
Spring, summer

The mainly oak–ash woodland, lying on heavy clay above slopes of limestone grassland, includes both small-leaved lime and hornbeam, with alder in the wettest places, above a wide range of smaller plants. Over 500 species of fungi occur and the blend of wood and grassland has attracted 52 species of butterfly. Nightingale and woodcock are among the breeding birds.

Great Wood Walk

ST 165360; 8km; STNC
Circular walk chiefly in FC woodlands
Booklet from STNC
Spring, early summer

This Quantock walk through coniferous woods and parkland offers the possibility of seeing red deer.

Ham Hill Country Park

ST 478167; 62ha; Yeovil DC
Disused quarries and spoil heaps
Booklet from Yeovil DC
Spring, summer

Limestone quarrying has left spoil heaps and hollows, together with old quarry faces of rock, which combine to give a variety of wildlife interest from plants such as common rock-rose, autumn lady's-tresses, musk thistle and ploughman's-spikenard to birds such as kestrel and yellowhammer or butterflies such as small copper, marbled white and dingy skipper.

Holford

Permit only; 5.3ha; STNC reserve
Ancient woodland
Spring

Also known as the Kelting reserve, this oak–ash woodland with alder, willow and thorn scrub lies at the downstream end of Holford Glen.

Horner Wood

SS 897454; 405ha; NT
Mixed woodland
Permit only off pathways
Spring, early summer

In early spring a cold wind blows across the higher slopes of Exmoor but the valley woodlands, like Horner Wood, are well sheltered.

Most of the wood is several thousand years old, indicated by the presence of ivy-leaved bellflower, bilberry, goldenrod, scaly male-fern, Cornish moneywort, slender St John's-wort, lesser skullcap, wood spurge and bitter vetch. These plants are part of a suite of woodland species which do not colonise easily in the west; the presence of one or two is not conclusive, but that of most of the species is very strong evidence for ancient woodland. The wood, of course, has not remained unchanged but has been strongly modified by centuries of management and it is a mosaic of different types. Horner is now mainly high-forest, grown on from the old coppice stools, but the patterns of previous management give it a varied appearance.

Hazel and holly or birch and rowan make up most of the understorey while the ground cover is often a dense spread of bramble; but an interesting change may be seen as the woods climb higher and bracken and bilberry show in the higher oakwoods which merge into heather and gorse as they meet the open moor.

The streams attract typical birds such as dipper and grey wagtail while the variation of the site is answered by woodland species which include the western trio of wood warbler, redstart and pied flycatcher with many other commoner birds. The most dramatic of the mammals is undoubtedly the red deer and Horner Wood is one of their three main winter strongholds.

The wood holds a very fine lichen flora, with over 10 species recorded including many that are rare. The aerial epiphyte *Usnea articulata*, now confined to south western England, is present and the species occurring are representative of the ancient woodland in north western Europe.

Hurscombe (Wimbleball Lake)

SS 974317; 18.6ha; STNC reserve
Reservoir-side old farmland
Access only on public rights of way
Leaflet from STNC or site dispenser
Spring, early summer

Farmland, reverting to scrub and marsh, an old larch plantation and hedges, provide a good variety of habitat, while the reserve already attracts several species of wintering duck.

Langford Heathfield

ST 100236; 91.5ha; STNC reserve
Lowland heath, ancient woodland
Permit only off pathways
Spring, summer

A fine variety of habitat, oak woodland, birch and willow scrub, dry and wet acid heathland, attracts birds and butterflies to the reserve. The wildlife interest, the richness of warblers, of wetland sedges and other plants, will be illustrated by a nature trail as soon as this is established.

Mascall's Wood

Permit only; 4.8ha; STNC reserve
Ancient woodland and grassland
Spring, early summer

A fine variety of trees such as ash, hazel, holly, small-leaved lime, field maple, oak and yew above a rich ground cover contrasts with the sunlit limestone grassland which adds to the range of butterflies and other animals.

Mendip Nature Conservation Area

ST 482545; 586ha; STNC reserves
Cheddar limestone reserves represented by Black Rock,
Long Wood, Velvet Bottom and others
Leaflets from STNC
Spring, early summer

Black Rock, Long Wood and Velvet Bottom reserves lie around the winding drove in a beautiful and fascinating complex of woodland, scrub, grassland and craggy rocks.

Long Wood contains a good variety of tree species but ash is probably the most successful, with an understorey of hazel and hawthorn and the lime-loving group of dogwood, privet, spindle, wayfaring-tree and field maple. The limestone influence is underlined by rich-woodland plants such as dog's mercury and enchanter's-nightshade with the unusual herb-Paris, while recent coppicing encourages a brilliant show of flowers in spring. Steep, rocky slopes are thickly ferned, a wonderful green spread of hart's-tongue, male-fern and lady-fern, polypody, broad buckler-fern, maidenhair spleenwort and hard shield-fern, while the valley bottom is damp enough for meadowsweet and willow species along the stream bed. During the summer the stream disappears into a swallow hole, emerging again below the Cheddar Gorge.

The shoulder of the drove outside the wood is rich in downland plants where scrub with bracken and foxglove opens out. Primrose and eyebright, lady's bedstraw, common rock-rose, slender St John's-wort, quaking-grass, carline thistle, dwarf thistle and small scabious all occur.

Velvet Bottom is a narrow grassy valley, hummocked and pitted at first by old lead workings, then dropping in levels, below, where lead was filtered out. The valley sides are rich in limestone plants but the bottoms are still so highly contaminated that intensive grazing is dangerous and the grassland is deep and coarse. The twisting valley is sheltered and rich in butterflies.

Black Rock reserve, a slope above the drove, is chiefly steep grazed grassland, with a block of planted conifers and areas of native woods, a rich reserve with over 200 tree and flower species recorded. The limestone flowers again appear, and the scrub is good for butterflies and birds.

The complex's special interests probably lie in the geological features shown in the quarries, in archaeological features such as Rhino Cave in Long Wood, where hyaena and woolly rhinoceros teeth have been found, and in the ecological significance of the lead-contaminated Velvet Bottom which was worked from pre-Roman times until the 1880s.

Mill Water

Permit only; 0.8ha; Tony Parsons, Barnfield,
Tower Hill Rd, Crewkerne, Somerset
Small wetland
Spring, summer

A pond, the old millstream, a fine area of reed-swamp and a spread of scrub make up a most attractive small reserve with a good range of insects and birds, protected and recorded by the enthusiasm of its owner.

Mounsey

Permit only; 57ha; STNC reserve
Ancient woodland and marshes
All year

Many rare lichens and bryophytes are associated with this very important western oak and ash wood in the Barle Valley. Redstarts, pied flycatchers and wood warblers all breed in high numbers. The valley meadows support interesting plant and butterfly populations.

North Hill Nature Trail

SS 968474; 5km; ENPC
Foreshore-to-moorland circular walk
Booklet from ENPC
Spring, summer

The trail climbs from the harbour up the landslipped cliffs through planted woodlands and tangles of bramble, ivy, honeysuckle and madder, to the moorland where gorse and western gorse flower high above the Bristol Channel and bilberry and heather blow in the fresh upland breeze.

North Lodge Copse

ST 397123; 0.5ha; WdT reserve
Mixed woodland
Spring, summer

A small roadside wood with a good variety of tree species.

Otterhead Lakes

ST 224141; 8ha; STNC reserve
Woodland, marsh and lakeside
Nature trail leaflet from STNC or on site
All year

The reserve surrounds two lakes managed by Wessex Water Authority as a fishery and water-supply source. The marsh and woodland are of interest for birds, dragonflies and bog plants.

Park Wood Nature Trail

ST 551458; c.3km. Wells Nat. Hist. and Arch. Soc.
Circular walk from Wells centre through woodland
Booklet from Wells Museum
Spring, early summer

The trail passes the moat of the Bishop's Palace and crosses, through meadowland, to a good damp woodland nearby.

Bridgwater Bay: the Parrett Estuary.

Perry Mead

Permit only; 2.5ha; STNC reserve
Meadowland
Summer

A small area of meadows which adjoins the River Cary and has a good wetland flora.

Priddy Mineries

ST 547515; 49.2ha; STNC reserve
Wetland and limestone grassland
Permit only off rights of way
Spring, summer

An area of former mineral workings, the reserve includes limestone grassland while large pools provide a wide range of interest such as breeding great crested newt and a variety of dragonflies and water beetles.

Quants

ST 189876; 14ha; STNC reserve
Mixed woodland, scrub and rough grazing
Spring, summer

The reserve is a mosaic of woodland, scrub and rough grazed heathland, partially damaged prior to purchase by woodland felling and conifer plantings. Part of the wood however is ancient with a rich ground flora including adder's-tongue. There are a number of interesting lichens with several rare species on the old oak and ash standards. The remaining woodland areas are secondary consisting of birch, with some oak ash and sycamore, and support breeding birds such as garden warbler, blackcap and nightingale. The heathland has been partly invaded by bracken, but bell heather, bilberry and heath spotted-orchid survive and nightjars have been recorded.

Rodney Stoke

Permit only; 35ha; NCC reserve
Limestone woodland and some grassland
Leaflet from NCC
Spring, early summer

Chiefly ash woodland, the reserve also supports a wide range of other species and a good ground flora including nettle-leaved bellflower, meadow saffron and purple gromwell. The woodland, scrub and grassland encourage some 30 butterfly species.

Screech Owl

Permit only; 25ha; SCC reserve
Disused brickpit
All year

The wetland reserve, part of a group of old brickpits, is centred on a pond rich in invertebrate species together with a fine stand of common reed. The reedbed provides a winter roost for large numbers of starling and is a site at which uncommon birds such as little gull and spotted crake have been recorded; duck such as shoveler may often be seen on the marshy ground near the river.

Pinkworthy pond: the stillness of dawn at an Exmoor pool.

Searts Copse

ST 671302; 0.3ha; WdT reserve
Deciduous wood
Spring, summer

Despite its small size, the copse – with large oaks and a hazel understorey – is rich in plants and insects. There is an interesting wet area.

Shapwick Heath

Permit only; 221ha; NCC reserve
Remnant of Somerset Levels fenland
Spring, summer

Marsh and fen on rich peatlands, most of which have now been destroyed by drainage or cutting, the reserve contains a rich variety of plants such as marsh fern and an outstanding range of insects.

Somerset and North Devon Coast Path

SS 793487–971467; 25km; CC
Part of long-distance coastal footpath
Booklet from CC or HMSO bookshops
Spring, summer

From County Gate to Minehead the path, part of the South West Peninsula Coast Path, undulates from sea level to the hills above the Bristol Channel providing a wealth of wildlife interest.

South Hill

Permit only; 2.8ha; STNC reserve
Limestone grassland and scrub
Spring, summer

The old quarry, where rock was worked for limestone flags, has been colonised by a fine variety of lime-loving plants and scrub, and attracts both breeding birds and butterflies.

Street Heath

Permit only; 7.6ha; STNC–SCC reserve
Lowland heath
Spring, summer

Old peat diggings, wet heath and birch woodland combine to provide a wide range of habitats, but suffer from a lowered watertable caused by continued peak extraction nearby. Despite this, many attractive insects and birds may be found. The plant life includes species such as bog asphodel, common and pale butterwort, lesser butterfly orchid, heath spotted-orchid and least bur-reed.

Sutton Bingham Reservoir

ST 543095; 1.6ha; WWA
Reservoir and marshy fringes
All year

Throughout the year a good variety of water birds may be seen on and around this reservoir on the Somerset/Dorset border.

Swell Wood

ST 361238; 30ha; RSPB reserve
Deciduous woodland
Spring, summer

On the south side of WEST SEDGEMOOR wetland reserve lies this strip of woodland. A deciduous wood with a good variety of trees and shrubs, the site is most important for its heronry. Over 60 pairs of herons have been counted, making it one of the largest colonies in southern England. Jackdaws, marsh tits, nuthatches and woodpeckers also nest in the mature oaks, while nightingales, blackcaps and garden warblers are found in the open areas with a dense shrub layer.

Tealham Moor

Permit only; 45ha; STNC reserve
Grazing marsh in ten blocks
Spring, summer

A splendid example of the Somerset Levels marsh-lands, the reserve holds a fine range of typical plants and wetland breeding birds. An artificial scrape increases the interest for waterbirds and in winter attracts a variety of wildfowl and waders.

Thurlbear Wood

Permit only; 10.4ha; STNC reserve
Rich mixed woodland, limestone scrub and grassland
Spring, early summer

The upper woodland is chiefly old coppiced hazel with field maple and hawthorn below oak and some ash standards, as well as at least one huge wild cherry tree. Wide areas carpeted with ivy have clumps of stinking iris, wood spurge, dog's mercury, and small violets. Beneath the trees is a bright mosaic of woodland plants including bugle, enchanter's-nightshade and wild strawberry with a variety of grasses and sedges.

Below the slope an old lime kiln still stands, now capped with trees and shrubs. Dogwood and wayfaring-tree add to the understorey with traveller's-joy at the woodland edges. An area of grassland containing a range of downland species is hummocked with rounded ants' nests and hedged with open scrub.

Vigo Wood

Permit only; 14ha; STNC reserve
Mixed woodland
Spring, early summer

The oak–ash woodland contains some unusual pollarded trees and stands above a rich ground cover. Areas of bracken and scrub attract a good range of breeding birds and the reserve is notable as a wintering ground for woodcock.

Wellington Castlefields

ST 139175; 10ha; STNC reserve
Woodland, wet grassland and scrub
Spring, summer

The very attractive reserve below the Wellington Monument overlooks the Vale of Taunton Deane. The woodland shows an interesting range from dry acid oak to wetter ash, maple and alder, and has a similarly varied selection of flowering plants. Dyer's greenweed, devils'-bit scabious, sneezewort and meadow thistle abound in the wet grassland which is full of butterflies.

Wells Conservation Centre

ST 564458; 1ha; STNC reserve
Wildlife education centre
Group visits by arrangement
All year

An old cemetery and chapel restored as a wildlife garden, display centre and educational facility.

Westcombe

Permit only; 4.8ha; STNC reserve
Mixed woodland
Spring, summer

Despite the decline of otters in the bordering river Westcombe still holds the fascination of a typical mixed woodland.

Westhay Heath

Permit only; 6ha; STNC reserve
Peat workings, reedbed and scrub
Dangerous site, permit must be obtained from STNC
Summer

Worked-out peat excavations have been flooded to create open water pools, reedbeds and fringing marsh vegetation supporting waterrail.

Westhay Moor

Permit only; 39.8ha; STNC reserve
Remnant of raised bog
Spring, summer

Only two small areas of the Somerset peat moors have been saved from peat extraction and Westhay Moor demonstrates, with a mix of species such as *Sphagnum* mosses, cottongrasses, deergrass, heather and cross-leaved heath, much of the beauty that has been lost. The reserve also contains a large area of worked-out peatland which is being developed into prime wetland wildlife area.

West Sedgemoor

ST 361238; 373ha; RSPB reserve
Wet grazing marsh and woodland
All year

Probably the most important spring passage site for whimbrel in all Britain and one of the richest for breeding waders in south west England, the reserve consists of low-lying meadows intersected by ditches where curlew, black-tailed godwit, lapwing, redshank and snipe breed. In winter the shallow pools attract golden plover, mallard, teal and occasional Bewick's swan, together with huge numbers of lapwing.

Withial Combe

ST 576375; 7ha; STNC reserve
Ancient woodland
Spring

The steeply incised gully and waterfall has fringing woodland of oak, ash and small-leaved lime, but parts have been decimated by Dutch elm disease. There is a rich ground flora.

Wyndham Woods

Permit only; 16.6ha; STNC reserve
Ancient woodland
Spring, summer

Two wet, low-lying woods near Williton which support a rich ground flora with several typical ancient woodland indicator plants.

Light and shade in Ashen Copse, Somerset.

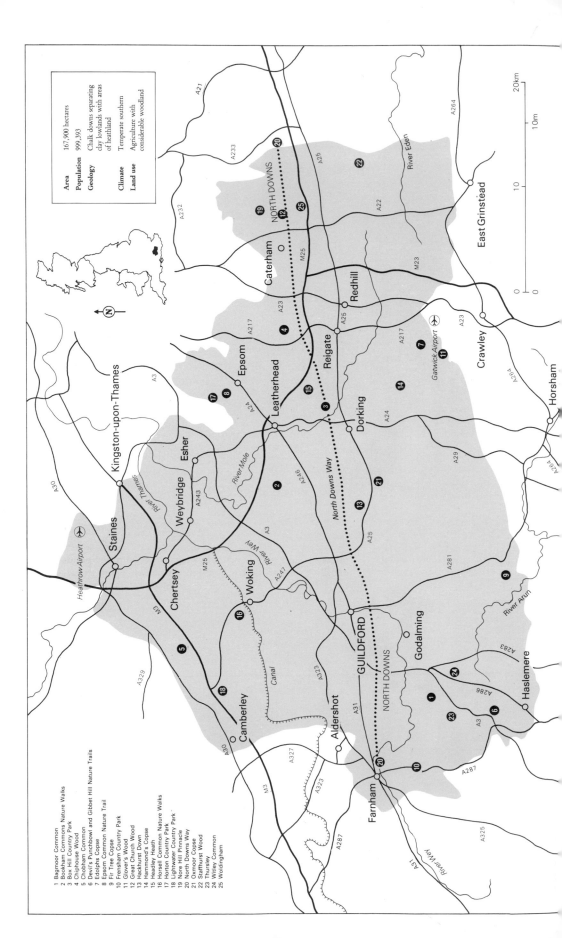

Area	167,900 hectares
Population	999,393
Geology	Chalk downs separating clay lowlands with areas of heathland
Climate	Temperate southern
Land use	Agriculture with considerable woodland

1 Bagmoor Common
2 Bookham Commons Nature Walks
3 Box Hill Country Park
4 Chipstead Wood
5 Chobham Common
6 Devil's Punchbowl and Gibbet Hill Nature Trails
7 Edolphs Copse
8 Epsom Common Nature Trail
9 Fir Tree Copse
10 Frensham Country Park
11 Glover's Wood
12 Great Church Wood
13 Hackhurst Down
14 Hammond's Copse
15 Headley Heath
16 Horsell Common Nature Walks
17 Horton Country Park
18 Lightwater Country Park
19 Nore Hill Pinnacle
20 North Downs Way
21 Oxmoor Copse
22 Staffhurst Wood
23 Thursley
24 Witley Common
25 Woldingham

Surrey

Surrey is not what it seems. It looks like a predominantly woodland county, just as it was for centuries past; but the abundance of trees hides the facts that about half Surrey's total area is urbanised, and that it has a higher density of population than almost any other county save the Metropolitan areas. However, this does not mean that wildlife has been squeezed out. On the contrary, much of the urbanisation includes relatively low-density, residential properties, in which wildlife is often encouraged. Moreover, many areas of industrial land include exhausted mineral workings which are often of very considerable wildlife value. For example, there are over 1000ha of flooded gravelpits in north Surrey alone. Together with some large and shallow reservoirs, these constitute a major wetland component, rich in wildlife and important at the national level for breeding and migrating birds. The urban areas of north Surrey have extensive parks and open spaces, and are penetrated by the radially arranged railway routes into London. These allow wildlife access well into the heavily built-up outskirts of the metropolis. The county is also traversed north–south and east–west by new motorways, the margins of which may, in the future, also prove to be important habitats and dispersal routes for plants and animals.

The more rural parts of Surrey, the south and west, are characterised by small farms and villages, abundant hedgerows and copses, small streams and ponds. There are no really extensive or unbroken areas of any single habitat; even the forestry plantations are relatively small. Thus, what characterises the landscape and wildlife of Surrey is not so much the apparent domination by trees and woods, but the extraordinary variety of small and diverse fragments, dominated by direct human influence.

These two factors, diversity and development, are interlinked. The development has been continuous for thousands of years: grazing, coppicing, digging, clearing and cultivation, and building. All have left their mark and contribute to the diversity. This in turn owes a lot to the varied geology of Surrey. The chalk hills of the North Downs form a transverse ridge right across the

county. To the north are the clays and aggregates of the Thames Basin; to the south lie more sands and clays of different types, forming the Weald. In places the greensand ridge is higher than the Downs – as at Leith Hill, which (at 295m) is the highest point in south-east England. Some of the sandstones are hard enough to have been used for building purposes, and the old sandstone mines are the nearest thing in the south-east to natural caves – important sites for hibernating bats and other subterranean life. The chalk has been quarried, mainly for making cement, leaving interesting sites for plants and insects. Removal of sand has left pits suitable for colonisation by sand martins and the little ringed plover. Digging clay for a great variety of bricks and tiles, so typical of Surrey's houses, has resulted in wet, overgrown claypits ideal for amphibians, including the great crested newt. The Weald's ironstone was at one time the basis of a major smelting industry which left a legacy of 'hammer ponds', constructed to provide a head of water to drive machinery. These tree-fringed waters, now often heavily silted up, are rich habitats for insects and the birds that feed upon them. Iron smelting was supported by extensive exploitation of coppiced woodland for charcoal, which was also needed for domestic fuel and for making gunpowder. Today large areas of woodland remain in the Weald, including much old coppice with a high content of dead wood. These are excellent sites for forest insects and mammals, the latter including deer and dormice.

The different geological deposits that underlie the Surrey landscape have given rise to very varied soils. These include clays and fertile sands, which are heavily cultivated, but also nutrient-deficient soils, ranging from very acid to very alkaline. These are of little economic value and have therefore often escaped extensive interference, leading to a rich and varied flora and fauna. This is especially true of the dry, thin and highly calcareous soils that cover the chalk. The downland turf that has developed here has its botanical specialities, including many beautiful orchid species, but it needs constant grazing to suppress the growth of taller vegetation and ultimately the spread of scrub and woodland. This process of succession shades out the smaller plants and also prevents the sun warming the soil – an important factor for the insects in this habitat, many of which are completely dependent on certain species of chalk grassland plants. In the past the grazing was by sheep and rabbits, but the latter were decimated by myxomatosis in the 1950s and 1960s and sheep farming is no longer an economic way of using the land. Consequently the maintenance of this important open downland habitat has become the responsibility of conservationists, but not before large areas have been lost to encroaching woodland.

In the west of the county, forest clearance several thousand years ago, followed by leaching of the sandy soils by rain, has created the heathlands that are perhaps Surrey's most important habitat type. The sun-warmed, well-aerated and nutrient-poor sands offer a set of environmental conditions found only here and in a few other areas of southern England. The associated flora and fauna are of particular interest and include national rarities such as the sand lizard and Dartford warbler. The heaths also have wet areas with acidic peat bogs, dominated by *Sphagnum* moss and supporting interesting plants such as the insectivorous sundews and butterwort.

Shallow heathland pools are inhabited by many plants and insects (especially dragonflies) that are rare elsewhere. Like the downlands, these heaths suffer change and serious threats. There is little or no grazing now to stop the advance of birch and Scots pine scrub, and in places this process has been accelerated by conifer planting. As open spaces near to centres of population, the fragile heathlands are subject to heavy recreational use, which leads to erosion of the soft sandy soils. Fires are frequent, killing many animals and causing the development of a degraded habitat dominated by gorse or bracken. These can cope with being burnt but are less interesting than the ericaceous community that they replace. Frequent fires also mean that heather is burnt before it is old enough to form old woody clumps – the preferred habitat of sand lizards and an important source of insect food. Active conservation efforts include scrub clearance, relocation of threatened sand-lizard colonies and an attempt to re-establish the natterjack toad in suitable heathland pools.

There is only one National Nature Reserve in Surrey – THURSLEY heath and bog – but there are many small local reserves, including those managed by the Surrey Wildlife Trust.

P. MORRIS

Alders

Permit only; 2ha; SWT reserve
Wet woodland
Spring, early summer

The small area of wet woodland lies within old quarry workings with the added wildlife interest of a number of pools including a sizeable colony of water-violet.

Bagmoor Common

SU 926423; 13.6ha; SWT reserve
Mixed woodland
Spring, summer

An acid woodland of birch and pine with mature oak and scrub areas, the reserve is notable for butterflies with over 23 species recorded, including white admiral and purple emperor.

Bay Pond

Permit only; 6.8ha; SWT reserve
Lake and alder swamp
Can be overlooked from footpath at TQ 353516
All year

The lake is fringed with attractive wetland plants, such as marsh-marigold, yellow iris and purple-loosestrife, beneath tall stands of bulrush, together with more uncommon species such as skullcap, lesser water-parsnip and golden dock. Over 100 bird species have been recorded here, with breeding birds including little and, occasionally, great crested grebe and visiting birds such as heron, kingfisher, grey wagtail and several duck species.

Bookham Commons Nature Walks

TQ 121567; various lengths; NT
Woodland, scrub and grassland
Leaflets from the Warden, Merrit's Cottage,
Bookham Common, Leatherhead or NT
Spring, summer

The walks are set in 180ha of oakwood and scrub-invaded grassland which, with the added interest of old fishponds, holds a wealth of animal life and a range of plants in which well over 500 species have been recorded.

Box Hill Country Park

TQ 179513; 253ha; NT
Chalk downland and woodland
Spring, summer

Although it is not strictly a nature reserve, and although parts of it suffer enormous public recreational pressures, the Box Hill area of chalkland remains a dramatic and fascinating place.

The steep sweep of woodland on the slope above the River Mole gives the great shoulder of chalk its name, for it is filled with box – box and yew over young box. At the upper and lower woodland levels, where light strikes in most easily, smaller plants are able to survive; woodland species such as common twayblade or lime-loving plants such as deadly nightshade show beneath the trees.

The slopes beside the woodland are scrub and grassland – a scrub community of ash and birch, gorse, hawthorn and oak, wayfaring-tree, whitebeam and yew. There is open scrub over wild rose and lime-loving flowers such as marjoram, milkwort and salad burnet, horseshoe and kidney vetch and the vivid pink-rose pyramids of sainfoin. In some areas the scrub shelters species such as stinking hellebore, ploughman's-spikenard and the strange, small man orchid, while orchids of the grassland include autumn lady's-tresses with bee, musk, pyramidal and fragrant orchid.

On the plateau above, where a capping to the chalk begins to develop, woodland shows again. Beech, with oak, ash and wild cherry, stands above an understorey of holly, yew and box with a variety of other species which include large-leaved lime, over a varied ground cover of typical woodland plants. A further woodland type, ash over yew, box and elder laced with traveller's-joy, spreads above a rich-wood ground cover below the slopes of box.

The animals of the area include edible snail, a very large land snail imported by the Romans. Apart from any climatic consideration, it is limited to chalk or limestone areas by the need for calcium to build its shell. Butterfly species are numerous and include chalkhill blue and silver-spotted skipper.

Chiphouse Wood

TQ 260570; 8ha; WdT
Deciduous woodland
Spring, summer

The reserve consists of mature oak woodland and newly planted trees. The planting has been designed to link areas of existing woodland while leaving wide rides and glades for the benefit of wildlife and visitors.

Chobham Common

SU 965648; 198ha; SCC reserve
Wet and dry heathland
Spring, early summer

The dry heath is characterised by heather, purple moor-grass and the generally more western bristle bent, together with a considerable invasion of birch and pine. Wet areas have bog plants such as hare's-tail cottongrass and round-leaved sundew. The common is of outstanding interest for its spiders and insects, one species of ant being found nowhere else but the ISLES OF SCILLY (Cornwall), and one species of spider nowhere else in the British Isles.

Colekitchen

TQ 085489; 2.6ha; SWT reserve
Downland
Permit from SWT
Summer

The characteristic chalk grassland of this North Downs reserve supports plants such as marjoram, basil, common and greater knapweed, field scabious, salad burnet, rock rose, yellow-wort and autumn gentian. The excellent variety of flowers attracts a good range of butterflies including green-veined and marbled white, and common, chalkhill and Adonis blue.

Cucknells Wood

Permit only; 10ha; SWT reserve
Mixed woodland
Spring, early summer

Set on the spring-line where sandstone meets clay, the wood shows the variation from dry to damp, from more acid to enriched ground conditions which this circumstance implies. Woodland birds include marsh and willow tit with all three native woodpecker species.

Devil's Punchbowl and Gibbet Hill Nature Trails

SU 890357; 3 and 4km; NT
Two circular walks
Leaflets from site or Hon. Sec., Hindhead Committee, Littleshaw, Hindhead
Spring, summer

Superb views from the Chilterns to the South Downs together with the wildlife interest of heathland or woodland characterise these trails.

Edolphs Copse

TQ 236425; 23.6ha; WdT
Deciduous woodland
Spring, summer

The attractive ancient oak and ash woodland has an understorey of hazel and hornbeam coppice with carpets of bluebells and other flowers.

Epsom Common Nature Trail

TQ 196609; 3.5km; Epsom and Ewell BC
Circular walk in ancient common land
Leaflet from E and EBC Parks Dept
Spring, early summer

The trail passes through woodland and scrub with heathland and meadow grassland and the wetland interest of a stream-fed pond.

Fir Tree Copse

TQ 023350; 5.7ha; SWT reserve
Woodland
Spring, early summer

Carpets of bluebells interspersed with clumps of primroses, wood anemones and yellow archangel flower beneath mixed oak, ash and hazel coppice.

Frensham Country Park

SU 849406; 311ha; NT–Waverley DC
Heath, woodland and ponds
Leaflets from interpretative centre or WDC
Spring, early summer

An example of the Surrey heaths, the country park has a range from dry heath with heather, bell heather, bracken, gorse, western gorse, birch and Scots pine to wet heath characterised by purple moor-grass, *Sphagnum* mosses and plants such as bog asphodel, white beak-sedge and round-leaved sundew. The Great and Little Ponds contain reedbeds of bulrush, yellow iris, common reed

Seale Chalk Pit: plants recolonise the quarry.

and sweet-flag which attract a variety of birds including a good population of reed warbler. There is an interesting conservation trail.

Glover's Wood

TQ 230410; 25.5ha; WdT
Deciduous woodland, bog
Spring, summer

The reserve is an excellent example of the Wealden woods. It lies across the valley of Welland Gill. On the steep side of the gill there is extensive hornbeam coppice with a scattering of other species, such as ash, wych elm, maple, hazel, small-leaved lime and wild service-tree. Here the ground flora is dominated by bluebells, yellow archangel and dog's mercury. This part of the wood is possibly primary – that is, ancient woodland that has never been cleared – whereas the plateau area is woodland of oak, birch and hazel which has developed more recently on abandoned fields. There is also an area of *Sphagnum* bog.

Godstone Reservoirs

Permit only; 18ha; SWT reserve
Two small reservoirs
Can be overlooked from footpath at TQ 362511
All year

A good variety of waterbirds may be seen on the reservoirs, with wintering duck, occasional passage migrants and breeding water and waterside birds such as great crested grebe, little ringed plover and a colony of sand martin.

Gracious Pond

Permit only; 12ha; SWT reserve
Mixed woodland
Spring, early summer

Formerly a monastic fishpond, Gracious Pond now consists mainly of dry and wet woodland above heather and its associate heathland species. A good range of dragonflies and water-associated spiders occurs.

Graeme Hendrey

Permit only; 10ha; SWT reserve
Mixed woodland
Spring, early summer

The mixed deciduous wood set within an old sand quarry makes an interesting contrast with CUCKNELLS WOOD which shows the transition from sandstone to damper clay. Here flowering plants include large numbers of bird's-nest orchid with a colony of common wintergreen while several varieties of ferns flourish here including hart's-tongue and hard fern.

Great Church Wood

TQ 369548; 5ha; WdT
Deciduous woodland
Spring, summer

The attractive ancient woodland contains a wide range of trees and shrubs, and many interesting flowers including herb-Paris, small teasel and several uncommon orchids. It is important both historically and as a local amenity.

Hackhurst Down

TQ 096486; 32ha; SCC–NT reserve
Chalk downland
Spring, summer

A good chalkland plant life, including round-headed rampion and autumn lady's-tresses with more common species such as cowslip and horse-shoe vetch, encourages an interesting variety of butterflies including a colony of chalkhill blue.

Hammond's Copse

TQ 213442; 29ha; WdT
Mixed woodland
Spring, summer

This ancient woodland consists partly of hazel coppice with oak standards and a rich, varied ground flora. The rest of the wood has been cleared and replanted with conifers. However, many of the planted trees have failed and natural regeneration of native species is taking over.

Headley Heath

TQ 204538; 112.8ha; NT
Heathland, woodland and chalk grassland
Leaflet from NT
Spring, early summer

Until at least the early 1930s, the site was an open spread of sheep-grazed heathland, with only a scattering of birch. During World War II the area was used for tank-training exercises and the torn-up heath was churned into a perfect seed-bed for the tiny airborne seeds of birch. In the absence of sheep grazing, rabbits were not enough to control the spread of the trees and, in 1954, myxomatosis practically removed even that slight control on their growth. Sweeping fires were also encouraging bracken invasion and the heath looked set for complete destruction.

Fire is now used to assist the return of the heathers, for the charred birch stumps are removed from the ground and gorse and bracken mown above the height of regrowing heather until the latter is strong enough to shade out its competitors. Belts and spinneys of birch and oak are retained as windbreaks and as a habitat for heath-edge animals, while a few natural hollows show a scatter of pools.

The wide horizon beyond the heath gives way to a smaller country where the curving sides of old dry valleys are thick with scrub or woodland. Blackthorn and hawthorn, dogwood, ash and yew, crab apple, holly and sycamore are tangled with wild rose and laced with swathes of traveller's-joy. With wild thyme and common rock-rose, tall mulleins, tiny milkworts, the delicate musk mallow, marjoram, eyebright, common bird's-foot-trefoil and viper's-bugloss, the grassland slopes are gardens of wild flowers.

Although the warblers and songbirds of the chalky scrub and woodland may be more obvious, many warblers breed on the heath above. Linnet, redpoll and meadow and tree pipit may be seen, together with more uncommon birds such as woodcock and nightjar. Winter flocks of goldfinch and siskin visit as well as occasional passage migrants or predators such as owls and shrikes.

A good range of butterflies includes chalkhill blue, green hairstreak and dark green fritillary with several skipper species, while there is a great variety of moths including orange underwing. This is also a noted site for Duke of Burgundy.

Headley Warren

Permit only; 31.2ha; SWT reserve
Chalk grassland and woodland
Spring, summer

The reserve lies on the slopes of a dry valley where a shallow soil has developed over the curves

Pools where dragonflies breed add to the habitat range at Thursley.

of chalk. Much of the woodland is coniferous plantation but areas of native woods contain yew, juniper and box with ash, buckthorn, dogwood, field maple, privet, spindle, wayfaring-tree and whitebeam. Other species include wild cherry and guelder-rose with tangles of traveller's-joy, bramble and wild rose. This variety gives a wide range of habitat from deep shade beneath the yews to well-lit grassland around the scrub. Woodland plants include yellow archangel, nettled-leaved bellflower, white and broad-leaved helleborine, woodruff and moschatel, but the greatest glory of Headley Warren lies in its herb-rich grassland.

Here there is a pattern of colour which shows the full beauty of the chalkland. Mounded anthills vary the slopes, each a cushion of small herbs such as wild thyme, sweet and hairy violet, eyebright and common bird's-foot-trefoil. The grassland itself is a mosaic of species – cowslip, common rock-rose, horseshoe and kidney vetch, yellow rattle and yellow-wort, milkwort and chalk milkwort, small scabious, clustered bellflower, marjoram, squinancywort and restharrow, wild basil and basil thyme – alive with the vibrant colour of all number of butterflies and the constant buzz of bees.

Here are strange small plants such as adder's-tongue and uncommon species such as wild candytuft, wild liquorice and grass vetchling. The reserve contains a splendid range of unusual plants such as the rare green hound's-tongue, while a good variety of orchids is also found which includes bee, man and pyramidal orchid.

This profusion of plant life in a warm and sheltered site is obviously rich in insects and a butterfly list of some 35 species includes dark green and pearl-bordered fritillary, brown, green and white-letter hairstreak with Adonis blue, Duke of Burgundy and the migrant clouded yellow.

Horsell Common Nature Walks

TQ 989605, SU 002605, 007593 and 015611; each 2.4km; Horsell Common Preservation Soc.
Four varied walks
Booklet from HCPS or STNC
Spring, summer

The walks are set in 280ha of mainly sandy heathland invaded by birch and Scots pine. Wetter areas contain cross-leaved heath, cottongrasses and round-leaved sundew while the heather, bell heather, dwarf gorse and scrub attract a good range of heathland birds.

Horton Country Park

TQ 191618; 99ha; Epsom and Ewell BC
Meadowland and woodland
Leaflet from E and EBC
Spring, early summer

Since no herbicides are used, the hay meadows are rich in spring and summer flowers while the woodlands and hedges attract birds such as treecreeper, blackcap and chiffchaff.

Lightwater Country Park

SU 921622; 48ha; Surrey Heath BC
Woodland, heathland and wetland
Leaflet from SHBC
Spring, early summer

A nature trail has been laid out in the park which shows the habitat range from Scots pine and mixed woodland, through gorse and heather heathland, wet acid heath and bog, with *Sphagnum*, bog asphodel, cross-leaved heath, round-leaved sundew and purple moor-grass, to open pools fringed with bog myrtle where mallard, coot and moorhen feed.

Moor Park

Permit only; 6.8ha; SWT reserve
Wet alder woodland
Can be overlooked from footpath at SU 867459
Spring, early summer

The deep alder swamp lies in a curve of the River Wey. Rich in characteristic plant species, such as sedges, in spring it is filled with the sound of songbirds. Breeding species include water rail.

Nore Hill Pinnacle

TQ 378576; 0.2ha; SCC reserve
Geological site
All year

The chalk pinnacle is of great geological interest as an example of a form of weathering unique in the British Isles.

North Downs Way

SU 844467–TQ 429561; 72km; CC
Long-distance way
Booklet from CC or HMSO bookshops
Spring, summer

Starting from Farnham and ending at Dover in Kent, the way mainly follows the crests of the downland in Surrey, with spectacular views across the lower farmland and with all the colour and beauty of chalk turf and woodland.

Nower Wood

Permit only; 43.3ha; SWT reserve
Mixed woodland
Spring, early summer

Nower Wood has long been noted for its show of spring flowers, particularly for its spread of bluebell. The wood has been much altered from its natural state, with planted species such as sweet chestnut and rhododendron, Scots pine, larch and Norway spruce, but it still contains a fine range of native trees and shrubs.

The lower areas, on or near the chalk, are characterised by trees, such as ash, beech, field maple, wild cherry and yew, and show typical rich-wood plants including enchanter's-nightshade, bugle, woodruff and yellow archangel.

Hornbeam and wood-sorrel indicate the change through birch and bluebell to the oak, holly, honeysuckle and bracken which characterise the higher acid woodland; rowan is also present. Where the clay with flints is damp, small bright plants such as yellow pimpernel flourish and the wetter areas may contain spreads of willow swamp with wetland plants such as soft rush and lesser spearwort. Ash, too, enjoys the wetland edge and the pools form an unexpected feature this high up the hill.

The largest, topmost, pond is overlooked by a hide, which also overlooks the swamp below, an ideal spot for woodland clearing birds such as spotted flycatcher. The evening visitor might see a roe deer or a mallard, or hear a nightingale's song across the pool.

Badger live in the wood and some 35 species of breeding birds have been recorded. There are interesting populations of dragonfly and a good range of moths and butterflies.

Oxmoor Copse

TQ 097467; 1.2ha; WdT
Deciduous woodland
Spring, summer

Large oaks, hazel coppice and abundant bluebells indicate that the reserve is probably a remnant of a much larger ancient woodland. It occupies a prominent position in a picturesque valley.

Seale Chalk Pit

Permit only; 1.2ha; SWT reserve
Disused chalk quarry
Spring, summer

The small quarry is being recolonised by chalkland plants including both bee and fly orchid, and its sunny position on the southern flank of the Hog's Back encourages a good variety of butterflies.

Staffhurst Wood

TQ 412483; 38ha; SCC reserve
Mixed woodland
Spring, early summer

Old oak pollards, hornbeam coppice and some fine wild service-trees indicate that this is probably an ancient woodland relict, a remnant of the old Weald clay forests. Oak and beech are the main standards above a varied ground cover, with the continuity of woodland here ensuring a habitat for an excellent variety of insects.

Thundry Meadows

SU 898440; 15.2ha; SWT reserve
Damp and wet meadowland, some woodland
Bog areas are dangerous
Spring, summer

A variety of wetland habitats contains a fine range of plants including bogbean and fen bedstraw, common marsh-bedstraw and marsh cinquefoil, with petty whin and dyer's greenweed, with heath spotted-orchid and early marsh-orchid. Butterflies include woodland species such as purple emperor and pearl-bordered fritillary.

Thursley

SU 900399; 250ha; NCC reserve
Bog, heath and woodland
Leaflet from NCC
Spring, early summer

The dry heath is coloured with heather, bell heather, gorse and dwarf gorse, with areas of sand and stands of birch. Wetter heath is characterised by purple moor-grass grading into bog where *Sphagnum* mosses spread beneath cross-leaved heath and common cottongrass, where southern marsh-orchid shows in early summer and fascinating bog plants grow. The wet heath and the bog afford habitat for bog asphodel, white and brown beak-sedge, cranberry and both oblong-leaved and round-leaved sundew, while the open pools within the bog are rich in species such as bogbean, lesser bladderwort, bottle sedge and marsh St John's-wort.

The range of woodland, heath and bog is rich in bird life with over 140 species recorded. Some 65 breed on the reserve, with good numbers of redstart, with locally uncommon species such as curlew and with national rarities such as Dartford warbler. The heath is noted as a raptor site with records of 10 different species of falcon or hawk, including breeding sparrowhawk and kestrel, regular visiting hen harrier and occasional Montagu's harrier, merlin, osprey and peregrine. Great grey shrike are regular winter visitors.

Somewhere between 5000 and 10,000 insect species are present, including both silver-studded blue and grayling butterflies and the heather-feeding emperor moth. Of outstanding interest to entomologists, the reserve contains no fewer than 26 dragonfly species, probably more than any other single site in southern Britain.

Vann Lake

TQ 157394; 11.2ha; SWT reserve
Lake and woodland
All year

The old hammer pond is surrounded by mixed mainly deciduous woodland including wild service-tree, with a good ground cover of plants such as bluebell, primrose, common cow-wheat, early-purple orchid and common spotted-orchid. There is an exceptional variety of fungi, including over 560 species, one unknown to science before its discovery in 1973. Over 100 bird species have been recorded including waterbirds on the lake and songbirds such as nightingale in the woodland.

Wallis Wood

TQ 121388; 13.2ha; SWT reserve
Woodland and grassland
Spring, early summer

Oak and ash stand above hazel coppice, now being restored by active management, which together with a block of hornbeam contains a wide range of woodland plants including species such as common centaury and broadleaved helle-

Birch scrub and gorse above great sweeps of heather typify the colourful Surrey heathlands.

borine. A good range of bird life may be seen, together with butterflies such as white admiral, purple emperor and dark, green, silver-washed and small pearl-bordered fritillary.

Witley Common

SU 936409; 150ha; NT
Large area of typical Surrey heathland
Nature trail leaflets from information centre
Spring, early summer

Great spreads of woodland and heather heathland demonstrate the plants and animals characteristic of the area, including heather, bell heather and gorse, whinchat and stonechat, together with adder and heathland insects.

Woldingham

TQ 374538; 20.6ha; NT reserve
Grassland and scrub
Summer

The reserve consists of four separate blocks of chalk downland on the south-facing slopes of the Surrey Downs – Oxted Downs, South Hawke, Hanging Wood and Tandridge Hill. The grassland, which is ungrazed except by rabbits, has been invaded by scrub but still includes a wide variety of flowers such as autumn gentian, ploughman's-spikenard and basil-leaved thyme. There is a good variety of butterflies, grasshoppers and harvestmen, while the areas of scrub are important for birds and also provide refuge for badgers.

Sussex

A great horseshoe-shaped rim of chalk hills encompasses an area in south east England called the Weald. Some 55km long by 23km broad, it comprises a large part of Kent and Surrey and almost the whole of Sussex (now administratively divided into East and West). Its long axis runs approximately WNW–ESE; the south east corner, isolated some 8000 years ago by the formation of the English Channel, now forms the Bas Boulonnais in the country around Calais. The Wealden geology conspires to make Sussex a region of strong contrasts, covering downland, sandstone hills, clay vales and alluvial plains.

The chalk hills of the South Downs rise from the sea to form an impressive line of cliffs, the SEVEN SISTERS, some 11km long between BEACHY HEAD in the east and SEAFORD HEAD in the west. West of Brighton the Downs swing inland until at the Hampshire border their southern edge lies about 10km from the sea. In a letter dated 1773 and written during one of his frequent visits to Sussex, the famous naturalist Gilbert White describes the South Downs as 'that chain of majestic mountains'. Impressive though they are, the Downs can hardly be dignified as mountains since at only three points do they exceed 260m! The range extends for over 90km from Beachy Head to the county boundary, and is broken up into five blocks by four rivers that breach the escarpment: from east to west the Cuckmere, the Ouse, the Adur and the Arun. East of the Arun the Downs are largely unwooded, while to the west lie large areas of fine beechwoods as well as more recent conifer plantations.

In 1761 a farmer from Hartfield near the Kent border moved to Glynde where he set about improving the polled, black-faced, speckled-leg-ged sheep of the eastern Downs to produce what was to become the most famous of all breeds of sheep, the Southdown. The close-cropped turf of the southern chalk must be among the richest botanical habitats in Europe – it is possible to find more than 20 different species of flowering plant in a piece of ground 30cm square. Many of these, such as round-headed rampion and early spider-orchid, are confined to the southern chalk in Britain. The insects are no less exciting and include the now rare and threatened Adonis blue butterfly, whose caterpillar feeds on another chalk plant, horseshoe vetch.

Sheep farming has progressively declined on the Downs since World War I and much old downland pasture has been converted to arable land, much of it used for intensive barley production. Other areas of abandoned sheep walk are rapidly becoming invaded by coarse grasses and scrub. A survey by the Nature Conservancy Council has revealed that between 20 and 25 per cent of the area of old chalk grassland in the two counties has been lost in recent years.

North of the South Downs the Weald comprises a complicated series of alternating clays and sandstones. They culminate in the forest ridges of the High Weald, dominated by the large expanse of ASHDOWN FOREST, the biggest single tract of undeveloped countryside in southern England east of the New Forest. Lowland heath is one of the most rapidly disappearing of all habitats in western Europe, and the 25 sq.km of heath, bog and valley woodlands which represent the remains of John of Gaunt's medieval royal park are protected by their own Act of Parliament.

The Weald has traditionally produced the finest oaks in the kingdom, and East and West Sussex still form the most wooded area of almost the least wooded country in Europe. The wooded, deep, steep-sided rocky ravines of the High Weald, known locally as ghylls, are more reminiscent of Welsh oakwoods or parts of Exmoor than the populous south east. The similarity does not end there as they contain an extraordinary assemblage of both animals and plants, such as hay-scented buckler-fern and Tunbridge filmy-fern, that are far more characteristic of the oceanic west and are probably persisting in the south-east as relics of the Atlantic forest period of 5000–6000 years ago.

The Weald clay country of West Sussex still has hundreds of hectares of mature oak forest including several well-known woodland nature reserves such as THE MENS and EBERNOE COMMON. These are the stronghold of many of Britain's rarest woodland butterflies, and the beautiful wild service-tree is a characteristic feature.

In common with other parts of the British coastline, the Sussex coast has experienced major changes in sea level over the last thousand years or so. In the extreme east the county boundary ends in that most extraordinary of British coastal features, the vast shingle expanse of the Dungeness foreland. As one travels eastwards the coastline is punctuated by a series of alluvial flats, each dissected by extensive systems of drainage dykes. Starting with the western edge of Romney Marsh and the area around Camber Castle south of Rye, this is followed by the Pevensey Levels to the east of Eastbourne and then the flood plains of the Sussex rivers: the Lewes Brooks, Adur Levels and AMBERLEY WILD BROOKS. With the reclamation and deterioration of areas such as the Somerset Levels and the Norfolk Broads these areas are now among the last remaining strongholds of our wetland flora and fauna.

Sussex is a county of paradoxes. In the north the tentacles of Gatwick Airport, with its attendant sprawl of industries, reach out into the countryside of the Sussex–Surrey borders. Sussex's 150km of coastline, with its holiday beaches and marinas, are the most developed in the British Isles. Yet the Weald itself, notwithstanding its proximity to London, can be counted among some of the last unspoiled landscapes in England.

DAVID STREETER

Adur Estuary

TQ 211050; 10ha; RSPB reserve
Mudflats and saltmarsh
Can be viewed from adjacent public footpaths
Leaflet available from RSPB South-East office
Winter

This tidal section of the River Adur within Shoreham-by-Sea is an excellent place to watch waders. Redshank, dunlin and ringed plover are common, while avocet, bar-tailed godwit, whimbrel and shelduck are occasionally seen. On the saltmarsh, sea-purslane, glasswort and sea aster grow.

Amberley Wild Brooks

Permit only; 5ha; SWT reserve
Rich flood meadows
All year

The surrounding areas are of most interest to birdwatchers, with good numbers of Bewick's swan, pintail, shoveler, teal and wigeon in winter. However in spring and summer the ditches are filled with arrowhead, bladderwort and frogbit, and are one of the last remaining strongholds for wetland flora in the county.

Arlington Reservoir

TQ 533073; 100ha; Eastbourne Waterworks
Company reserve
Open water
Access on footpath and bridleway only
Late summer, winter

Completed in 1971, the reservoir is particularly good for wildfowl. Canada geese, mallard, pochard, tufted duck and shoveler winter, while the migration brings in unusual waders such as spotted redshank.

Arundel Wildfowl Refuge

TQ 020081; 24ha; WT
Open water, wet grassland and reedbed
Information from entrance building or WT
All year

Many birds are attracted to the wild area where a lake, wader scrape, reedbed and two marshy fields may be viewed from the observation hides. Lapwing, redshank and teal breed, and passage birds include regular common and green sandpiper and greenshank. Winter duck may include many pochard, teal and tufted duck, shoveler and wigeon, together with bittern, bearded tit and Cetti's warbler.

Ashdown Forest

TQ 432324; 2560ha; Conservators of Ashdown Forest
Heathland and woodland
Spring, summer

This wide area of High Weald heathland, once a royal hunting forest, is a splendid mosaic of dry, damp and wet heathland with valley mires, streams, scrub and woodland. Reduced grazing has accelerated the spread of woodland and accidental fires may help the invasion of bracken, but fine heather moorland still remains. Gorse and dwarf gorse add colour and purple moorgrass varies the stands of heather here and there, while creeping willow, saw-wort, petty whin and dodder may be found.

The wetter sites, where *Sphagnum* mosses grow, are also defined by common cottongrass, bog asphodel and round-leaved sundew, while some iron-rich mires contain fen bedstraw and marsh fern, and stream-cut gullies may hold not only sheltered narrow woodlands but also lemon-scented fern and hay-scented buckler-fern. The woodlands themselves are considerably varied and include invasive birch, oak, willow and Scots pine with alder and alder buckthorn by some of the streams and areas where woodland, often beech, was enclosed against grazing pressure in earlier years.

Animals include an important population of fallow deer with badger, fox, stoat, weasel and typical small mammals together with a wide range of birds. Woodland birds – blackcap, willow warbler and nightingale, for instance – sing in the scrub, while woodcock may be seen at dawn or dusk, when nightjar may hawk after insects. Predators include kestrel, sparrowhawk and an occasional pair of hobbies.

The wet heaths provide breeding sites for a fine range of dragonflies, and the forest as a whole is rich in such insects as silver-studded blue, grayling, dark green, pearl-bordered, small pearl-bordered and silver-washed fritillary butterflies and the emperor moth, a feature of the heathlands.

Beachy Head Nature Trail

TV 586956; 2km; Eastbourne BC
Coastal chalk downland
Leaflet from natural history centre at site or EBC
Spring, early summer

The circular trail demonstrates the fascination of this spectacular chalk headland with its range of plants from kidney vetch to wayfaring-tree, and chalkland butterflies including five species of blue.

Beechland Wood

TQ 414205; 0.8ha; WdT
Deciduous wood
Spring, summer

A small valley oak woodland which has been augmented by the planting of native trees.

Bewl Bridge

No access; 51.4ha; SWA reserve
Part of Bewl Bridge Reservoir
Reserve may be overlooked from TQ 678318 and other rights of way
Leaflets from visitor centre at TQ 676337
Autumn, winter

Passage waders may be seen on the mud when the water level falls in autumn, while winter waterfowl include pochard, teal, tufted duck and wigeon with shoveler and great crested grebe.

Black Down Nature Trail

SU 921309; 2.4km; NT
Woodland and grassland walk
Leaflet from Haslemere Educational Museum and bookshops
Spring, summer

The trail, on the highest point in West Sussex, leads through woods of Scots pine and oak where fallow and roe deer are resident. Meadow pipit, linnet and yellowhammer may be seen outside the woods, where there are magnificent views of the South Downs.

Brock Wood

TQ 644250; 4.8ha; WdT
Deciduous woodland
Spring, summer

An attractive woodland reserve with many fine oak trees and hazel coppice.

Burton Pond

SU 979180; 31.2ha; WSCC–SWT reserve
Lake, wood, heath and bog
Leaflet from WSCC
All year

Extensive reedbeds, containing lesser bulrush, branched bur-reed and cowbane at its only Sussex locality, stand around a lake bright with yellow water-lily. To the west, birchwoods slope down to a wet alder wood and the lake margins. On the other side Black Hole, an alder carr containing cranberry, has been bridged by a viewing causeway. The higher ground is mostly covered by birch heath. Teal, tufted duck, great crested and little grebe, water rail and reed and sedge warbler all breed. Many pochard are present in winter.

Castle Hill

TQ 367074; 45ha; NCC reserve
Fine chalk grassland
Permit only off public footpath
Leaflet from NCC
Spring, summer

Superb chalkland flowers include dropwort, yellow-wort and small scabious with field fleawort, chalk milkwort and round-headed rampion. Corn bunting, meadow pipit and skylark breed on the slopes, while scrub contains linnet, whitethroat, yellowhammer and chalkland butterflies.

Chailey Common

TQ 386210; 173ha; ESCC reserve
Wet and dry heath
Spring, early summer

Despite invading bracken, heathland plants still include all three common heathers, tormentil, heath milkwort and petty whin. Scrub birch and woodland encourage a variety of birds.

Chailey Warren

Permit only; 2.5ha; SWT reserve
Damp and dry heath
Early September

The reserve protects a population of marsh gentian which flowers in early autumn.

Chichester Harbour

SU 775005; 1200ha; Chichester Harbour Conservancy reserve
Huge area of deeps, tidal mudflats and islands
All year

Twenty thousand dunlin can't be wrong: Chichester Harbour is fascinating in winter. At high tide

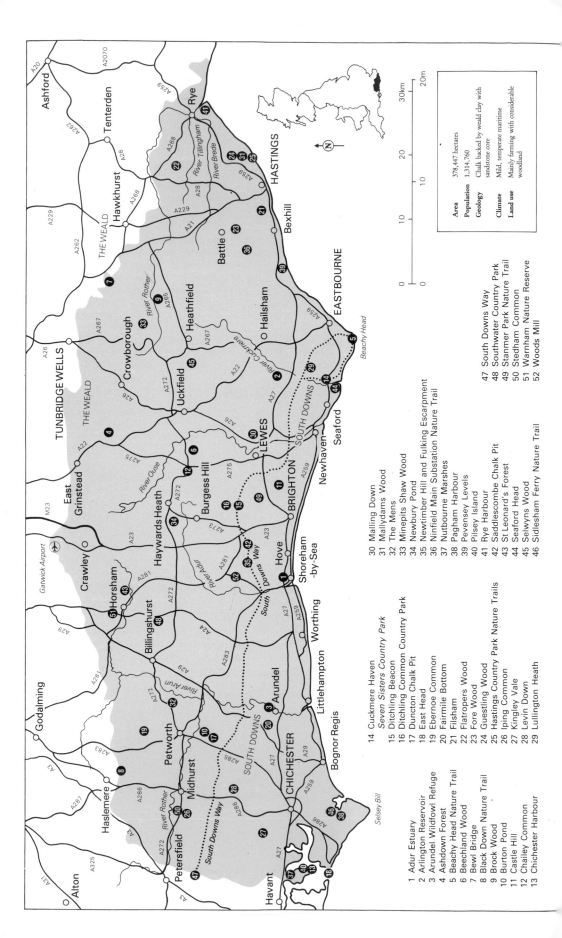

Area	378,447 hectares
Population	1,314,760
Geology	Chalk backed by weald clay with sandstone core
Climate	Mild, temperate maritime
Land use	Mainly farming with considerable woodland

1 Adur Estuary
2 Arlington Reservoir
3 Arundel Wildfowl Refuge
4 Ashdown Forest
5 Beachy Head Nature Trail
6 Beechland Wood
7 Bewl Bridge
8 Black Down Nature Trail
9 Brock Wood
10 Burton Pond
11 Castle Hill
12 Chailey Common
13 Chichester Harbour

14 Cuckmere Haven
    Seven Sisters Country Park
15 Ditchling Beacon
16 Ditchling Common Country Park
17 Duncton Chalk Pit
18 East Head
19 Ebernoe Common
20 Fairmile Bottom
21 Filsham
22 Flatropers Wood
23 Fore Wood
24 Guestling Wood
25 Hastings Country Park Nature Trails
26 Iping Common
27 Kingley Vale
28 Levin Down
29 Lullington Heath

30 Malling Down
31 Mallydams Wood
32 The Mens
33 Minepits Shaw Wood
34 Newbury Pond
35 Newtimber Hill and Fulking Escarpment
36 Ninfield Main Substation Nature Trail
37 Nutbourne Marshes
38 Pagham Harbour
39 Pevensey Levels
40 Pilsey Island
41 Rye Harbour
42 Saddlescombe Chalk Pit
43 St Leonard's Forest
44 Seaford Head
45 Selwyns Wood
46 Sidlesham Ferry Nature Trail

47 South Downs Way
48 Southwater Country Park
49 Stanmer Park Nature Trail
50 Stedham Common
51 Warnham Nature Reserve
52 Woods Mill

the rising waters drive the birds off the mudflats to huddle, thousands strong, on roosts such as Thorney Island where they stand, head to wind, waiting until their feeding grounds are uncovered again.

The tide fills and drains through the channel east of Hayling Island where EAST HEAD lies like an opened door, a narrow spit of sand dunes. In the late 1780s the land lay almost out to Hayling Island but, slowly, since that time, it has been worn back north and eastwards: the spur of East Head has swung back as if it were on a hinge.

East Head and NUTBOURNE MARSHES between them hold examples of much of the habitat of the harbour. The main habitat is the huge area of estuary muds, the lime-rich silts which hold the wealth of marine worms, molluscs and crustaceans that feed the winter waders. The mudflats also form low-tide grazing meadows where dark-bellied Brent geese feed on the eel-grass and *Enteromorpha* and some 8000 birds may be seen within the harbour. Large numbers of redshank, curlew, bar-tailed and black-tailed godwit, grey plover and sanderling may be present, with several thousand shelduck, with wigeon, mallard, pintail and teal, and with goldeneye and red-breasted merganser diving in the channels. Severe weather may see pochard and tufted duck fly in from the frozen gravelpits inland or, perhaps, a flock of white-fronted geese, spiralling down on to the mudflats.

The plant life of the Nutbourne Marshes mud is mainly restricted to eel-grass, the green alga *Enteromorpha* and common cord-grass, but East Head contains a number of interesting and typical plants. The saltmarsh is characterised by glasswort, sea-lavender, thrift and sea aster which grade into duneland sea bindweed and evening-primrose. Sea couch, marram, lyme-grass and sea rocket show in the open dunes, while specialities such as golden samphire and sea-heath also occur.

Breeding birds include common and Sandwich tern, and the only Sussex breeding colony of black-headed gull, together with ringed plover, redshank and shelduck. Smaller birds include a good population of reed bunting, and two woodlands nearby contain heronries.

The interest of the harbour is increased by its continuity with LANGSTONE HARBOUR (Hampshire). Together they form the largest area of estuarine mudflats on the south coast of Britain, of exceptional importance to wintering waders and wildfowl.

Cuckmere Haven

TV 519995; 392ha; ESCC–Lewes DC
Chalkland estuary, cliffs and downland
Leaflets from visitor centre, ESCC or LDC
Spring, summer

If you look towards BEACHY HEAD from the western side of the Haven, some of the finest chalk coastland in the country lies before you. Rank upon rank of smoothly curving hillsides have been guillotined to form sheer white cliffs, the Seven Sisters, topped by a close green turf; below, the Haven itself is a wide meadow valley where the old river meanders form winding pools beside the now straightened course of the River Cuckmere. The SEVEN SISTERS COUNTRY PARK and the SEAFORD HEAD reserve make up the area called Cuckmere Haven.

After the last ice age the hills lay inland, higher above the deep-cut valley than now. The sea was

Smooth curves of chalkland: the Cuckmere Valley below Firle Beacon.

further south, and some 30m lower, so that the cutting effect was considerable and, in the case of the main valley, sliced deep into the hills to form the basis of the shape of the present Haven. As the sea rose towards its modern level, the deep channel became silted up.

A shingle bank has been thrown up in the mouth of the Haven, formed mainly from flints which have washed out of the chalk; the bank provides a habitat for sea beet, yellow horned-poppy and sea-kale, and behind it an islanded lagoon provides nesting sites for ringed plover and common tern. The lagoon and the marshland beyond are a feeding point for migrant waders and winter wildfowl, while the marsh holds glasswort, sea aster, sea-purslane and sea worm-wood, and the alluvial grassland adder's-tongue and marsh-mallow.

Chalk grassland curves up from the valley floor and caps the cliffs, a pattern of short and tall, species-rich swards, varied by shallow scrub, which stretches to Beachy Head. Early-purple and pyramidal orchid, common spotted-orchid and autumn gentian occur among typical chalkland salad burnet, common centaury, carline and dwarf thistle, squinancywort and wild thyme, while deeper grassland holds wild carrot, wild mignon-ette, viper's-bugloss, weld, yellow rattle and red bartsia.

Only three of the Seven Sisters lie wholly within the Country Park, but the coastal footpath runs on to Beachy Head and within this length of the highest chalk cliffs in Britain are several unusual plants. Field fleawort, burnt orchid and round-headed rampion bring splashes of colour to the grassland while coastal plants such as rock sea-lavender and sea radish may be found. Moon carrot, least lettuce and small hare's-ear occur, the last found elsewhere in mainland Britain only on the limestone cliffs of Devon.

Jackdaw, herring gull and fulmar nest on the cliffs, meadow pipit and skylark on the grassland, while the scrub, particularly on Seaford Head, is rich in small birds. Resident species include stonechat while spring brings redstart, blackcap, chiffchaff, common and lesser whitethroat, grass-hopper and willow warbler and a host of passage-birds. Ring ouzel and pied flycatcher pass through, en route for the moors and western woodlands, while more uncommon visitors might include bluethroat and ortolan bunting, red-breasted fly-catcher, hoopoe and wryneck.

Waders using the river as a migration route may pause to feed on the marshes or visit the lagoon and river meanders, where cormorant, heron, mute swan and shelduck are commonly to be seen, and winter brings further waterbirds such as little grebe, mallard, teal, tufted duck and wigeon.

The Haven is a place of contrasts, acid enough above Seaford Head for such insects as emperor and oak eggar moths, rich enough on the down-land for chalkhill blue butterflies; the dry chalk slopes contrast with the water meadows below, and there is a further range of contrast between the saltmarsh and shingle ridge.

Ditchling Beacon

TQ 329133; 19.6ha; SWT reserve
Steep chalk grass and scrub
Spring, summer

A very steep north-facing scarp of the South Downs: from the top of the reserve there are enormous views clear across the Weald to the far North Downs. An excellent range of plants covers the slope, while scrub provides cover for bird life and grades into young ash woodland. Butterflies include chalkhill blue and brown Argus.

Ditchling Common Country Park

TQ 336181; 76ha; ESCC
Wealden common
Leaflet from site or ESCC
Spring, early summer

Oak woodland, scrub, spreads of gorse and bracken-filled grassland are supplemented by a sizeable lake. Spring brings a fine show of bluebell and wood anemone to contrast with tall bulrush round the lake. Birds include blackcap, stonechat and linnet while butterflies include small pearl-bordered fritillary and green hairstreak.

Duncton Chalk Pit

SU 961162; 2.4ha; SWT reserve
Disused chalk quarry
Spring, summer

Chalk woodland and scrub contain such interest-ing species as narrow-leaved everlasting-pea and wild liquorice.

East Head

SZ 765985; 30.4ha; NT
Dunes, saltmarsh and sandy foreshore
Leaflet from NT
All year

Part of CHICHESTER HARBOUR

Ebernoe Common

SU 976278; 71.6ha; SWT reserve
Ancient beech–oak woodland
Spring, early summer

A superb example of high-forest woodland, the common contains many huge old beech trees with younger oak woodland, an area of scrub and old ponds. This variation encourages a good range of birds including nightingale and woodcock, and of insects including white admiral, purple emperor and silver-washed fritillary.

Fairmile Bottom

SU 991095; 53ha; West Sussex CC
Chalk grassland and woodland
Leaflet on site
Early summer

The chalk downland has a rich variety of plants including several species of orchid. There is some scrub and woodland with fine yew trees.

Filsham

No access; 17.1ha; Hastings BC–SWT reserve
Wetland
Overlooked from right of way at TQ 775098
All year

The area of reedbed, water meadows and drainage ditches is rich in spring and summer with arrowhead, yellow iris, marsh-marigold, water mint and water-soldier. Passage and winter waterbirds, including mallard, shoveler, teal, wigeon, snipe and jack snipe, ensure the year-round interest of the site.

Flatropers Wood

TQ 862229; 34.8ha; SWT reserve
Mixed woodland
Spring, early summer

Mainly oak, with birch and coppiced sweet chestnut over bluebell, bramble and honeysuckle, the reserve contains many characteristic woodland birds and has good populations of pearl-bordered and small pearl-bordered fritillary.

Fore Wood

TQ 756128; 55ha; RSPB reserve
Mixed woodland
Spring, early summer

Where NAP WOOD is an acid central Wealden woodland and THE MENS a fine high forest on Wealden clays, Fore Wood is an interesting mix on clay and sands, like neither reserve but with echoes of both.

From a study of the plants it seems likely that Fore Wood is a primary woodland site, that woodland cover has been maintained, although much altered by management, for many years.

Roughly half the reserve is sweet chestnut coppice, a fast-growing tree probably imported by the Romans for its crop of edible nuts. Oak and birch occur rather sparsely throughout the area, while the dense shade and slow decomposing leaf litter limit the ground cover to spring bluebell and wood anemone with a later spread of bracken, bramble and ivy. By contrast the hornbeam coppice is much more varied. The spring show of flowers is chiefly wood anemone and the ground cover is later mainly honeysuckle, bramble and ivy, but oak standards are more plentiful and the hornbeam coppice is varied with ash, aspen, birch, field maple and grey willow. Other smaller areas include blocks of scrub, of alder, of oakwood, with standard and coppiced oak, of mixed woodland with an understorey of blackthorn, hawthorn, hazel and holly, elder, wild rose and guelder-rose over dog's mercury, yellow archangel and pendulous sedge.

An attractive facet of the reserve is its steep-cut ghylls, tree-lined along the stream bed and rich in ferns and mosses. An artificial pond, too, adds to the interest and, although much of the woodland floor is shaded and poor in species, small numbers of primrose, woodruff, wood spurge, wood-sorrel, moschatel and early dog-violet add to the springtime show. Orchids include common spotted-orchid, common twayblade and broadleaved helleborine, while among other interesting plants are tutsan and butcher's-broom.

The birds are chiefly those of woodland, woodland edge and scrub; they include some six species of tit, all three native woodpeckers, nuthatch, treecreeper and tawny owl. Hawfinch have probably bred in some years and sparrowhawk have certainly done so. Many other species should breed in or visit the reserve as the habitat range is further increased by sympathetic management.

Guestling Wood

TQ 863144; 12.4ha; WdT
Mixed woodland
Spring, early summer

The varied woodland includes areas which are to be allowed to develop to high forest to contrast with the sweet chestnut coppicing which has been the traditional management.

Hastings Country Park Nature Trails

TQ 860118; various lengths; Hastings BC
Sandstone sea cliffs, valleys and heathland
Leaflets from interpretative centre or HBC
Spring, early summer

The trails are laid out variously to demonstrate the interest of the cliffs where seabirds nest, the gorse and heather heathland, and the cool, damp, fern-rich glens or valleys.

Hooe Common

Permit only; 1.7ha; SWT reserve
Rushy meadow with willow and gorse scrub
Spring, summer

The marshy area includes a variety of typical and attractive plants together with an interesting range of wetland insects.

Iping Common

SU 853220; 77ha; WSCC
Dry and wet heathland
Spring, summer

Lying beside the busy A272, the acid heathland of Iping Common is highly susceptible to fire. Woodland, of course, would be the natural climax here, and seedling birches demonstrate how readily the change might come. Heather and bracken can both survive burning, due to their deep-buried roots, and bare ground is quickly recolonised by mosses and plants such as sheep's sorrel. Large-scale fires can, however, deplete the populations of ground insects, amphibians and reptiles unable to move quickly to unburnt areas.

Small pockets of bog have developed in the dips and hollows of the common, marked by the white plumes of hair's-tail cottongrass, by the paler purple where cross-leaved heath takes over from bell heather and by clumps of sedges and rushes and tussocks of purple moor-grass. The wettest places are vivid with *Sphagnum* mosses

Kingley Vale: the chalk valley holds one of the finest yew woodlands in Europe.

and plumed with common cottongrass. The bogs and pools provide a fascinating contrast with the drier parts of the common, where fine grasses and small plants such as tormentil and heath bedstraw line the edges of the paths.

The plant life, however, modifies the dryness, giving shade and shelter to a wide variety of animals. Over 100 species of spider have been recorded, including a number of rarities, and other heathland animals, such as common lizard, find suitable habitats here. Breeding birds include reed bunting, meadow pipit, skylark and yellow-hammer while the woodland fringe adds its own range of characteristic species.

Kiln Wood

TQ 527203; 3.6ha; WdT
Deciduous woodland, grassland
Spring, summer

A fine oak wood with a number of other tree species, including birch, beech, holly and willow, and a shrub layer composed of coppiced horn-beam, chestnut and hazel. There is an adjacent area of rough grazing.

Kingley Vale

SU 824088; 146ha; NCC reserve
Yew woodland, chalk scrub and grassland
Leaflets from reserve centre or NCC
Spring, summer

Above the great horseshoe curve of Kingley Vale a memorial stone to Sir Arthur Tansley, first chairman of the Nature Conservancy, overlooks the view which he is said to have considered the finest in Britain: the view across land and water,

across woodland, farmland, coastal lagoons and sea, past the landmark of Chichester Cathedral, clear across to the Isle of Wight.

Sir Arthur's personal preference may have many rivals but the naturalist's eye is unlikely to disagree with the claim of the yew wood below to be one of the finest in Europe. Great yews, gnarled and twisted, slopes of straight young yews, yew varied with ash, whitebeam and oak – from the deeper soils on the valley bottom the trees have spread to cover the steep chalk slopes in a strange, dark, mysterious forest.

Besides the woodland proper, spreads of scrub, of hawthorn, blackthorn, buckthorn, dogwood, juniper, spindle, wayfaring-tree, of a fascinating mix of varied species, laced with traveller's-joy, bramble, white bryony and thorned with wild rose, cluster the woodland edges and pattern the slopes. Chalk heath, too, where heather and bell heather, acid plants, grow mixed with lime-loving species, adds to the variation of the site.

Nothing grows on the chalk beneath the yews; these are the climax trees, the end of the suc-cession, slow powerful trees that make their own cathedral-cool climate on even the hottest day. But if the succession ends with bare chalk under the shade of the yews, it starts with the open downland, bright with sunlight: small herbs and grassland colonise the chalk, filling it with colourful plants before the scrub moves in to begin the change to woodland.

Kingley Vale has just that herb-rich grassland, maintained by grazing to hold it at that stage. Within the grassland plants such as common bird's-foot-trefoil and horseshoe and kidney vetch are food plants for butterflies and add to the richness of colour. Common rock-rose, hawkbit and hawkweed contrast with chalk and common milkwort, harebell, clustered bellflower and round-headed rampion. Eleven orchid species have been recorded, including fly, bee and frog orchid, and autumn lady's-tresses.

The reserve is as rich in animals as in plants, with fallow and roe deer, a great variety of birds, with adder and common lizard, with spiders, beetles such as glow-worm and many species of moth. The butterflies include four blues, five fritillaries and five skippers, together with white admirals and a record of purple emperor.

Levin Down

SU 886134; 10ha; SWT reserve
Chalk grassland and scrub
Spring, summer

The speciality of the reserve is a fine colony of juniper, but it also contains a most attractive range of chalkland flowers such as kidney vetch and common rock-rose, together with a rich and varied scrub which has developed around tiny secret lawns of herb-rich grassland. Scrubland birds are plentiful and the warm southern aspect is excellent for the characteristic chalkland butterflies.

Lullington Heath

TQ 545018; 62ha; NCC reserve
Chalk heathland
Permit only off rights of way
Leaflet from NCC
Spring, early summer

Chalk heath occurs where shallow acid soils occur on the chalk, producing neither acid heath nor chalk downland but a mix of many species from both habitats. Heather and salad burnet, for instance, might grow side by side. In spite of the fact that gorse has invaded a considerable part of the reserve it still remains an area of great interest to botanists.

Malling Down

TQ 430108; 43ha; SWT reserve
Chalk grassland and scrub
Dogs must be kept on leads as reserve is grazed
Spring, summer

Part of the reserve is a series of chalk pits and spoil heaps renowned for their varied communities of chalkland flowers. The remainder is a deep and steep-sided dry valley with flourishing colonies of chalkland butterflies. The scrub provides a rich diversity of bird species.

Mallydams Wood

TQ 857122; 24ha; RSPCA reserve
Mixed woodland and heath
Booklet from field centre or RSPCA
Spring, early summer

A very wide range of habitat characterises this mainly educational reserve where heather heath and small areas of *Sphagnum* mosses contrast with the woodland rides rich in gorse, broom and spreads of common spotted-orchid, the birch woodland over bluebell and bracken or the old pollards of oak and sweet chestnut. The underlying sandstone is shown in a stream-cut ghyll, typical of High Weald woodlands, and, even though much modified by earlier management, the reserve demonstrates much that is characteristic of East Sussex woods.

The Mens

TQ 024236; 155ha; SWT reserve
Mixed woodland
Leaflet from SWT
Spring, early summer

The Mens (extending its title to cover the seven continuous woods which combine to form the reserve) has generally been common land where grazing rights prevented coppicing because the animals would have cropped the growing shoots. From time to time trees must have been felled for timber, for few of the present trees are more than 100 years old, but the woodland has not been intensively managed since the nineteenth century and now all stages, from seedling to forest tree, may be seen growing naturally here.

Where the Wealden clays are lighter, huge beech trees tower above a tangle of holly and young beech, a dense understorey beneath which little can survive: just here and there a tree has fallen and the open glade allows more plants to grow.

Heavier clays are more varied, with oak and beech, a more open canopy, with an understorey of holly, yew and hazel, of Midland hawthorn and crab apple, with ash and spindle and an equally rich ground cover. Wood anemone, bluebell and bugle may be found, with wild rose, sanicle, violets and wood spurge. Other interesting plants occur, such as butcher's-broom, wood melick and pendulous sedge, and the woodland structure is varied with more open areas of birch and bracken or richer spots where ash stands over spiny tangles of blackthorn.

The Mens: bluebells beneath high-forest beech.

There is a good population of true woodland birds, exemplified by all three woodpeckers and woodland butterflies abound. The white admiral, the insignia of the SWT, occurs here but pride of place must go to the purple emperor, a rare and beautiful butterfly which flies in the sunlight round the upper branches of the taller oak trees.

Roe deer are abundant and their tracks may be found on the paths, while fallow and muntjac deer may be seen from time to time. Parts of the reserve are among the finest in the country for their fungal flora with more than 40 *Russula* species recorded.

Minepits Shaw Wood

TQ 607280; 3.8ha; WdT
Deciduous woodland
Spring, summer

This neglected coppice-with-standards wood contains a mixture of oak, ash, field maple, hazel and hornbeam. An attractive steep-sided stream with a small waterfall runs through the reserve.

Nap Wood

Permit only; 44.5ha; NT-SWT reserve
Mainly oak woodland
Access on Sundays April-October only
Leaflets from SWT
Spring, early summer

By contrast with the heavier clays of THE MENS, Nap Wood lies mainly on the acid sandstone of the Tunbridge Wells sands; instead of the close high-forest woods of The Mens, much of Nap Wood consists of almost park-like oak trees over sloping bracken.

On the higher slopes of the wood the oak trees could never reach a tall maturity because of the poorness of the soil, hence they were coppiced, particularly for bark for the tanning trade; here birch and rowan have invaded above a ground cover of bracken and bluebell. Lower down, on the deeper clay, oak was grown as standards. A richer understorey could develop: hazel for coppicing, crab apple, hawthorn, yew perhaps and holly, occasional wild cherry above a tangle of bramble and honeysuckle with further spreads of bluebell. Lower still the wet clays of the valleys encourage a growth of alder, hard, ideal for clog-making, and a range of heavy-soil plants such as ramsons, yellow archangel and pendulous sedge with damp shade-loving plants such as mosses and ferns. Sweet chestnut and Scots pine, both planted, add a further range of habitat.

The mammals of Nap Wood include fox and badger. The birds include most of those typical of lowland oakwoods, with migrant species such as redstart and wood warbler.

A fascinating aspect of the wood is that the damp valley bottoms, less variable in humidity and temperature than the rest of the Weald, hold certain Atlantic plants which have probably survived here for thousands of years. Plants such as hay-scented buckler-fern are generally limited to the west, and would not be expected here.

Newbury Pond

TQ 306243; 0.5ha; SWT reserve
Small pond
Spring, summer

Consisting of a small pond together with a marsh, the reserve contains an interesting variety of water plants, marsh plants, and insects associated with this kind of habitat.

Newtimber Hill and Fulking Escarpment

TQ 242112; 61ha; NT
Grassland and scrub
Summer

An exceptionally rich area of chalk grassland on the steep scarp slope of the South Downs, the more interesting plants include dropwort, horseshoe vetch, autumn gentian, round-headed rampion and a number of species of orchid. On the summit of Newtimber Hill, there is a small area of chalk heath where the calcareous soils give way to clay-with-flints where plants of acid and alkaline soils mix. The scrub provides excellent habitat for birds and a small number of juniper bushes occur – the most easterly site for this species on the Downs.

Ninfield Main Substation Nature Trail

TQ 725117; 2km; CEGB
Circular trail around boundary of substation
Restricted to educational visits
Booklet from CEGB
Spring, early summer

The grazing meadows, water meadows, stream-sides, pools and woodlands through which the trail passes demonstrate some of the interest of the East Sussex countryside.

Nutbourne Marshes

SU 766051; 360ha; Chichester Harbour Conservancy reserve
Salting, creeks and tidal mudflats
Access along sea wall rights of way only
Autumn, winter

Part of CHICHESTER HARBOUR

Pagham Harbour

SZ 857965; 440ha; WSCC reserve
Tidal saltmarsh and surrounding land
Leaflets from information centre
All year

With a great range of sand, shingle, saltmarsh and coastal plant life, including one national rarity, the reserve has attracted over 200 bird species and is rich in insects such as butterflies and moths. The larger area of CHICHESTER HARBOUR may be better known as a winter bird site but the mudflats and the sheltered Ferry Pool often contain a wealth of birds difficult to rival. The Sidlesham Ferry nature trail follows part of the western edge of the harbour and illustrates much of the wildlife.

Pevensey Levels

TQ 667056; 44ha; NCC reserve
Meadows and drainage ditches
Permit only, obtained from NCC SE office
Spring, summer, autumn

The reserve represents one of few remaining areas of undrained land on the marsh and consists of a series of undrained fields intersected by drainage dykes. The aquatic flora of the dykes is very rich, and species such as frogbit, bur-reed and reedmace are common, whilst rarer plants such as narrow-leaved water-plantain may also be found. Invertebrates, too, are an important aspect of the ditches. Dragonflies and water beetles are well represented, and the site is one of the best in Britain for freshwater molluscs. Breeding birds include reed and sedge warbler, reed bunting and yellow wagtail. In winter, high water levels attract a wide variety of waterfowl such as shoveler, teal and wigeon, as well as waders like snipe and golden plover. Short-eared owl and hen harrier are also common. The traditional management of grazing cattle and sheep, together with periodic dyke maintenance, ensures that the variety of habitats is conserved.

Pilsey Island

SU 770008; 18.2ha; MOD-RSPB reserve
Estuarine island
Access limited, check with RSPB South-East Regional Office. Can be viewed from footpath on Thorney Island
Winter

This small island off the southern tip of Thorney Island is the largest wader roost in CHICHESTER HARBOUR. Huge flocks of dunlin, Brent geese and oystercatchers congregate there in winter.

Powdermill Wood

Permit only; 1.9ha; SWT reserve
Wet woodland
Spring, early summer

The small reserve protects an interesting area of wet coppiced alder woodland and sedges, and is noted for its bird life.

Rye Harbour

TQ 942187; 356ha; ESCC reserve
Foreshore, shingle, saltmarsh, meadows and lagoon
Leaflets from warden
Visitors should keep to footpaths
All year

Looking inland from the shingle at the mouth of the River Rother, a low line of hills can be seen some 5km away. Between 3000 and 4000 years ago this was the coastline of Britain and the raised land represents the old sea cliffs of the time. Gravel extraction in the new land has given rise to a widespread series of pits, one of which lies within the reserve while the others may all be overlooked. It is these pits, together with the shingle ridges and foreshore, that form the most interesting and important features of the site.

Most visitors will probably come to see the spectacular bird life, the winter wildfowl, the passage birds and the colonies of terns, but the plant life of Rye Harbour is equally varied. The small saltmarsh shows all five native species of glasswort together with sea aster, sea-purslane and sea-heath, while the shingle carries a wide range of plants from yellow horned-poppy to biting stonecrop, from viper's-bugloss to sea pea, seakale and sea wormwood. The diversity of plants found on the reserve includes lesser bulrush, lesser centaury, henbane, blue fleabane, green-winged orchid, musk mallow, rock samphire, bladderwort and least lettuce.

In winter large numbers of waders – dunlin, lapwing, oystercatcher, golden plover, with curlew, ringed plover, redshank, sanderling and snipe – may be seen together with a congregation of coot, mallard, pochard, shoveler, tufted duck, wigeon, eider, goldeneye, gadwall, shelduck and teal. Spring brings many birds of passage including bar-tailed godwit, grey plover, turnstone and whimbrel, and sees the arrival of summer breeders such as common and little tern. Other breeding species include ringed plover, oystercatcher, redshank, black-headed and herring gull, little grebe, pochard, shelduck, tufted duck, yellow wagtail and wheatear, while heron may often be seen stalking their prey at the gravelpits.

In autumn several thousand hirundines use the reedbeds as a roost and attract hobbies on passage as well as the resident sparrowhawks.

Among the other animals of note are the introduced marsh frog, released on Romney Marsh in 1935, and the brown-tailed moth, a characteristic south eastern species.

Saddlescombe Chalk Pit

TQ 267122; 0.6ha; SWT reserve
Disused chalk quarry
Spring, summer

The reserve was established chiefly to protect a population of juniper but also contains a variety of downland plants.

St Leonard's Forest

TQ 208299, 216303 and 212308; 5.2ha; SWT reserve
Three small woodland areas
Spring, early summer

Representatives of three specialities of the old central Wealden forest are contained within these sites. One is an area of old beech woodland with a block of standard oak and coppiced birch, one is a protected area of lily-of-the-valley, while the last is a narrow sandstone valley containing unusual bryophytes forming a link between this and the wetter areas of western Britain.

Seaford Head

TV 505980; 112ha; Lewes DC reserve
Chalk cliffs, grassland and scrub
Spring, summer

Part of CUCKMERE HAVEN.

Looking across the mouth of Cuckmere Haven: Seaford Head to the Seven Sisters Cliffs.

Selwyns Wood

TQ 552205; 11.2ha; SWT reserve
Mixed woodland, heathland and stream valley
Spring, early summer

The mixed deciduous wood consists mainly of coppiced sweet chestnut on the acid Ashdown sands. Active coppicing is intended to ensure and demonstrate the continuance of this form of management.

Seven Sisters Country Park

TV 519995; 280ha; ESCC
Chalk cliffs, downland, shingle and estuary
Leaflets from information centre
Spring, summer

Part of CUCKMERE HAVEN.

Sidlesham Ferry Nature Trail

See PAGHAM HARBOUR.

South Downs Way

SU 762193–TV 600972; 129km; CC
Long-distance way
Leaflet from CC or booklet from HMSO bookshops
Spring, summer

The route of the long-distance way follows the South Downs clear across the county from the Hampshire border to the coast at Beachy Head. The wildlife includes that of the superb chalk cliffs and of open herb-rich downland.

Southwater Country Park

TQ 158256; 22ha; Horsham DC
Lakes, grassland and woodland
Leaflets from information cabin
Spring, autumn

This reclaimed brickworks with two lakes, grassland and woodland has a good variety of the more common animals and plants.

Stanmer Park Nature Trail

TQ 337097; 1.6km; Brighton BC
Woodland and parkland
Leaflet from BBC
Spring, early summer

The circular trail shows an attractive range of spring flowers in an area rich in wildlife: mature trees attract birds such as great spotted woodpecker and there is a resident population of badger.

Stedham Common

SU 855219; 35ha; SWT reserve
Wet and dry heathland
All year

Parts of the reserve have reverted to their woodland origins but regular and accidental fires have kept this change in check in other areas, allowing heather and gorse to flourish. The reserve is predominantly dry heath, but some small areas of wet heath result in a wide range of plant species. Heathland bird species such as stonechats, tree pipits and nightjars are present but the most noteworthy group of animals is the invertebrates, with the rich spider fauna a particular feature.

Vert Wood

Permit only; 3.2ha; SWT reserve
Mixed woodland
Spring, early summer

Areas of scrub and a glade, together with a small pond, add to the variety of the woodland reserve which contains a good range of birds and insects.

Waltham Brooks

Permit only; 42.4ha; SWT reserve
Flood meadows
Winter

The winter floods encourage a good variety of wetland birds including Bewick's swan, shoveler, teal, wigeon and snipe. In spring the reserve is colourful with marsh-marigold, followed by a bright show of yellow iris. Redshank, lapwing, gadwall and shelduck may be seen.

Warnham Nature Reserve

TQ 168323; 61ha; Horsham DC reserve
Woodland, grassland and pond
Access to mill pond area only
All year

The richest part of the reserve is the mill pond with its fringing reedbeds and willows. Canada geese, heron and kingfisher can be seen throughout the year and are joined by cormorant, teal, wigeon and goosander in winter.

West Dean Woods

Permit only; 15.4ha; SWT reserve
Old oak woodland on chalk
Spring, early summer

A fascinating relict woodland with areas of high forest and of hazel coppice under oak standards, the reserve is rich in species such as wild daffodil and bluebell growing on the non-calcareous mantle which covers the chalk. Early-purple orchid and toothwort are among the varied plants of the woodland floor, while bird and insect life includes woodcock and silver-washed fritillary. Fallow and roe deer may be present.

Woods Mill

TQ 218137; 6ha; SWT reserve
Woodland, grassland, marsh and lake
Leaflets from information centre
Spring, summer

The reserve buildings house not only the headquarters of the SWT but also an excellent information centre. The reserve itself contains a small example of a damp wealden clay wood, but is most notable as a fine wetland area where lime-rich waters draining from the South Downs encourage a fine variety of plants and animal life.

Small though it is, the wood contains much of interest. It was managed as coppice with standards, oak and hazel, although only a few of the standards still remain and, except for a demonstration area, coppicing is no longer practised. Birch has invaded the wood but there is still a good mixed range of trees, with ash, beech, field maple, hawthorn, holly and wild service-tree above a rich ground cover of wood anemone, bluebell, lesser celandine and primrose, of early dog violet and moschatel, saw-wort, wood spurge, wood millet and wood sedge, with wood-edge banks of dogwood, stands of common spotted-orchid and sprays of male-fern and hart's-tongue.

The wetland areas are various – streams and ditches, an old water tank, the lake, marsh and reedbed. The water tank, a rectangular pool, is dipped into for invertebrates during educational demonstrations, and is also a water garden of species such as bogbean, bulrush and water dock, marsh-marigold, water mint and water-plantain. The marsh and lake edge are rich in plants such as meadowsweet and great willowherb, with wild angelica, bulrush, branched bur-reed, cuckoo-flower, hemp-agrimony, yellow iris and yellow loosestrife. Alder and willow stand upon the banks with brown and grey sedge, while yellow water-lily shows on the lake itself. Near the lake a small reedbed, edged with banks of bramble, adds to the variety of the wetland.

Kingfisher and heron visit the lake and the alders draw winter flocks of goldfinch, redpoll and siskin. In winter, too, redwing and fieldfare, thrushes from northern Europe, may be seen feeding on the hedges and fields around the reserve. Reed bunting and sedge warbler breed in the reed-bed area, while the woodland affords nest sites for many species including several tits, nuthatch and treecreeper.

As with most wetlands, the area is particularly rich in insect life, in attractive dragonflies, including the broad-bodied libellula with its blue-bodied male and orange-bodied female, and damselflies such as common ischnura, azure and large red. Butterflies include peacock, small tortoiseshell, red admiral and comma.

Autumn gentian is one of the treasures of the chalk grassland of Cuckmere Haven.

View from Blackdown, towards Telegraph Hill, looking southwards with Chanctonbury Ring in the background.

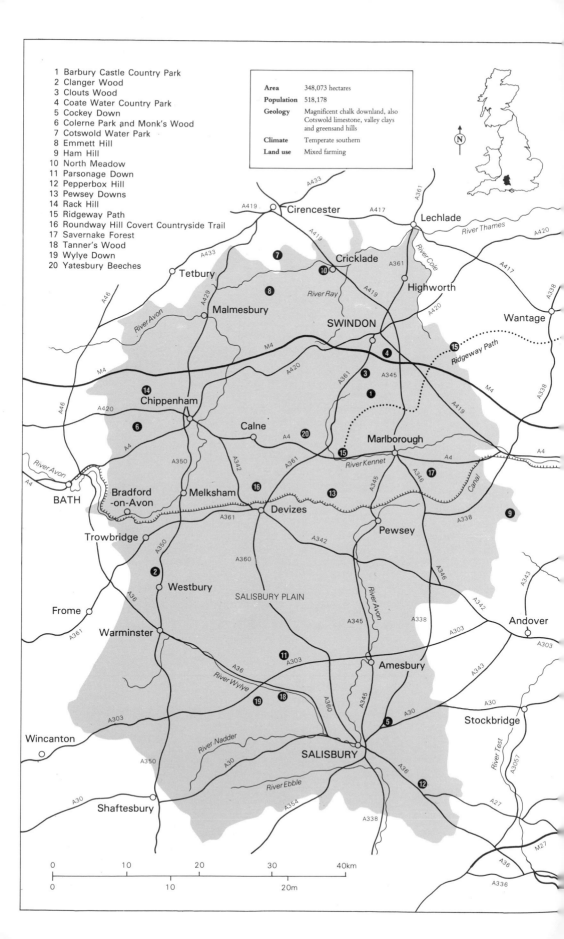

1 Barbury Castle Country Park
2 Clanger Wood
3 Clouts Wood
4 Coate Water Country Park
5 Cockey Down
6 Colerne Park and Monk's Wood
7 Cotswold Water Park
8 Emmett Hill
9 Ham Hill
10 North Meadow
11 Parsonage Down
12 Pepperbox Hill
13 Pewsey Downs
14 Rack Hill
15 Ridgeway Path
16 Roundway Hill Covert Countryside Trail
17 Savernake Forest
18 Tanner's Wood
19 Wylye Down
20 Yatesbury Beeches

Area	348,073 hectares
Population	518,178
Geology	Magnificent chalk downland, also Cotswold limestone, valley clays and greensand hills
Climate	Temperate southern
Land use	Mixed farming

Wiltshire

Better known for its archaeological treasures than for its wildlife, Wiltshire nonetheless possesses a surprising variety of habitats and species of great interest to the naturalist. The county is well worth inspection by those who might otherwise pause only briefly to look at Stonehenge, Avebury or Salisbury Cathedral on their way to the holiday beaches and harbours of the West Country.

Since the earliest continental settlers left their traces at Windmill Hill, the history of Wiltshire has been one of forest clearance, with settlements put on the high ground, and then later at the major river crossings and confluences along the springs of the greensand. The county's chief industry has always been agriculture, and traditionally Wiltshire was known as the 'land of chalk and cheese' because of the two main types of grassland: the fine grasses of the chalk downland supported flocks of sheep, while the lusher meadows of the clay vales provided grazing for the cows whose surplus milk was converted into cheese.

Geologically, two-thirds of Wiltshire consists of chalk, either directly exposed or overlain by superficial deposits of varying thickness. Salisbury Plain and Marlborough Downs are the two distinct areas that make up the chalk downs. Limestone of another type, Jurassic, forms a border along the county's north west boundary. This part of the Cotswolds is separated from the chalk by the clay vale, which includes Oxford and Kimmeridge clays. In the south west of the county an eroded anticline exposes more Jurassic rocks in the Vale of Wardour. The Portland stone quarried from here was used in the construction of most of the important buildings in the south of the county, including Fonthill Abbey, Longford Castle and Salisbury Cathedral. Finally, in the south east of the county, a layer of tertiary deposits overlies the chalk and allows the development of some oak-with-hazel coppice woodlands.

Wiltshire's most notable and fiercely protected habitat is undoubtedly the chalk downland, which comprises almost three-quarters of what remains of this habitat in Britain. Developed over hundreds of years, first by forest clearance and then by intensive grazing by rabbits and sheep, this habitat is now under threat from demands for increased agricultural productivity. When ploughed, chalk downland is very good for growing cereal crops, and when 'improved' with fertilisers the number of grazing cattle that a piece of land will support can be greatly increased. Agricultural improvement, however, involves the encouragement of coarse grasses and the elimination of the dozens of finer herbs and grasses that give the downland its distinctive character.

Typical good downland can contain up to 40 plant species per square metre, and these may include up to a dozen species of orchid, ranging from the rare lizard orchid through the uncommon musk orchid and marsh helleborine to the abundant early-purple orchid and common spotted-orchid. Other attractive flowers include milkworts, scabious, rampion (found only on the Marlborough Downs), gentian, stemless and tuberous thistle (the latter is one of Wiltshire's specialities), and numerous trefoils, including bird's-foot-trefoil and horseshoe vetch.

Horseshoe vetch is the link to the downland's other attractive feature, the butterfly population, because it is the chief food plant for several species of blues. The powder-blue chalkhill blue, the increasingly rare Adonis blue, and the common and little blues may be found flying freely on sunny days alongside the commoner browns and marbled white and the day-flying burnet moth, whose pupal cases form such a distinctive feature on the larger flowering grass stalks.

In many parts of the county the downland is also under threat from the development of scrub, following the permanent reduction in the rabbit population after myxomatosis and the great decrease in the number of sheep kept. Although this scrub is being actively managed in many parts of Wiltshire, there are one or two sites where a sequence of progression through juniper and hawthorn scrub to ash wood can be clearly demonstrated. Mention must also be made of the role of the Ministry of Defence in the preservation of Wiltshire's downland, for a significant proportion of it comes within the boundaries of the army ranges, and hobby, stone curlew and the herds of deer on Salisbury Plain, as well as the much more plentiful skylark and lapwing, benefit greatly from this protection.

Woodland is comparatively uncommon in Wiltshire. Virtually no woods grow directly on chalk, although some fine old woodlands flourish on the clay-with-flints deposits on top of the chalk ridge between the valleys of the Wylye and the Nadder, and the largest ancient wood in the county, SAVERNAKE FOREST near Marlborough, is established on a similar deposit. On the Jurassic limestone of the north west, woods flourish which contain Bath asparagus and yellow star-of-Bethlehem, whereas the woods on the tertiary deposits south of Salisbury support many butterflies, including silver-washed fritillary, white admiral and the increasingly rare purple emperor.

Wiltshire offers three major river systems, a canal and several artificial lakes. The Salisbury Avon drains Salisbury Plain; the Bristol Avon drains the clay vale; and the Kennet drains Marlborough Downs and flows eventually into the Thames. The Salisbury Avon and the Kennet are typical chalk streams, supporting a rich fish, insect and plant life. Associated with these two rivers, especially the Avon, are the functioning remains of several old water-meadow systems, which originally operated by being periodically flooded in winter to encourage the growth of grass. The Kennet and Avon Canal crosses the county, and though still in the process of being restored it offers many undisturbed stretches where wildlife may be observed quietly. The main lakes in Wiltshire belong to the large estates, such as those at Fonthill, Bowood, Longleat and Stourhead. In the extreme north of the county the headstream of the Thames runs through some meadows growing over gravel deposits. Here, in some carefully managed reserves, grow the last Wiltshire remnants of fritillary, once so much more widespread.

The archaeological interest in Wiltshire has already been referred to, but to the all-round naturalist these historical sites often have a biological interest too. The tumuli, Iron Age forts and even the huge mound of Silbury Hill are clothed with good chalk turf. The standing sarsens of Avebury and Stonehenge bear a rich lichen flora, and the old droveways on the downs and the chalk ridges offer an abundance of plant and animal interest to the walker.

JOHN PRICE

Barbury Castle Country Park

SU 157761; 52ha; WCC
Chalk downland
Spring, summer

An Iron Age encampment set high on a north-facing scarp of the Marlborough Downs, Barbury Castle is an example of grazed downland and has superb views across the landscape round Swindon.

Blackmoor Copse

SU 234293; 31.2ha; WTNC reserve
Woodland and coppice
Spring, summer

Blackmoor Copse stands on a spread of clay with flints, a damp heavy soil contrasting with the thin chalk soils of the neighbouring downs. It is a splendid example of mixed woodland – its ecology indicates that the northern part represents original forest while, in the southern part, woodland has recolonised ancient fields.

Most of the fine oak standards were felled in the 1940s and the wood was then left derelict. Thickets of birch invaded the wood, altering its traditional structure, but some fine oaks still remain. The hazel understorey is varied with shrubs such as dogwood and hawthorn, while chalk must be close to the surface in one small corner where wild privet, field maple, spindle and wayfaring-tree grow together with sanicle, wood melick and lime-loving traveller's-joy. Damp wide rides and clearings are filled with plants such as greater bird's-foot-trefoil and bugle, meadow-sweet, yellow pimpernel and ragged-Robin, and edged with woodland species: violets, primrose, woodruff and wood spurge.

The woodland is rich in animal life, from dormouse to roe deer, from warbler to woodcock, but its particular interest, and the reason for which it was originally acquired, is its wealth of woodland butterflies. Pride of place belongs to the purple emperor, but other attractive species occur, including white admiral, purple hairstreak and silver-washed fritillary. On a fine July day all four should be on the wing, although both purple emperor and purple hairstreak tend to fly around the topmost branches of the oaks. The damp rich clays are well suited to purple emperor since they also encourage the growth of willows, essential as its larval food plant. Like the white admiral, a related species which feeds on honeysuckle, it hibernates as a caterpillar, stitching a hammock from a leaf of its chosen food plant.

Chilmark Ravine

Permit only; 55ha; MOD
Caves and quarries
All year

The original source of stone for Salisbury Cathedral, 30km east, it is now one of the most important sites for bats in Britain with 10 out of 16 native species including Bechstein, and greater and lesser horseshoe.

Clanger Wood

ST 873538; 52.5ha; WdT
Mixed woodland
Spring, summer

This reserve was formerly broadleaved woodland, but has now been substantially replanted with mixed conifers. However, blocks of the original oak woodland remain. The wood is renowned for its wildlife and is an especially rich site for birds and butterflies. In spring and summer the ground is covered with a mass of woodland flowers.

Clouts Wood

SU 136795; 13.2ha; WTNC reserve
Mixed woodland
Nature trail leaflet from WTNC
Spring, summer

The mainly deciduous woodland of oak and ash and some hazel coppice lies on a steep chalk hillside. The rich ground cover contains spiked star-of-Bethlehem, herb-Paris, green hellebore, wood vetch and yellow archangel.

Coate Water Country Park

SU 178820; 45.8ha; Thamesdown BC
Wetland bird sanctuary
Permit only to hides
Leaflet from site
All year

An interesting variety of birds has been recorded here, including red-throated diver, woodlark, little stint and hobby.

Cockey Down

SU 172329; 6.4ha; WTNC reserve
Chalk downland
Summer

This north-west facing grassland supports a superb range of downland plants including field fleabane, bastard-toadflax, chalk milkwort, autumn gentian and abundant fragrant orchids. There is also a good variety of butterflies with populations of chalkhill blues, dingy skippers, green hairstreaks and possibly breeding marsh fritillary.

Colerne Park and Monk's Wood

ST 835725; 44.4ha; WdT
Mixed woodland
Spring, early summer

In this fine example of old coppiced oak and ash woodland on limestone, the ground flora is notable for plants such as Solomon's-seal, angular Solomon's-seal and lily-of-the-valley.

Cotswold Water Park

Most of the park lies in Gloucestershire, under which county it is described.

Emmett Hill

SU 009901; 5ha; WTNC reserve
Hay meadow
Spring, early summer

The two traditionally managed meadows are separated by a stream and a small area of scrub. Before the hay is cut in July, the northern field is a mass of colour with dyer's greenweed, cowslip, saw-wort, betony, meadow thistle, pepper saxifrage and common spotted-orchid; the unusual adder's-tongue can also be found in this meadow. The southern field lies on more acid soils and contains a surprising predominance of pignut.

Great Cheverell Hill

Permit only; 9ha; WTNC reserve
Chalk grassland
Spring, summer

The downland turf of Great Cheverell Hill is a reminder of what the chalk downlands must have been like when they were grazed by sheep, not ploughed for arable crops.

The reserve is particularly rich in plant species because the soil is shallow on the slope, but even the deep-grassed plateau is full of yellow rattle, greater knapweed and clusters of colourful vetches. The bank itself is a colourful tapestry shaped to the slope of the hill: white is picked out by oxeye daisy or the tiny eyebrights which often cushion the ant-hills; vivid yellow is everywhere: tall spikes of agrimony, common bird's-foot-trefoil, lady's bedstraw, cowslips. Dazzling sprays of ragwort attract bright butterflies and stand above the paler yellow of common rock-rose or horseshoe and kidney vetch, important food plants for some of the butterfly larvae. Yellow-wort is strikingly plentiful on the thinner, barer soils. Shades of pink, blue-purple, purple-red, a subtle show of colours can be seen in common centaury, restharrow, squinancywort, in clustered bellflower and harebell, in small scabious, selfheal, dwarf thistle and scented cushions of wild thyme.

Bee and pyramidal orchid add their special beauty to the slope and, in early summer, there is the clear white of star-of-Bethlehem. One of the most spectacular plants at Great Cheverell Hill is woolly thistle, while among several species of note bastard-toadflax, burnt orchid and lesser butterfly-orchid occur. The reserve also supports a good variety of butterflies, including chalkhill, Adonis and small blue, green hairstreak and the beautifully marked marsh fritillary.

Ham Hill

Permit only; 2ha; WTNC reserve
Chalk grassland
Late spring, summer

The steep, north-west facing grassland is particularly important for orchids and butterflies. There are also small areas of scrub and secondary ash woodland, and a deep cutting, formerly an old coach road, runs through the centre of the site.

Jones's Mill

SU 168614; 12ha; WTNC reserve
Small valley fen
Spring, summer

A shallow damp valley with a waterlogged peaty soil in a basin of clay, the reserve lies on ground once farmed as a water-cress bed. It is now managed in two halves, one a head-high fen, the other a marshy meadow astride a stream. The meadow may be grazed by cattle; the fen is fenced, sheltered and surrounded by trees.

The marshy meadow is rich in waterside plants such as water forget-me-not, water figwort and water mint, with water-cress in the clear fast-

Chalkhill blue butterfly is found only in the south, usually near its food plant, horseshoe vetch.

running stream. Marsh-marigold in the spring is followed later by comfrey and spiny-leaved marsh thistle. The meadow is often thick with rushes and plants such as square-stalked St John's-wort, a foretaste of the richness of the fen.

The fen is thick with tall plants such as bulrush, great horsetail, great willowherb and meadowsweet or spread with a lower cover of sedges where more acid areas occur. The stream, in fact the Salisbury River Avon, meanders through the fen, encouraging the show of wetland plants. Among and around the taller plants, such as yellow iris, ragged-Robin, common valerian and hemp-agrimony, greater bird's-foot-trefoil and marsh bedstraw climb.

Common spotted-orchid and southern marsh-orchid make a superb display among the sedges, but it is the acid-loving plants which are of greatest interest in this county of widespread chalk. Among the sedges is flea sedge, more commonly found on wet moors, bog pimpernel, a plant of wet peaty heaths, and bogbean, a typical plant of watery bogs. Many of the plants of the reserve are uncommon within the county and a number, such as marsh arrowgrass, have a somewhat local distribution in the country as a whole.

Breeding birds include insect-feeders which exploit the hatches so characteristic of wetland. Several species of warbler breed here and the fen and marshy meadow provide suitable habitats for water rail and snipe or hunting grounds for sparrowhawk and kestrel. Among the varied selection of insects which can be spotted, the butterflies include marsh fritillary.

Kingsettle Wood

Described under Dorset.

Nadder Island

Permit only; 0.4ha; WTNC reserve
Wooded island
Spring, early summer

The island, which is within the city of Salisbury itself, was formed artificially when a new channel was dug to drain a development area. It is now thick with willow species, banks of common nettle and stands of common reed.

The grazed chalk grassland of Pewsey Downs, an example of ancient pasture.

North Meadow

SU 099944; 39ha; NCC reserve
Old-meadow grassland
No access off public rights of way
Leaflet from NCC
May, mid-June

An exceptionally fine ancient meadow, the reserve contains a rich mix of meadow plants: adder's-tongue, great burnet, cowslip, oxeye daisy, southern marsh-orchid and common meadow-rue. It is, however, most famous for fritillary, with perhaps 80 per cent of the total British population.

Oysters Coppice

ST 895261; 6ha; WTNC reserve
Mixed woodland
Spring, summer

Oysters Coppice lies on upper greensand although standard ash trees among the oak-over-hazel suggest slightly less acid conditions, except where holly and rowan grow. The ground cover, with wild daffodil and bluebell, is more characteristic of western woodlands. A variety of mammals frequent the reserve and birds include a summer breeding population of wood warbler.

Parsonage Down

SU 045412; 276ha; NCC reserve
Chalk downland
Permission required from warden
Spring, summer

This area of downland is unusual in that it is gently undulating and is normally grazed by cattle. The diversity of plants in relation to the topography is the most interesting feature of the reserve. There is a varied invertebrate fauna and the Adonis blue butterfly occurs.

Pepperbox Hill

SU 212248; 34ha; NT
Rough chalk grassland and scrub, woodland
Spring, summer

The grasslands of PEWSEY DOWNS and GREAT CHEVERELL HILL are a richness of short-grazed herbs. Pepperbox Hill, in contrast, marks the progression towards woodland which, uncontained by man, would eventually cover these hills. The tiny scented herbs have faded away, drowned by the deep rank grassland, but in exchange are thickets of colour with sheltered suntraps where butterflies bask and yellowhammers sing. Dogwood, hawthorn, wild privet, wayfaring-tree and whitebeam are clustered together, barbed with wild rose, set among and around the dark contrast of yew and juniper.

Beneath the scrub, although small plants such as squinancywort and wild thyme only occur on ant-hills or in the paths, taller plants rise above the grasses. Pyramidal orchids occur, as do a host of other plants: agrimony, wild basil, lady's bedstraw, harebell, greater knapweed, wild mignonette, wild parsnip, ragwort, small scabious

and dwarf thistle, plants which attract marbled white and gatekeeper butterflies or vivid burnet moths.

Beech has not yet spread from the woodland nearby, but it is interesting to note that the sunlit edges of the wood contain the same lime-loving shrubs as the grassland scrub contains, with the addition of elder and guelder-rose as well as more typical woodland species such as ash and holly, but without juniper. The ground cover is essentially that of woodland and varies from virtually nothing in the more densely shaded areas to spreads of ivy, dog's mercury, and enchanter's-nightshade, with wood melick, sanicle, violets and woodruff.

Peppercombe Wood

SU 038575; 0.8ha; WTNC reserve
Mixed woodland
Spring, early summer

Coppiced hazel under standards of oak, ash and wych elm grows above a ground cover of species such as bluebell, moschatel and snowdrop. The elms are diseased and have been replaced with a wider variety of trees.

Pewsey Downs

SU 115635; 166ha; NCC
Open chalk downland
Leaflets from NCC
Spring, summer

No one who travels in southern England can fail to be impressed by the sweep of chalkland which dominates so much of the area. For many centuries this was the land of sheep, of huge flocks which spread across the downland. Today most of the sheep have gone or graze on reseeded pastures and the woods are kept at bay by the work of widespread arable farms. In a few areas, however, the herb-rich turf of unimproved grassland remains and Pewsey Downs is a splendid example of this very special downland.

Compared with ASTON ROWANT (Oxfordshire) Pewsey is far more exposed and has had a longer continuous record of grazing, with only a small plantation on a patch of superficial drift in contrast to the rich beechwoods of the Chilterns reserve.

The reserve is, typically, a sward of red and sheep's fescue with plentiful glaucous sedge, salad burnet and dwarf thistle, with upright brome but rather little tor-grass, and contains a particular range of plants which indicates its importance. Just as some woodland plants find it difficult to recolonise secondary woodland, so certain grassland species are unable to return if they have been driven out by ploughing or use of chemical fertilisers. The plants indicating the ancient turf at Pewsey include bastard-toadflax, field fleawort, chalk milkwort, burnt orchid and horseshoe vetch, while the betony, saw-wort and devil's-bit scabious found here are rare on any chalk outside Wiltshire and Dorset.

These key species are part of a superb pattern of colourful plants which is spread across the downland and includes clustered bellflower, cowslip, hoary plantain, quaking-grass, yellow rattle and spiny restharrow, sainfoin, squinancywort, small scabious, kidney vetch and musk thistle. The slopes are often mounded with ant-hills which provide one of the special pleasures of chalklands, for each ant-heap becomes a tiny garden thick with small flowers such as lady's bedstraw, common bird's-foot-trefoil and eyebright, harebell, mouse-ear hawkweed, common rock-rose and wild thyme.

Besides burnt orchid, the reserve protects a range of other orchid species, including common spotted-orchid and bee, frog, fragrant, greenwinged and pyramidal orchid. The strange-looking knapweed broomrape, which grows as a parasite on greater knapweed and is plentiful on the downlands of Salisbury Plain, is also found in the reserve. Here, too, are a number of uncommon plants – round-headed rampion near its western limit, early gentian and the rare hybrid between dwarf and tuberous thistle. Early gentian is mainly found on the southern central chalk and, unique among British gentians, does not occur in northern Europe, while the tuberous thistle is even more restricted in its British range and grows in only two other districts in the country.

The wealth of plants supports a wide range of insects including large populations of downland butterflies. By early July the down may be enlivened by brown Argus, chalkhill and little blue and the fast-flying marsh fritillary which occurs here because of its food plant, devil's-bit scabious. Similarly, the others require common rock-rose, horseshoe vetch and a range of small trefoils and clovers and it is this close relationship between food plant and range which provides much of the fascination of these beautiful butterflies.

Prescombe Down

Permit only; 47ha; NCC reserve
Chalk downland and scrub
Spring, summer

The reserve contains uncommon species, such as meadow saxifrage, saw-wort and early gentian, as well as commoner plants of chalk grassland and distinctive plants of the Wiltshire and Dorset Downs, such as dwarf sedge. The mixed scrub attracts breeding birds such as corn bunting, willow warbler and whitethroat.

Rack Hill

ST 844763; 10.6ha; WTNC reserve
Limestone grassland and scrub
Permit only off right of way
Spring, summer

The rich mosaic of limestone downland is interspersed with blocks of scrub and some secondary woodland. Horseshoe vetch, clustered bellflower and devil's-bit and small scabious add colour to the rich downland turf which also supports colonies of chalkhill blue, dark green fritillary and green hairstreak. The scrub attracts good numbers of warblers and finches.

Ridgeway Path

SU 118681–259833; 30km; CC
Long-distance way
Booklet from HMSO bookshops
Spring, summer

The footpath, starting near Avebury, occasionally deflects from the ancient Ridgeway but follows the same line along the crest of the Downs to IVINGHOE BEACON (Buckinghamshire).

Roundway Hill Covert Countryside Trail

SU 005647; 2km; FC
Mixed woodland trail
Leaflet from FC
Spring, early summer

The trail circles through mixed woodland with an understorey of box above a high steep slope replanted with beech trees. Small clearings full of chalkland plants form platforms from which there are wide views across the countryside.

Savernake Forest

SU 225667; 1000ha; FC
Mixed woodland
Spring, early summer

A spread of ancient woodland on the clay-with-flints soil south east of Marlborough, Savernake Forest was held from Norman times until the sixteenth century as a royal hunting forest. Much of it has now been planted with conifers but some huge old trees remain: considerable areas are retained as broad-leaved woodland and some have been planted with young broad-leaved species including oak.

Some parts of the forest are dominated by beech, with a thin understorey of young beech and little ground cover but fallen leaves, although well-lit clearings may be carpeted with close grassland, mosses, rosebay willowherb and bracken. Other woodland blocks are far richer, with oak, ash, rowan and sycamore above a more varied herb layer, a contrast with the planted stands of beech, oak or conifers.

In common with many ancient parkland woods, the ground flora is often rather limited and the greatest variation of plants may be found in the rides and ride-edges. Here grassland plants as agrimony, lady's bedstraw and meadowsweet, ragwort and hairy St John's-wort, selfheal and tormentil grow with species such as wood avens, enchanter's-nightshade, dog's mercury, wood spurge and wood-sorrel. As the dampness and type of top-soil change so do the woodland plants and, in autumn, meadow saffron may show in some of the richer areas, an uncommon, beautiful flower with a rather limited range in England.

Grassland fields within the forest add to the habitat range which encourages a diversity of insects and other animals. Woodland birds include kestrel and sparrowhawk, while among the forest mammals are fallow and lesser numbers of red, roe and muntjac deer.

Somerford Common

SU 024863; 2.4ha; WTNC reserve
Mixed woodland
Spring, early summer

Somerford is a remnant of the medieval Braydon Forest. The wood was clear-felled in the late 1950s and is now managed to provide the greatest range of variation. The ground cover includes primrose, cowslip and their hybrid, with a number of orchids, under a mixed shrub-layer with standard oak and ash. Birds are varied, and butterflies include speckled wood and white admiral.

Tanner's Wood

SU 033373; 1ha; WdT
Derelict woodland
Spring, early summer

The wood has been devastated by Dutch elm disease and is being replanted with a mix of tree species.

Upper Waterhay

Permit only; 2.7ha; WTNC reserve
Old-meadow grassland
May

The reserve was established to protect a fine display of fritillary, which is unusual because most of the plants have white flowers.

Whitesheet Hill

ST 79935; 2.5ha; WTNC reserve
Disused chalk quarry
Leaflet from WTNC or NT
Spring, summer

The Hardway and Long Lane are remnants of the ancient drove-road which led from Castle Cary to Salisbury, and ran close by the chalk quarry at the foot of the Whitesheet Downs. Now long-abandoned, the quarry has largely returned to grassland and, with a range of habitat from open chalk scree to the short-cropped grassland above, has become a valuable nature reserve.

The small chalk scree slope is largely populated by colt's-foot, a well-known primary coloniser, growing on bare ground anywhere, provided the soil is not too acid. The spring-time yellows of colt's-foot, cowslip and primrose make a beautiful display on the slopes around the entrance to the quarry, followed later by many of the characteristic chalkland plants such as lady's bedstraw, common bird's-foot-trefoil, salad burnet, harebell, yellow rattle and wild thyme.

The spread of many of the plants is clearly related to habitat, with plants such as carline thistle and quaking-grass more plentiful in the shallow turf near the open chalk and with taller plants such as meadow crane's-bill growing where the soil is deeper. Deeper soils, too, carry a developing scrub, where ash, blackthorn, hawthorn, wild privet and willow provide singing posts and nesting sites for birds. The shallow slopes beside the drove-way are brilliant with common rock-rose in summer, while the reserve as a whole holds good numbers of common spotted-orchid, together with bee and pyramidal orchid, common twayblade and, later, autumn gentian.

There are signs that fox and badger visit the reserve and it is frequently hunted by kestrel, while smaller birds include skylark, meadow pipit, willow warbler, corn bunting and yellowhammer. The sheltered slopes full of colourful flowers attract many butterflies, including both marsh and dark green fritillary, with a colony of marbled white.

Wylye Down

SU 002363; 34ha; NCC reserve
Chalk downland
Permit only off right of way
Leaflets from NCC
Spring, summer

The rich grassland contains much dwarf sedge, a species characteristic of south Wiltshire and Dorset but rare elsewhere, together with many chalkland plants. Less common species include bastard-toadflax, field fleawort, dyer's greenweed, meadow saxifrage, saw-wort and a range of orchid species.

Yatesbury Beeches

SU 060714; 0.4ha; WdT
Roadside beeches
Spring, summer

The trees provide both shelter to the roadway and a sanctuary for birds and insects.

Abbreviations Used in the Guide

Note: county councils are given in the following form, e.g. ACC for Avon County Council; the county is always the same as the section title unless otherwise stated, and these abbreviations do not appear in the list below. All county names beginning with the letter N are spelt out to avoid confusion with the NCC (Nature Conservancy Council); CC alone stands for the Countryside Commission. For convenience the managing body named in line 1 of each entry is sometimes given an obvious abbreviation in line 3, when indicating for instance the availability of a leaflet (e.g. KAMT for Kenneth Allsop Memorial Trust). Such abbreviations are not listed below.

AWA	Anglian Water Authority
AWT	Avon Wildlife Trust
B and HWT	Bedfordshire and Huntingdonshire Wildlife Trust
BBNPC	Brecon Beacons National Park Committee
BBONT	Berkshire, Buckinghamshire and Oxfordshire Naturalists' Trust
BC	After a place name: Borough Council
BR	British Rail
BTCV	British Trust for Conservation Volunteers
BWB	British Waterways Board
BWT	Brecknock Wildlife Trust
CC	Countryside Commission/after a place name: County Council
CCT	Cheshire Conservation Trust
CEGB	Central Electricity Generating Board
CPRE	Council for the Preservation of Rural England
CTNC	Cornwall Trust for Nature Conservation/Cumbria Trust for Nature Conservation (according to context)
CWT	Cambridgeshire Wildlife Trust/Cleveland Wildlife Trust (according to context)
DBWPS	Devon Bird Watching and Preservation Society
DC	After a place name: District Council
DNPA	Dartmoor National Park Authority
DNS	Deeside Naturalists' Society
DNT	Derbyshire Naturalists' Trust/Dorset Trust for Nature Conservation (according to context)
DWT	Devon Wildlife Trust/Durham Wildlife Trust/Dyfed Wildlife Trust (according to context)
ENPC	Exmoor National Park Committee
ENT	Essex Naturalists' Trust
ESCC	East Sussex County Council
FC	Forestry Commission
FSC	Field Studies Council
GTNC	Gloucestershire Trust for Nature Conservation
GWT	Glamorgan Wildlife Trust/Gwent Wildlife Trust (according to context)
H and IOWNT	Hampshire and Isle of Wight Naturalists' Trust
H and MTNC	Hertfordshire and Middlesex Trust for Nature Conservation
HNT	Herefordshire Nature Trust
HIDB	Highlands and Islands Development Board
HMSO	Her Majesty's Stationery Office
H and MWT	Hertfordshire and Middlesex Wildlife Trust

IOW	Isle of Wight
IWCC	Isle of Wight County Council
JCNS	Jersey Conservation and Naturalists' Society
KTNC	Kent Trust for Nature Conservation
L and RTNC	Leicestershire and Rutland Trust for Nature Conservation
L and SHTNC	Lincolnshire and South Humberside Trust for Nature Conservation
LDSPB	Lake District Special Planning Board
LNR	Local Nature Reserve
LTNC	Lancashire Trust for Nature Conservation
LWT	London Wildlife Trust
MBC	After a place name: Metropolitan Borough Council
MMNT	Manx Museum Naturalist Trust
MNCT	Manx Nature Conservation Trust
MOD	Ministry of Defence
MWT	Montgomery Wildlife Trust
NCC	Nature Conservancy Council
NNR	National Nature Reserve
NNT	Norfolk Naturalists' Trust
NOA	Norfolk Ornithologists' Association
NT	National Trust
NTJ	National Trust for Jersey
NTS	National Trust for Scotland
NWA	Northumbrian Water Authority
NWNT	North Wales Naturalists' Trust
NWT	Northamptonshire Wildlife Trust/Northumberland Wildlife Trust/Nottinghamshire Wildlife Trust (according to context)
NWWA	North Western Water Authority
NYMNPC	North York Moors National Park Committee
PC	After a place name: Parish Council
PCNPA	Pembrokeshire Coast National Park Authority
PPJPB	Peak Park Joint Planning Board
RC	After a place name: Regional Council
RSNC	Royal Society for Nature Conservation
RSPB	Royal Society for the Protection of Birds
RSPCA	Royal Society for the Prevention of Cruelty to Animals
RWT	Radnorshire Wildlife Trust
SNCT	Staffordshire Nature Conservation Trust
SNPC	Snowdonia National Park Committee
SSSI	Site of Special Scientific Interest
STNC	Shropshire Trust for Nature Conservation
SWT	Scottish Wildlife Trust/Suffolk Wildlife Trust/Surrey Wildlife Trust/Sussex Wildlife Trust (according to context)
SWWA	South Western Water Authority
TWA	Thames Water Authority
UWG	Urban Wildlife Group
UTNC	Ulster Trust for Nature Conservation
WARNACT	Warwickshire Nature Conservation Trust
WdT	Woodland Trust
WNCT	Worcestershire Nature Conservation Trust
WSCC	West Sussex County Council
WT	Wildfowl Trust
WTNC	Wiltshire Trust for Nature Conservation
WWA	Welsh Water Authority/Wessex Water Authority (according to context)
YDNPC	Yorkshire Dales National Park Committee
YWT	Yorkshire Wildlife Trust

Addresses

The following is a list of the major wildlife organisations in The South of England, together with those owners and managing bodies from whom information and/or permits may be obtained, but whose addresses are not already given in the text. All requests should be accompanied by a stamped addressed envelope, and readers should understand that permits may be refused at the managing bodies' discretion.

The nature conservation trusts of Southern England

Avon Wildlife Trust
The Old Police Station
32 Jacob's Wells Road
Bristol BS8 1DR

Bedfordshire and Huntingdonshire Wildlife Trust
Priory Country Park
Barkers Lane
Bedford MK41 9SH

Berkshire, Buckinghamshire and Oxfordshire Naturalists' Trust (BBONT)
3 Church Cowley Road
Rose Hill
Oxford OX4 3JR

British Trust for Conservation Volunteers
2 Mandela Street
London
NW1 0DU

Cornwall Trust for Nature Conservation
Dairy Cottage
Trelissick, Feock
Truro
Cornwall TR3 6QL

Devon Wildlife Trust
35 New Bridge Street
Exeter
Devon EX4 3AH

Dorset Trust for Nature Conservation
39 Christchurch Road
Bournemouth
BH1 3NS

Gloucestershire Trust for Nature Conservation
Church House
Standish
Stonehouse
GL10 3EU

Hampshire and Isle of Wight Naturalists' Trust
8 Market Place
Romsey
Hampshire
SO5 8NB

Kent Trust for Nature Conservation
The Annexe
1a Bower Mount Road
Maidstone
Kent ME16 8AX

London Wildlife Trust
80 York Way
London N1 9AG

LWT can provide information on all sites within the GLC area, regardless of management

Somerset Trust for Nature Conservation
Fyne Court
Broomfield
Bridgwater
TA5 2EQ

Surrey Wildlife Trust
Hatchlands
East Clandon
Guildford
GU4 7RT

Sussex Wildlife Trust
Woods Mill
Henfield
West Sussex
BN5 9SD

Urban Wildlife Trust
131–133 Sherlock Street
Birmingham
B5 6NB

Wiltshire Trust for Nature Conservation
19 High Street
Devizes
Wiltshire SN10 1AT

Other organisations

Avon County Council
Avon House
The Haymarket
Bristol BS99 7DE

Batsford Estate Office
Moreton-in-Marsh
Gloucestershire
GL56 9QF

Bournemouth Borough Council
Town Hall
Bournemouth
BH2 6DY

Bracknell District Council
Easthampstead House
Town Square
Bracknell
RG12 1AQ

Brighton Borough Council
Town Hall
Bartholomews
Brighton
BN1 1JA

Bristol City Council
Council House
College Green
Bristol BS1 5TR

Bristol Naturalists' Society
c/o Bristol City Museum
Queens Road
Bristol
BS1 5AQ

Bristol Waterworks Co.
Recreations Dept
Woodford Lodge
Chew Stoke
Bristol
BS18 8XH

British Waterways Board
Melbury House
Melbury Terrace
London NW1 6JX

Buckinghamshire County Council
County Hall
Aylesbury
HP20 1VA

Central Electricity Generating Board
The Surveyor
Sudbury House
15 Newgate Street
London EC1A 7AU

Cornwall Bird-Watching and Preservation Society
c/o 13 Tregellas Road
Mullion
Helston
Cornwall

Cornwall County Council
County Hall
Truro
TR1 3AY

Countryside Commission
John Dower House
Crescent Place
Cheltenham
Gloucestershire
GL50 3RA

Dartmoor National Park Authority
Parke
Haytor Road
Bovey Tracey
Newton Abbot
Devon
TQ13 9JQ

Devon Bird Watching and Preservation Society
14 Parkers Way
Totnes
Devon TQ9 5UF

Devon County Council
County Hall
Topsham Road
Exeter
EX2 4QD

Dorset County Council
County Hall
Dorchester
Dorset
DT1 1XJ

Eastbourne Borough Council
Town Hall
Eastbourne
BN21 4UG

East Sussex County Council
Pelham House
St Andrew's Lane
Lewes
BN7 1UN

Epsom and Ewell Borough Council
PO Box 5
Town Hall
The Parade
Epsom
Surrey
KT18 5BY

Exmoor National Park Committee
Exmoor House
Dulverton
Somerset
TA22 9HL

Information centre
Minehead and West Somerset
Publicity Association
Market House
Minehead
Somerset

Forestry Commission

Headquarters for England, Wales and Scotland
231 Corstorphine Road
Edinburgh
EH12 7AT

West
Avon Fields House
Somerdale
Keynsham
Bristol
BS18 2BD

Gloucestershire County Council
Shire Hall
Gloucester
GL1 2TG

Gosport Borough Council
Town Hall
Gosport
Hampshire
PO12 1EB

Hampshire County Council
Recreation Dept
North Hill Close
Andover Road
Winchester
SO22 6AQ

Hastings Borough Council
4 Robertson Terrace
Hastings
East Sussex
TN34 1JE

Her Majesty's Stationery Office

Government bookshops
Southey House
Wine Street
Bristol
BS1 2BQ

49 High Holborn
London WC1V 6HB

Horsell Common Preservation Society
Fairbanks
Pembroke Road
Woking
Surrey
GU22 7DP

Isle of Wight County Council
County Hall
Newport
Isle of Wight
PO30 1UD

**Isle of Wight Natural History and
Archaeological Society**
66 Carisbrooke Road
Newport
Isle of Wight
PO30 1BW

Isle of Wight Tourist Board
The Old Town Hall
Leigh Road
Eastleigh
Hampshire
SO5 4DE

Jeffery Harrison Memorial Trust
Sevenoaks Wildfowl Reserve
Tadorna
Bradbourne Vale Road
Sevenoaks
Kent
TN13 3DH

Kenneth Allsop Memorial Trust
via Wincanton Press National School
North Street
Wincanton
Somerset BA9 9AT

Landmark Trust
Shottesbrooke
Nr Maidenhead
Berkshire
SL6 3SW

Lewes District Council
Lewes House
Lewes
East Sussex
BN7 2LX

Ministry of Defence
Lands Dept
Tolworth Tower
Ewell Road
Surbiton
Surrey
KT6 7DR

National Trust
42 Queen Anne's Gate
London
SW1H 9AS

*There are also 15 regional offices in England and
Wales: their addresses are obtainable from the address
above*

Nature Conservancy Council

Headquarters
Northminster House
Peterborough PE1 1VA

South East
Zealds
Church Street
Wye
Ashford
Kent
TN25 5BW

South
Foxhold House
Thornford Road
Crookham Common
Headley
Newbury
Berkshire
RG15 8EL

South West
Roughmoor
Bishop's Hull
Taunton
Somerset
TA1 5AA

Newbury District Council
Council Offices
Market Street
Newbury
Berkshire
RG14 5BJ

Oxford City Council
Recreation Dept
Town Hall
Oxford
OX1 1BX

Royal Society for Nature Conservation
The Green
Nettleham
Lincoln
LN2 2NR

Royal Society for the Protection of Birds

England and Wales
The Lodge
Sandy
Bedfordshire
SG19 2DL

**Royal Society for the Prevention of Cruelty
to Animals**
Causeway
Horsham
West Sussex
RH12 1HG

Selbourne Society
89 Daryngton Drive
Greenford
Middlesex
UB6 8BH

Somerset County Council
County Hall
Taunton
TA1 4DY

South Somerset District Council
Council Offices
Brympton Way
Yeovil
Somerset
BH20 2DH

South West Water Authority
Peninsula House
Rydon Lane
Exeter
EX2 7HR

South Wight Borough Council
41 Sea Street
Newport
Isle of Wight
PO30 5DN

Surrey Heath Borough Council
Surrey Heath House
Knoll Road
Camberley
Surrey
GU15 3HD

Thames Water Authority
Nugent House
Vastern Road
Reading
Berkshire
RG1 8DB

Torbay Borough Council
Town Hall
Torquay
TQ1 3DR

Trust for Urban Ecology
South Bank House
Black Prince Road
London SE1

Wansbeck District Council
Council Offices
Newbiggin-by-the-Sea
NE64 6PL

Waverley District Council
Council Offices
The Burys
Godalming
Surrey
GU7 1HR

Water Authority reservoirs
See British Waterways Board

Wells Natural History and Archaeological Society
c/o The Museum
Wells
Somerset

Wessex Water Authority
Wessex House
Passage Street
Bristol
BS2 0JQ

West Sussex County Council
County Hall
Chichester
PO19 1RQ

Wildfowl Trust
England and Wales
Slimbridge
Gloucester
GL2 7BT

Wiltshire County Council
County Hall
Trowbridge
BA14 8JG

Wokingham District Council
Council Offices
Shute End
Wokingham
Berkshire
RG11 1BN

Woodland Trust
Autumn Park
Dysart Road
Grantham
Lincolnshire
NG31 6LL

Woodspring District Council
Town Hall
Weston-super-Mare
BS23 1UJ

Index